Out of the crisis

Evidence based communication programs for

managing world demographic problems

PhD Dissertation

By László Molnár

Budapest

October, 2006

Contents

Introduction

World demographic problems are strikingly increasing, and evidence based, scientifically grounded communication programs in managing these problems are common to find solutions to these problems. Current scientific research methods and communication programs and methods are considered in a vast amount of demographic projects worldwide to solve global earth problems.

The day when humanity starts eating the planet, say experts at the home page of the New Economics Foundation is 9 October, 2006. New research reveals rising consumption of natural resources is pushing the world into ever earlier ecological debt, or overshoot. New calculations show that from this date we will be living beyond our global environmental means. Humanity has used up what nature can renew this year and is now eating into its ecological capital. Each year, the day that the global economy starts to operate with an ecological deficit is designated as ecological debt day known internationally as overshoot day. From now on humanity will be in ecological overshoot, building up ever greater ecological debt by consuming resources beyond the level that the planet's ecosystems can replace, and this has been called the biggest issue you have ever heard of.

Part of the above processes is unsustainable demographic processes of global population. This is a serious risk for sustainability of human and earth ecosystems. Population growth, changing birth control, problems of migration, nuptiality, poverty, health crisis, ageing, mortality and various forms of inequality in these demographic processes are serious challenges to the human population as well as to the earth ecosystems. Managing these demographic processes is crucial from the point of sustainability. To make demographic processes sustainable scientific research and communication should be put in a new way and be used more effectively. To influence current demographic processes research and communication must be made effectively as it has already made by the POPLINE Staff of the INFO Project at the Johns Hopkins Bloomberg School of Public Health/Center for Communication Programs and is funded primarily by the United States Agency for International Development.

It is estimated that the world human population increase by about 200 thousand people daily. Uncontrolled population growth may lead to overpopulation. Conversely, a declining population may lead to an ageing society where the needs of the elderly are being cared for by a smaller group of working age people. Problems of overpopulation, increases in births and life expectancy, ageing societies and unsustainable use and depletion of resources are common problems of the world. Communication programs may effectively help in solving a series of demographic problems. These programs are related to ICT and adult education. New scientific research methods including multivariate and computer-intensive statistical techniques are indispensable part of developing social communication programs to alleviate increasing demographic problems.

Andrew Simms, NEF's policy director says: "By living so far beyond our environmental means, and running up ecological debts we make two mistakes. First, we deny millions globally who already lack access to sufficient land, food and clean water the chance to meet their needs. Secondly, we put the planet's life support mechanisms in peril." Earth ecosystem crisis and critical demographic processes cry for evidence-based risk management and proper risk communication supported by research-based feedback to slow down or stop critical processes.

General communication models

Communication is the process of exchanging information between various partners. Information can be exchanged through a common system of symbols or non-symbolically as in empathy. In a protocol, communication sent one-way is a message. Communication is also and academic discipline which studies communication.

Traditionally nine elements of any communication process is recognized, i.e. sender, receiver, encoding, decoding, message, media, response, feedback and noise. The sender is who is sending the message to another party. Encoding is the process of putting the intended message into symbolic form that will convey the message. The message is a set of word, pictures or symbols that the sender transmits. Media is the communication channel through which the message moves from sender to receiver, i.e. TV, radio, newspaper etc. Decoding is the process by which the receiver assigns meaning to the symbols encoded by the sender. Receiver is a person who is the targeted by the message. Response is the reaction or reactions of the receiver after being exposed to the message. Feedback is the receiver's response communicated back to the sender. In other words feedback should be collected to watch how much of the target population becomes aware of the things communicated. Noise is an unplanned static of distortion during the communication process, which results in the receiver getting a different message than the one the sender sent.

The communicator has to identify the target audience and its characteristics. Senders need to know what audiences they want to reach and what responses, i.e. attitude or action change they want. Therefore, encoding messages should be good to take into account how the target audience decodes or interprets them. Messages should be sent through media that reach target audiences and feedback channels should be developed to assess the response to the message. A simplified approach of communication is shown in Figure 1.

Figure 1. Simple form of communication

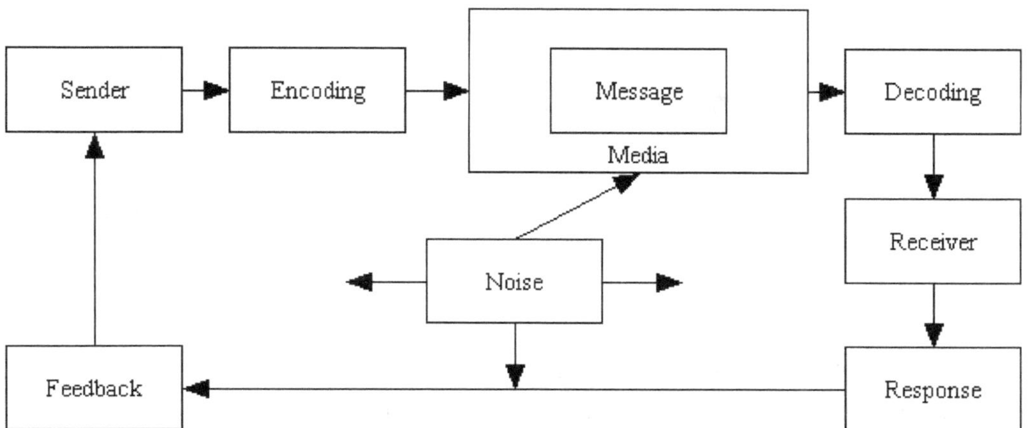

In real official communication processes managed by various organisations identifying the target audience is of crucial importance. To identify the target audience, instead of ad hod methods, the use of scientific methods is recommended for several reasons. Even more scientific research is common practice in every element of the communication process as shown in the Figure 2.

Once the target audience has been defined a decision should be made on the response sought. There can be interim and final responses as well. This brings us, again, to the scientific research, theory and methods of assessing the situation and scientific evaluation of processes.

In order to develop effective messages one should well define message content, i.e. what to say, message structure, i.e. how to say it logically, and message format, i.e. how to say it symbolically etc.

Figure 2. Role of research in official communication

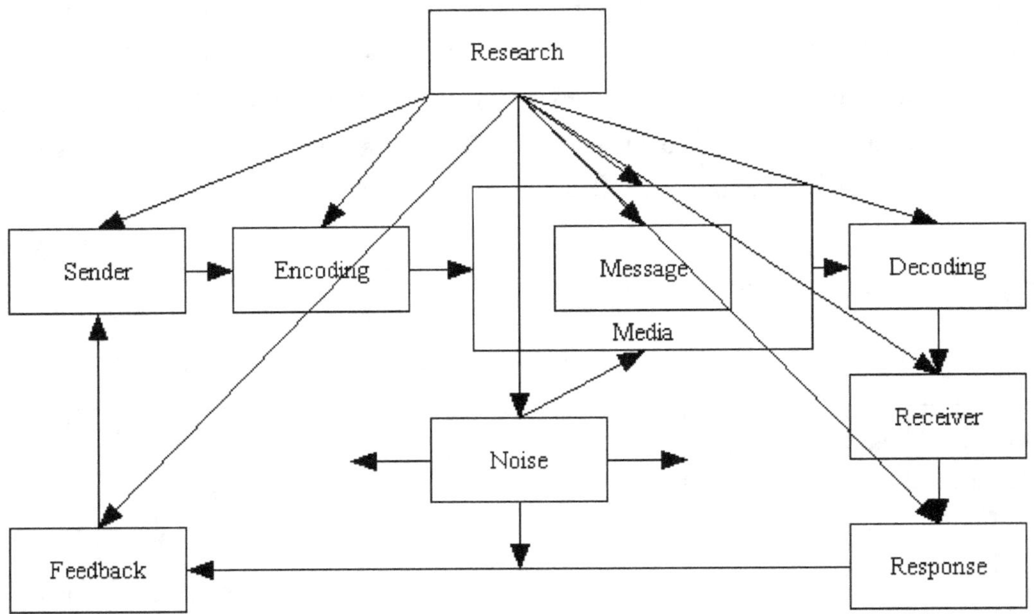

Communication not only needs a scientific approach in order to make it evidence based but is common practice. An amended and more realistic form of communication is shown in Figure 3.

This leads us to the realm of evidence based decision making and management. The first step in the preparation of a policy is a statement of what happens and then what should happen. Once a policy has been developed, systems must be designed to ensure that the policy is implemented. It has been proved in several occasions that evidence-based decision making has an important role in various policies, irrespective of the stage of the economic development of a given country.

The relevance of research as a tool for feedback remains true event if the decision maker's ignorance is, alas, related to the amount of available information as Ingelfinger put it, i.e. the larger amount the information, the larger the decision maker's ignorance (Ingelfinger, 1987). In addition, not only scientific knowledge tends sometimes to be misrepresented and misunderstood outside the boundaries of the scientific community, but scientists themselves do not always have a clear and consistent notion and understanding of what science covers, and often disagree profoundly on what it is telling us about the world – says John Zimon at the Cornell University (1992).

Figure 3. Role of research and communication in policy making

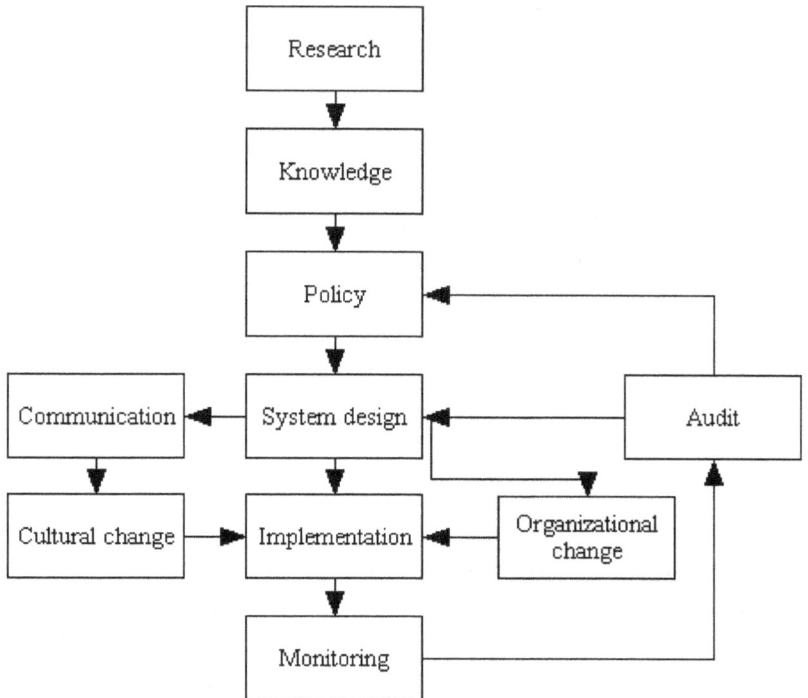

Research on population processes, e.g. migration, fertility etc. processes and decision-making resulted in a model developed by Fishbein and Ajzen that was then modified to include personal control. In this model not attitude but intention and behavior is in the focus. Behavior intention is predicted from three components: an attitudinal component or attitude toward performing the specific behavior, e.g. the use of a specific contraception, a normative component or the subjective norm, e.g. pertaining to a specific contraception, and a personal control element, i.e. a perceived behavioral control component. This model can be represented diagrammatically in a simple format (Figure 4).

Figure 4. Schematic representation of the Fishbein-Ajzen model adapted to include personal control

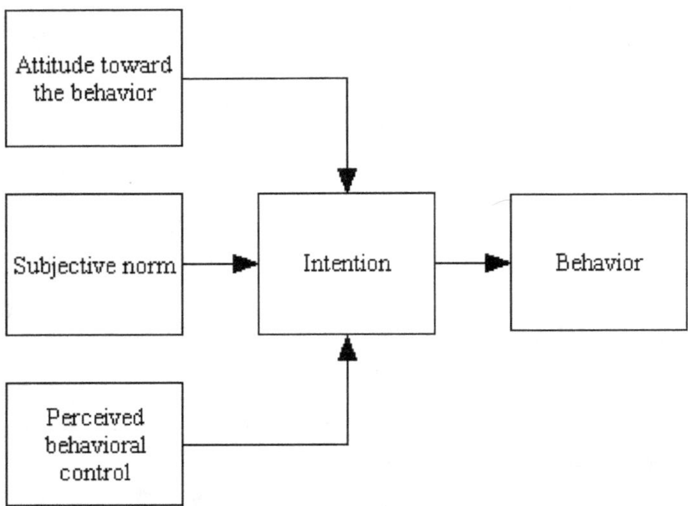

Social factors must also be incorporated in decision-making models, as they are to a certain extent in the Ajzen-Fishbein (or Fishbein-Ajzen) model. In addition to social influences, there are also individual factors that must be considered in decision-making. One of these individual factors is perceived control which also may be termed as controllability. So to the attitudinal and subjective norm component a perceived behavioral control component was added. For example individual considerations of the availability of contraceptive techniques should be entered into estimates of probabilities that contraceptive behavior will occur.

In order to reach the desired response to the message content there are three major types of appeal, i.e. rational, emotional and moral. Rational appeals are related to the audience's self interest, i.e. they show that the proposed attitude or action change will produce the desired benefits. Users of emotional appeals attempt to stir up emotions, negative or positive, that can motivate to change recent attitudes or actions. Moral appeals are directed to the audience's sense of what is right or proper.

Message structure should be decided if conclusions be drawn or left to the audience. Research results suggest that sometimes it is more effective to ask questions to stimulate involvement and motivate, and then letting them come to their own conclusions. Research results also suggest that a one-sided argument as opposed to a two-sided argument is more effective in many cases. However, presenting the strongest argument first gets strong attention but may lead to unfavorable ending.

Message format depends on the type of medium used. In printed format eye-catching pictures can make the message effective with great impact. A message carried over the radio the use of sounds and voices may be effective. On TV many different elements together with body language may be effective.

The effectiveness of the message source depends greatly on its credibility and attractiveness, and it is in the focus of ongoing research.

Two broad types of communication channels are personal and non-personal. In personal communication channels generally two or more people communicate directly with each other. Non-personal communication channels are media that carry messages without personal contact, i.e. newspapers, magazines, DM, radio, TV etc.

Important part of communication is social communication which primarily explores the ways information can be perceived, transmitted and understood, and the impact those ways will have on a society. Therefore social communication is politically and socially involved.

Computer-mediated communication is communication through computer-supported media (e-mail, chat, blogs etc.). This sort of communication, characterized with anonimity, privacy and security issues mainly focuses on social effects of different computer-supported communication technologies. Computer mediated communication has an effect on many different factors: impression formation, deception and lying behavior, group dynamics, disinhibition, and especially relationship formation.

A specific type of message presentation directly aims at influencing the opinion or behavior of people, rather than impartially providing information, in more and more subtle and insidious forms. Culturally it works in many different fields, including religions, politics, and economics in the form of mass communication.

Cross-cultural or intercultural communication is where people from differing cultural backgrounds communicate. Cross-cultural communication tries to bring together relatively unrelated areas e.g. cultural anthropology and communication in order to find a way of better communication of people from different cultures with each other (Béres I, Horányi Ö. 2001).

Global risk and fear from the future

Concerning global risk 9 October, 2006 is a special date, the day when humanity starts eating the planet, say experts of New Economics Foundation (NEF). New research reveals rising consumption of natural resources is pushing the world into ever earlier ecological debt, or 'overshoot'. New calculations show that from this date we will be living beyond our global environmental means. Research by the US-based Global Footprint Network in partnership with NEF and Best Foot Forward reveals that as of today, humanity has used up what nature can renew this year and is now eating into its 'ecological capital'. Each year, the day that the global economy starts to operate with an ecological deficit is designated as 'ecological debt day' (known internationally as 'overshoot day'). This marks the date that the planet's environmental resource flow goes into the red and we begin operating on a non-existent environmental overdraft. The fact that this year, ecological debt day falls on 9 October, only three quarters of the way through the year, means that we are living well beyond our environmental means. This leads, in effect, to a net depletion of the resources. From October 9 until the end of the year, humanity will be in ecological overshoot, building up ever greater ecological debt by consuming resources beyond the level that the planet's ecosystems can replace. This has been called, 'the biggest issue you've never heard of,' yet its causes and effects are simple and logical. If we eat more than we grow in any given year, we have to dip into reserves. If we cut trees faster than they grow back, then our forests become smaller than the year before. If we catch more fish than spawn each year, then there will be fewer fish in the sea.

The future of water and food is highly uncertain. "In the coming decades, the world's farmers will need to produce enough food to feed many millions more people, yet there are virtually no untapped, cost-effective sources of water for them to draw on as they face this challenge," say the authors of World Water and Food to 2025 research report (Coles 2003) at the International Food Policy Research Institute.

Plant and animal breeding programs in the Agricultural Experiment Stations brought major changes to agriculture in the twentieth century. In the first half of the twentieth century, these programs produced important productivity gains in the industrialized developed countries, with some achievements in sugar, tea, coffee, and spices in tropical developing countries, where both crop genetic improvement (CGI) and animal genetic improvement (AGI) gains were achieved. During the second half of the twentieth century (particularly after 1965), CGI gains in developing countries produced a "Green Revolution" affecting most developing countries. The Green Revolution and related agricultural productivity gains prevented a "Malthusian" outcome in global food markets in the wake of the major population expansion realized in virtually all developing countries after World War II. This Malthusian outcome in the form of high food prices and land scarcity, with attendant high land rents and prices, did not occur in the increasingly globalized economy. World prices of most agricultural crops in real terms declined after 1950. Many developing countries, particularly in Africa, however, have not realized a Green Revolution. These countries have also not achieved significant improvements in per capita income, although virtually all developing countries have realized improvements in child mortality rates, child malnutrition rates, and life expectancy. Increases in population density in rural areas were associated with changes in technology. A political "Boserup effect" was operative in many countries. This Boserup effect operated such that countries with low population densities invested little in CGI programs. As population increased, CGI investments increased. The Green Revolution is somewhat arbitrarily dated from 1965, when high-yielding or modern varieties (MVs) of both wheat and rice were first widely adopted in developing countries. These MVs are associated with the first two International Agricultural Research Centers (IARCs): the International Rice Research Institute (IRRI), located in the Philippines, and the International Center for the improvement of Wheat and Maize (CIMMYT), located in Mexico. But plant breeding programs in some developing countries were relatively advanced for some crops before 1965 (Evenson, 2004).

Several scholars, of whom Malthus is the most renown, hold the idea that a large, rapidly growing population is a factor associated with poverty. The difficult socioeconomic conditions in southern, developing countries together with their rapid population growth rates would seem to lend credibility to Malthusianism. It is important to know to what extent in developing countries populations can contribute to development. Thus, other authors, including Boserup, argue that it is often under challenging situations and constraints that societies are driven to conceive alternate strategies to improve their quality of life.

Populations are essentially forced to draw upon their creative powers in order to employ thus far underexploited, latent resources. The existence of a large market facilitates the growth of economies of scale at the population level, stimulates innovation, and therefore enables the growth of exchange and profit. Senegal is an example of a country constrained to continually do more to meet the health, education, nutrition, and labor needs of a large, young, and ever-growing population. Solutions to population problems in developing countries cannot be found in isolation (Lom, 1999).

Today, 800 million are starving because they cannot afford to buy food. However, 1.2 billion people lack access to safe water and 3 billion have inadequate sanitation. As a result 5 million people die from water-related diseases, including 2 million children younger than 5-years-old, according to the UN. Nearly two-thirds of world's people face water stress (Ashraf, 2003). "Unless potential water crises are averted, shortages of water could lead to future wars", warns a British cabinet official. Britain's International Development Secretary Clare Short said that nearly two-thirds of the world's population would be living in countries of significant water stress by the year 2025. "If we do not pay more attention to equitable water management we will see more conflict and war generated by water shortages," the secretary wrote in a report published by the Institute for Public Policy Research (Nearly… POPLINE. 2003 Mar-Apr).
Using sophisticated computer modeling, researchers created a `business as usual' scenario, showing projections to 2025 if present policy and investment trends continue. They also devised `water crisis' and `sustainable water' scenarios. Two of the three scenarios project a world where there is simply not enough water to go round Hodur (2003).

Unsustainable demographic processes of global population is a serious risk for sustainability of human and earth ecosystems. Population growth, changing birth control, problems of migration, nuptiality, poverty, health crisis, ageing, mortality and various forms of inequality in these demographic processes are serious challenges to the human population as well as to the earth ecosystems. Managing these demographic processes is crucial from the point of sustainability. To make demographic processes sustainable scientific research and communication should be put in a new way and be used more effectively. To influence current demographic processes research and communication must be made effectively as it has already made by the POPLINE Staff of the INFO Project at the Johns Hopkins

Bloomberg School of Public Health, Center for Communication Programs and is funded primarily by the United States Agency for International Development.

Control of demographic processes in order to ensure sustainability can be summarized in a simple diagram with an emphasis on research and communication (Figure 5).

The flowchart starts with a block, i.e. the philosophy of risk. In futurology, existential risk is both global and terminal. The term is used to describe disaster and doomsday scenarios caused by present sources of danger. The *end of the world* philosophers has spelt out the ways in which extinction of life might be the result.

Some say "God is dead" which is a widely quoted statement by Nietzsche. Others refer to the tragedy of the commons formulated in game theory, a class of phenomena that involve a conflict for resources between individual interests and the common good. Several other philosophical concepts may influence the various approaches to find a solution to the current demographic trends.

Long term demographic crisis is closely related to unsustainable population growth, uncontrolled birth, mass migration, poverty, and health crisis in the world. Risk communication is of crucial importance to manage long term demographic crisis.

Short term demographic crises often emerge. Around the wold, conflicts and natural disasters challenge health care providers to meet people's basic needs, including reproductive health care, under the most difficult conditions. Every year armed conflicts and natural disasters kill hundreds of thousands of people and inflict great suffering. Armed conflicts tear societies apart and disrupt people's lives, often for years. Natural disasters devastate whole regions without warning, as the December 2004 Asian tsunami, the August 2005 New Orleans hurricane, and the October 2005 Pakistan earthquake demonstrated. Health care systems, often struggling to meet people's needs in the best of times, can be quickly overwhelmed by the added burden of injury and infectious diseases.

At the same time, health systems themselves may be crippled by disaster or conflict. As of 2005 some 45 countries, predominantly in Africa and Asia, faced crises related to armed conflicts or natural disasters. Nearly 40 million people have fled their homes as a result of conflict and now are living as refugees outside their countries or, more often, as displaced people within their own countries.

Figure 5. Control of demographic processes with research and communication

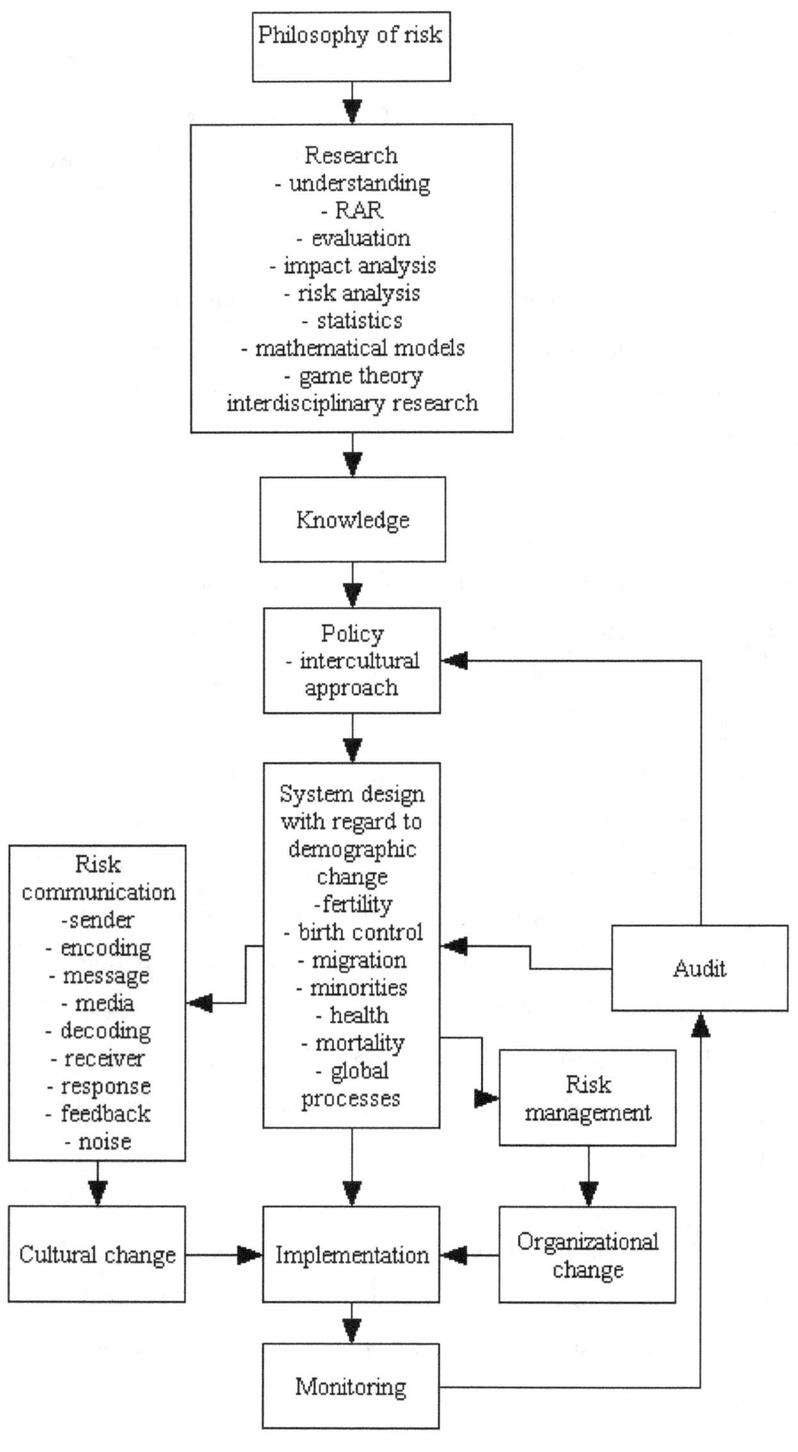

Natural disasters affect millions more. According to the United Nations refugees can formally be distinguished from internally displaced persons, according to whether or not they have crossed an international border. However, this distinction is not necessarily important from the point of risk.

Whatever their status, people who have been uprooted by armed conflicts or natural disasters have similar needs for protection, food, shelter, and health care, including reproductive health care. No international treaty defines responsibility for the protection of people displaced within their own country, however, as is the case for international refugees.

There is a common perception of refugees as people crowded into camps with few amenities. In reality, people living in refugee camps are usually better off than refugees who are dispersed within local communities. Food, water, and basic health care are more likely to be available in camps. Where refugees are dispersed, their status and needs are unknown, and it is more difficult for relief organisations to meet their emergency needs. Out of sight of international relief agencies, these people must depend on existing local services for health care and other needs.

Conventionally, in crisis situation, humanitarian and relief workers have focused on providing basic emergency services such as food, water, shelter, security, and primary health care, with a focus on controlling infectious diseases. These are priorities in a major emergency because many lives are at risk. Reproductive health care is also a serious public health issue in crises. More attention to reproductive health care, and to providing it immediately, particularly emergency obstetric care save lives in refugee settings.

Meeting a range of reproductive health needs in a crisis is crucial, including safe motherhood, protection from and response to sexual and gender-based violence, prevention and treatment of STIs including HIV/AIDS, family planning, and adolescent reproductive health. After the tsunami 400,000 refugees sought shelter in camps around Banda Aceh, Indonesia. An estimated 25,000 people of these were pregnant women. The local health care system could do little for them, however, because the tsunami had destroyed most of clinics and killed most of the midwives.

In many developing countries maternal mortality is one of the leading causes of death among women of reproductive age. In most crisis situations about 15 percent of pregnant women suffer life-threatening complications of pregnancy and delivery, about the same percentage as among pregnant women in general. But maternal complications are far riskier for women in crisis situations. The majority of refugee women are in countries where pregnancy can represent a serious health threat even in normal times. In crisis situations the need for emergency services to treat obstetric complications is acute, both because trauma, malnutrition, and psychological distress are widespread and because many health care personnel and facilities are no longer available.

Among Afghan refugees in camps in Pakisthan as compared to those who died other causes, those who died of maternal causes had faced *greater* barriers to health care. These barriers included failure to recognize the problem, the decision of family members not to seek care, lack of emergency transport to a health facility, and not receiving good quality, timely treatment.

Armed conflict and its aftermath unleash widespread sexual and gender-based violence, i.e. acts of violence committed against females because they are female and against males because they are male. Sexual and gender-based violence includes sexual violence, domestic violence, emotional and psychological abuse, sex trafficking, forced prostitution, sexual exploitation, sexual harassment, harmful traditional practices such as female genital cutting and forced marriage, and discriminatory practices.

The victims are most often women and girls, although men and boys are also subject to sexual violence. Violence occurs during all phases of conflicts, before and during flight, in camps, and during repatriation. In particular, rape used as a weapon of war has been documented in Algeria, Bangladesh, Bosnia and Herzegovina, Indonesia, Liberia, Rwanda, and Uganda.

While rape and other forms of sexual and gender-based violence take place in all societies at all times, conflicts often increase the incidence. The main factors behind increased sexual and gender-based violence are loss of security, psychological trauma, ethnic tensions, and the breakdown of family and community life. Other factors including overcrowding in camps and predominantly male camp leadership who do not see preventing gender-based violence as a high priority. In some instances peacemakers and humanitarian workers have been the perpetrators, exchanging food for sex by threatening to withhold food rations.

Domestic violence also wells up in many refugee settings. Men compensate for the loss of control over their lives by exerting violent control over their spouses. In some cases, domestic violence is more common than violence by those outside the family. For instance among conflict-affected population in East-Timor, nearly half of women reported abuse by intimate partners, both during the crisis and afterwards. By comparison, 24 percent of women reported violence by perpetrators outside the family during the crisis, and 6 percent after the crisis. During the crisis the perpetrators outside the family were mainly militia members, soldiers, and police. After the crisis about two-thirds of perpetrators were neighbors or other community members.

Conditions in refugee camps can expose women and girls to violence. In some camps women must wait in line to fetch water until late into the night, when they are vulnerable to attacks. Sexual attacks occur when women are doing other daily chores, too, such as collecting firewood in isolated areas, or when they have to use latrines in remote parts of the camp. Young children are also vulnerable to sexual predators when they are either separated from their families or are left unprotected in camps.

Of the 45 major crisis zones in the world, 28 are in Africa and 12 are in Asia. These are the continents where HIV/AIDS is most prevalent. Coupled with crisis situations, HIV and other STIs can spread rapidly, especially where HIV prevalence is already high. Poverty, powerlessness, food insecurity, and displacement often make refugees more vulnerable to sexual transmission of HIV. For example, in Liberia the prevalence of HIV was estimated at about 8 percent before the civil war. The war brought widespread sexual violence, including mass rapes and abduction of women and girls to act as sex slaves for soldiers. STI screenings after the war showed that 93 percent of male combatants and 83 percent of female combatants had at least one STI. Projecting from these high STI rates, health care providers in the country now estimate that HIV prevalence is much higher than before the war.

Family planning is as much in demand as it was beforehand. Yet refugees may have far less access to contraception because services and supplies have been disrupted. The result can be more unintended pregnancies and rising abortion rates. Also women who rely on contraceptive methods that require continual supplies, such as pills or injectables, may have to discontinue use abruptly when they flee their communities. Many women who use IUDs or implants no longer have access to safe removal and replacement.

Worldwide approximately 6.6 million adolescents are displaced by armed conflict. In crisis situations social support networks weaken and often break down entirely. Adolescents, especially girls, are at particular risk of forced sex and of sexual coercion in exchange for food, shelter, and protection.

In crisis situations unsafe sex and other risk-taking among youth often increase. In a refugee camp in the Republic of Congo, girls as young as 10 to 12 years old were reported to be sexually active, often with adult men. In a refugee camp in Kenya, despite the availability of free condoms and other reproductive health care about 70 percent of young men and women had unplanned sex without condoms.

What can local health care providers do when crisis strikes? Planning ahead, i.e. making emergency preparedness plans is of importance that consider staffing, logistics, supplies, infrastructure, establishing relationships with news media, and coordination with other organisations. Coordination is desirable but takes time, while health needs are urgent and great. It is very important to offer care immediately if a crisis occurs. Offer whatever skills, services, and knowledge is available. Focus should be made on refugees not living in camps. Refugees dispersed among the host communities need as much help as refugees in camps, and local organisations may be able to serve them better than relief agencies can. Some refugees may be health professionals themselves. Often they can contribute their skills to care for others. When the international relief workers leave, local health care organisations and providers take back the full responsibility for serving people's needs. With adequate support, capable health care services with a strong reproductive health care component can speed the transition from relief to recovery.

Formidable changes and challenges to the earth ecosystem and demographic processes has great impact on issues of philosophy, science, methodology and communication. Although empiricism, i.e. scientific knowledge that is closely related to experience, and induction, a basis of current scientific reasoning, does not give a solution to every problem of the earth. Modern scientific reasoning heavily relies on induction, i.e. data collection and statistical analysis of data. However, other sorts of scientific reasoning have their value as well. Although nontraditional approach in science could be useful in some cases in scientific research., the discussion of this in more detail would lead us far from our present topic of evidence based communication programs in managing world demographic problems.

Risk management

Practical management of risk is generally more detailed (Figure 6.) and fits in a global and local overall risk management framework.

Figure 6. Practical management of risk

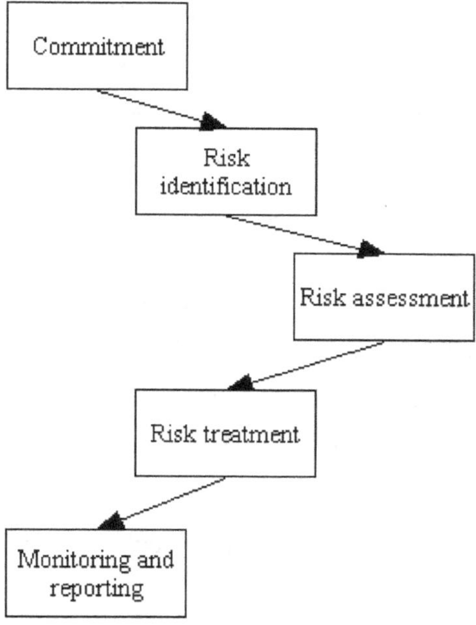

In risk management practice various types of generic risk is defined, and an attempt is made to manage these risks. For example strategy risk may be that a given strategy does not facilitate the delivery of services required and expected. Disaster risk is about external or environmental events adversely affecting continuity of activities. Human resources risk is about poor staff skills and inappropriate staff conduct that adversely affects performance. Information risk is about loss of integrity of data due to inaccuracy, delay or breach of confidentiality. Legal risk is about breach of legal requirements in the effective jurisdiction. Market risk is a direct or indirect loss resulting from the impact of market positions due to fluctuations in various market factors such as prices, interest rates and exchange rates etc. Operational risk is about the direct or indirect loss resulting from inadequate or failed internal processes, people and systems or from external events. Reputation risk is about a decline in reputation resulting in damaged credibility or loss of business. System risk about risk of errors or business interruption due to the failure of or lack of integrity on IT and other systems.

In risk management an assessment is made for risk considered in standard risk register in that the likelihood and consequence is listed. A consequence descriptor is also created with the amount of estimated consequence on estimated safety (minor injuries, major injuries, single fatality, multiple fatalities, i.e. 10s, multiple fatalities, i.e. 100s etc., and the nature of environmental, financial, reputation and legal losses. Also embedded monitors and early warning indicators are described that management rely on to determine whether their risk management activities are effective. Inherent and residual level risks are plotted separately on two different grids known as the profiling matrix. This matrix has rows and columns with the consequence and their likelihood to occur. Such a matrix show categorized urgent and less urgent fields of activity, and those fields that need to be monitored.

Risk treatment on the basis of structured above information generally means reduction of level of exposure by taking mitigating actions to reduce the impact or likelihood, sharing or transfer, i.e. by contracting out to a third party or via insurance, avoidance or elimination, i.e. by ceasing the activity or exiting the place, and ultimately acceptance. Detailed action plans should then be agreed and people made accountable for delivering. It is not recommended to behave in a way which suggests disparity between values of organisations and people, ignore risks from external parties, fail to act promptly if people raise concerns on matters, fail to act on feedback and shoot the messenger.

Risk communication

There is a special type of communication called risk communication which is of crucial importance from the point of controlling risk, which is related to several current processes including risk of the living earth and demographic processes. The concept of risk can be interpreted in at least two distinct ways. There are two positions in the philosophical debate over risk. Some people, the positivists think that risk is a purely scientific concept admitting complete characterization and analysis through data collection and quantitative methods.

Other people, the relativists think that risk is a purely subjective reaction to phenomena encountered in personal or social experience. The positivist interprets risk as referring objectively to the circumstances of the physical world. The relativist takes risk to a purely mental construct expressing emotional, moral or political reactions. Certainly both parties have its right. The positivists approach of risk can be primarily expressed in terms of probability and money loss. The relativists approach of risk can be better expressed in terms of psychological scales.

Risk communication has a strong link to communicating in a crisis. Establishing a relationship with the news media is critical. As part of disaster preparedness, governments and humanitarian agencies have or should have a plan of working with news media in crisis situations. In times of conflict and natural disaster, radio and other media can provide survivors with information about the security situation and about where to find shelter, food and water, and health services, including reproductive health care. The broadcast media may well be the only working means of communicating with the public.

Communication concerning demographic issues is related to adult education, which is the practice of teaching and educating adults. Educating adults differs from educating children in several ways. One of the most important differences is that adults have accumulated knowledge and experience which can either add value to a learning experience or hinder it. Another important difference is that adults frequently must apply their knowledge in some practical fashion in order to learn effectively; there must be a goal and a reasonable expectation that the new knowledge will help them further that goal.

A focus on community-based preparedness is replacing the conventional approach of training in imminent crisis situations. Disaster preparedness training can help international and local health care providers and government officials respond quickly and effectively when a disaster or crisis occurs. Many countries offer disaster preparedness training through the International Committee of the Red Cross. An example is the „Health Emergencies in large populations (H.E.L.P.) course, a three-week module focused on reproductive health that gives providers the tools to make decisions in large-scale emergency situations.

Information technology is widely used in communication. In particular, IT deals with the use of electronic computers and computer software to convert, store, protect, process, transmit, and retrieve information. The growth of use of information and communications technology (ICT) and its tools in the field of education has seen tremendous growth in the recent past.

However, communication in crisis is not easy, since crises pose enormous difficulties in the society. In a crisis situation services are disrupted. In a crisis situation transportation and communications are often disrupted, distribution networks dissolve, and infrastructure is partly or completely destroyed.

The local health care system itself may have suffered severely. Hospitals may have been looted, and medical staff may have fled or been killed. Providers may even face armed factions that want to take control of health care facilities. The post-conflict period often remains unstable, as security is lacking and permanent peace appears uncertain.

When a crisis strikes, reproductive health programs often cannot accomodate the huge numbers of refugees who urgently need services. For example, during the Great Lakes crisis in Africa in the early 1990s, one million Rwandans fled their homes in just a few days to surrounding Zaire, Tanzania, Burundi, and Uganda, countries that had limited health services to begin with. The sheer number of people was enough to overwhelm the capacity of any agency.

Crises come on top of existing problems. Since most conflicts occur in developing countries, where health conditions often are poor, many displaced groups already suffer from ill health, including malnutrition and STIs. Moreover, most refugees have few possessions left and cannot afford to buy health care, food, or much else.

Most communities are surprised by a natural disaster and have little chance of responding adequately, unless they have emergency plans, already in place. In contrast, conflicts usually result from worsening political or social conditions, which may provide warning before the situation deteriorates into violence and chaos.

Conflicts are unstable, preventing providers from responding effectively. Episodes of tension and violence can punctuate periods of relative calm. In contrast, in a natural disaster the extent of the damage can be determined, and relief workers and providers can respond more quickly.

Conflicts by definition involve groups fighting each other. One of more of the opposing sides, including the government, may have no regard for the health and welfare of the refugees. Refugee camps are not sanctuaries and have been attacked. Health care staff themselves can be the targets of armed groups. In contrast, a natural disaster often evokes an outpouring of support, and the government of the affected country takes on the responsibility of mounting a response. As a result, survivors of natural disasters often receive more aid and support than survivors of armed conflicts.

Conflicts force some people to live as refugees for years. In contrast, natural disasters displace most people for weeks or months rather than years, although the damage and disruption may take a long time to repair.

Improving organisation work

Managing world demographic problems include organising work often in developing countries in many different fields. These fields include organising the work of family planning, health care, relief and other organisations. These organisations in developing countries must do more with the same resources, and sometimes with fewer. Organising or reorganising their work for greater efficiency and better services in such circumstances is crucial. Improving the organisation of work need not be time-consuming, complicated, or expensive. A focus on meeting people's needs increasingly guides service delivery. Nine key elements of service delivery can be identified in which the organisation of work approach can be applied to better meet clients' needs, including services, health and reproductive health care needs.

1. Use of evidence-based practices. Organisations that base practices on the best available evidence can remove needless barriers to care and deliver better quality services.
2. Adaptability. Foresight and flexibility enable managers to deal with the fluctuations common to service delivery.
3. Links with other services and sites. Good referral systems help organisations provide access to a complete range of services.
4. Minimizing paperwork, maximizing information use. Collecting and using only those data necessary to make decisions reduces time-consuming paperwork.
5. Physical factors. Service providers can make better use of space and resources to ensure well-organised, well-stocked, and comfortable facilities.

6. Service hours and scheduling. Both clients and providers benefit when scheduling takes their needs into consideration.
7. Client flow. Improving how clients move through the health or other facility can shorten waits and provide more time for clients and providers to interact.
8. Division of labor and job design. Service providers and managers can be more productive and satisfied when all know their responsibilities and have authority to carry them out.
9. Social factors. Leadership, staff development, and open lines of communication motivate and support the staff, which is a key resource of the organisation.

From these nine key elements in the following parts evidence-based practices, minimizing paper-work, maximizing information use, and the social factors of communication will be considered briefly.

Use of evidence-based practices

Various demographic and health care programs increasingly use an evidence-based approach, i.e. they base guidelines, standards, and practices on scientific evidence of safety, effectiveness, and efficiency. Adopting evidence-based procedures and practices can eliminate unnecessary barriers to service provision and so deliver services better. Principles for using evidence-based practices include the use of most up-to-date interventions and approaches, avoidance of unproven practices, which waste time and resources, and adopt those that have an impact, and remove unnecessary barriers that hinder access to service or care.

The use of most up-to-date interventions and approaches means knowing and adopting approaches that are based on the best available evidence that enable organisations to provide the most effective services, health and reproductive health care efficiently. Evidence-based guidelines, i.e. norms, standards, protocols, and practice recommendations, help service providers make good decisions about specific aspects of care, such as diagnosing health problems or providing appropriate family planning methods.

The World Health Organisation (WHO) has developed the Medical Eligibility Criteria, which provide guidance regarding who can safely use contraceptive methods, as well as the Selected Practice Recommendations, which provide guidance regarding how safely and effectively use methods. This guidance is based on available evidence on the safety and use of contraceptives. It expands access to family planning services by helping ensure that people are not inappropriately denied a full choice of suitable methods.

Conclusive scientific studies of efficacy and safety are not always available to justify every health care practice. Organisations can try to stay up-to-date on whatever scientifically valid guidelines are available nationally, and then modify them to suit the local context and resources. In the absence of scientific evidence, organisations should continue to base practices on experience and logical assumptions or adapt practices used elsewhere.

The avoidance of unproven practices, which waste time and resources means, among other things, that programs that replace outdated guidelines with evidence-based practices can provide services more effectively. By using evidence-based practices, managers can avoid practices that do not work well or create unnecessary costs.

The adoption of those practices that have an impact means that examinations, standards, eligibility criteria, or practices that have no scientifically demonstrable value may be eliminated from practice. Unnecessary barriers that hinder access to service or care arise for many reasons. Service delivery guidelines that shape provider practices may be outdated. Providers may misinterpret or ignore service delivery guidelines and instead impose barriers based on gender or race or impose inappropriate contraindication to use a method.

Minimizing paper-work, maximizing information use means that collection of data what is needed, but no more is recommended. At every level of a health, reproductive health or related communication program, collecting up-to-date, reliable, and relevant information is crucial to analysing operations, solving problems, identifying trends, setting goals, and using resources wisely. However, collecting too much data can waste time, produce unnecessary paperwork, and obscure rather than illuminate decision-making.

The information that managers and service providers collect should directly be related to the decisions that they must make. Collecting only essential data reduces paperwork. Managers and service providers can decide what data to collect by looking at organisational objectives and selecting indicators that measure achievement of them. However, district or provincial program managers need more than just local data. Managers of larger organisations may need even more data and sophisticated data storage, data retrieval, data processing, and data communication methods, including database management, SQL queries, exploratory, confirmatory, multivariate, computer-intensive statistical methods, and the use of geographic information systems (GIS).

Managers should be able both to analyse the data they collect and to act on it. Once collected, the data should be tabulated and summarized in reports that facilitate access and analysis. To be useful, data must be converted into information that can be easily understood and delivered to the program staff who are able to apply it in decision-making.

The more relevant that data are to program staff members' job, the more that staff are likely to collect data accurately and on time. When they understand how program data can be used to identify problems or improve services, staff are more likely to make use of data. Charts and diagrams can help.

Managers can show service providers the importance and meaning of data by providing feedback on the data collected and used. Feedback also displays appreciation for staff efforts and motivates staff to maintain the information system regularly.

Social factors in communication for organising better services
The principles of social factors in communication for organising better services include the provision of leadership and motivation, development of staff potential, and enabling positive human relationships.

Leadership is vital to performance. Leaders inspire people through their own positive behavior, ethics, and values and thus serve as role models. Their shared vision provides staff with purpose and direction in their work.

Managers who are leaders motivate staff and encourage them to take responsibility for solving problems and improving services. They improve morale and performance by giving encouraging feedback and helping staff to see how their jobs benefit clients and enable the organisation to achieve its goals. They also organise people to work together collaboratively and effectively.

Program staff are more satisfied and perform better when they know that the organisation is committed to their personal and professional development. The organisation can encourage staff to improve their skills and their performance continually through training and job aids. Skills training can even empower staff to make decisions without the need for guidance from supervisors. Managers can also provide rewards and recognition for good performance.

Relevance of feedback in project management and communication

In management and communication for organising better services feedback is crucial. Even in small-scale projects to perform well, staff members need to know how they are doing compared with expectations for their job. Managers can clarify what is expected by preparing and distributing guidelines and by writing job descriptions and discussing them with staff. Feedback on job performance can come not only from supervisors' evaluations but also from clients' comments and from self- and peer-assessments.

Service providers need to be able to interact and communicate well with their clients, as well as with their supervisors and co-workers. When clients and service providers communicate openly, share information, and ask and answer questions freely, clients are more satisfied and understand and recall information better. Staff members who are able to communicate openly with their supervisors and co-workers can do their jobs better.

Without appropriate feedback management and communication will fail and the project will not be efficient and successful.

In large-scale demographic and communication projects the role and relevance of feedback is crucial. In large-scale projects vast resources are used and thousands or millions of people are affected. In such cases management and communication of the project cannot be made without appropriate feedback based on scientific research.

Improving organisation work in large-scale demographic and communication projects with feedback

In large-scale demographic and communication projects feedback of project management and project communication is provided by evidence. Evidence is given by the use of scientific methods. Scientific research methods include well-established data collection methods i.e.

sampling plans, sample size determination, statistical data analytic methods and other methods, all of them are subject to rigorous quality insurance criteria.

Feedback for risk management and risk communication is vital. Evidence-based communication in risk is of crucial importance since both on objective and subjective ground there are large challenges to sustainable development. Climate change, global warming, drought, acid rains, air pollution, diminishing of clear drinking water, destroyed natural habitats, threatened and extinct species, degraded soil, deforestation, highest in rate in history, polluted air and water, increasing amount of hazardous waste material production, increasing global population growth, increasing consumption, propelled by new technologies and globalization, ageing populations and increasing poverty pose serious dangers and risk to earth ecosystems. In such case communication can only be made on scientific grounds and with appropriate feedback. This feedback relies heavily on research and research methods.

Feedback for management and communication of critical demographic processes

Current methodology tackles traditional research methods in such a way that they be able to be used even in crisis situations. For example the Rapid Assessment and Response Technique (RAR) is a method to assess and rapidly respond to issues especially in situations where there is scarcity of information and data are needed very quickly. Instead of using the heavy and traditional armament of traditional scientific method RAR uses, among other things the triangulation method, which is a process of collecting and cross-checking information. From time to time research resources deal with useful inference from nonrandom samples. Creative and critical voices are worth considering when scientific research is applied (Stimson et al., 2003).

Rapid Assessment and Response

The Rapid Assessment and Response Technique is a method to assess and rapidly respond to a wide range of issues. It is particularly useful for complex issues, where individual and group behaviors are major factors.

Rapid assessment methods have the potential to give information which can be used to plan and develop various policies and programs, and to deliver and improve services. This approach is typically used in situations where data are needed very quickly.

RAR is used to help make decisions about appropriate interventions for various demographic, social and health issues. Rapid Assessment and Response (RAR) is a technique for the assessment of an issue in a particular study area, including the characteristics of the problem, population groups affected, settings and contexts, demographic, social, health and risk behaviors, and social consequences. It identifies existing resources and opportunities for intervention, and helps plan, develop and implement interventions. Until quite recently there was no structured framework for guiding such assessments. However, rapid assessments offer such a solution. Historically, it was typical for external consultants to be recruited by various organisations to undertake assessments, drawing on their past experience and receiving guidance from local individuals. The product of the assessment generally was a report with recommendations. Reports varied in scope, content, quality and perspective depending on the consultant and the approach.

In social and health projects various problems often emerged faster than conventional research or surveillance could map them, and conventional research was often feasible due to little research capacity.
RAR can be undertaken within a locality, i.e. city, country region, country or region.

Demographic, social and health issues are diverse and vary from country to country, between areas, between social groups, and can change over time. They are influenced by social, cultural, political, religious and economic factors. Views on public health, and means for delivering public health interventions, also vary. Interventions developed in one place may need to be modified to be used elsewhere. Therefore, before investing in interventions and policy changes it is essential to understand the nature of problems, affected populations and settings, and factors influencing them, identify resources and identify socially, culturally, religiously, politically and economically appropriate interventions. (An intervention is any action that is taken to help reduce a problem, help an affected population, change a particular setting, or change a risk behavior.) Interventions may be inappropriate unless developed from a proper assessment of the situation, perhaps with the RAR methodology. RAR is undertaken when there is already a commitment to intervene. RAR also has a role in that the research itself can alert governments and communities about the need for action, and the kinds of interventions that may be implemented.

RAR uses a simple model to identify the different levels of influence on risk behaviors. This is important for identifying the levels of assessment and levels at which interventions may be developed. Levels generally are structural, i.e. social, economic, political legal, religious, cultural environment, community, i.e. local networks, setting culture, norms, and individual, i.e. knowledge, attitudes, preferences, behaviors.

Structural factors are generally beyond the influence of the community or the individual and include social, economic and political conditions, laws, religion, and the culture of the society. Interventions at the structural level include: laws, policies, taxation, health systems and health systems financing (including how resources are allocated for health).

Community factors are external to the individual but located in their immediate environment, such as the social networks to which they belong; the norms, beliefs and values that are shared with friends and other local people. At the individual level there is the person's social-psychological situation including their knowledge, attitudes, behaviors and so on. Interventions at the individual level include: treatment and care.

Many community problems occur in settings where there is little assessment capacity. Some problems can emerge, develop and change quickly. Many of the major problems facing the world today are linked with culturally sensitive behaviors or occur in groups that are hard to contact. Conducting proper assessment and developing appropriate responses therefore raises major challenges. It is necessary to: assess the extent and nature of problems and associated health behaviors, risks and harms identify resources and opportunities for intervention identify socially, culturally, politically, and economically appropriate interventions identify factors that impede or enhance the effectiveness of interventions develop action plans for interventions and implement them conventional demographic, social and health surveillance have limitations that prevent appropriate and timely interventions, including long term perspective, high cost, slow or delayed response, production of information that is difficult to communicate to policy makers and inappropriate for developing interventions, lack of engagement with, and participation of, local communities, affected populations and other stakeholders, inability to translate findings into action. RAR addresses these limitations by producing rapid results, bridging the gap between assessment and public health response, building local alliances through involving local communities, affected populations and other stakeholders, initiating sustained action and developing local capacity for assessment and intervention development.

RAR has certain features or principles that distinguish it from conventional scientific surveillance. Time is vital when tackling social and health problems, which may occur more rapidly than can be assessed by public health surveillance or in the time it takes to undertake conventional research. A typical RAR is completed within 12 weeks or a relatively short time period.

RAR uses techniques that have a high output of information in relation to input of research effort. There is a preference for readily available or cheaper sources of information, rather than expensive surveillance systems and large surveys.

RAR is used to assist the development of interventions. The utility of a RAR may be judged by its adequacy for decision making, rather than increasing scientific knowledge for academic purposes.

RAR identifies and involves local stakeholders, including those with a responsibility for developing interventions. RARs encourage community participation to increase the practical relevance and applicability of the assessment.

New data gathering exercises such as surveys are undertaken only where the existing sources of information are inadequate. RARs use existing information to describe and understand the local situation and use this description to identify gaps in knowledge. The gaps are then filled using other research methods to collect new data.

RAR combines methods and sources of data. A single method or source of data cannot encompass all aspects of complex social problems, particularly those that are sensitive and tend to be hidden.

RARs do not only aim to answer a series of set questions in a particular order, or test a number of predetermined hypotheses in a set way. Instead, a RAR will usually consider and investigate questions and hypotheses as they emerge during the collection of data. This process of critically examining and responding to the data collected is ongoing. In this way, it differs from some forms of research that adopt a more strictly linear or pre-planned approach. Flexibility through induction, which is the process of drawing conclusions and developing hypotheses from the data collected, and searching for information that confirms, denies or modifies these conclusions and hypotheses, is a vital part of the RAR process that is often overlooked. A more traditional approach to research (defining a hypothesis and testing it according to a set procedure or protocol) is of less value to understanding complex health behaviors than a more flexible, inductive approach.

There is a need to see the problem in the social, cultural, religious, political and historical context. RARs commonly move across several levels of investigation, i.e. individual, community and structural in order to identify different levels for intervention. All societies are in a state of dynamic change, particularly those in developing countries. Problems may be emerging or rapidly developing and may be linked beyond the community level with structural and economic features of these countries.

Findings and conclusions are established through cross-checking multiple sources of data, sometimes referred to as data triangulation. (Triangulation is a process of collecting and cross-checking information throughout the RAR. Triangulation compares information collected by different methods and from different data sources until the researcher is confident of the validity and representativeness of the information, and of the diversity, conflicts and contradictions within a society.) RAR methods are potentially more rigorous, reliable and valid, than investigations that use a single research method or data source.

RAR is made with generally accepted scientific methodology well known from many other sources. It consists of the traditional steps of needs assessment, team formation, planning, identifying priority for action, initial community consultation, identification of parameters of RAR, establishment of community consultation process, building and training the RAR team, conducting advocacy, development of RAR plan, undertaking the field work, and translating the findings into action plan. This is in line with the flexible and investigative nature of the RAR methodology. Identification of the issue as a priority for action includes examination of data that may demonstrate a significant demographic problem, an identification of significant gaps (e.g. limited services etc.), demands from the public or specific interest groups, funding for a specific activity, politicians, community groups or other decision makers raising the issue. RARs may be initiated by a variety of interest groups or stakeholders, such as international, government or local government organisations, non-governmental organisations, research institutions, service providers or by members of the affected group. Translating findings into actions is a sensitive field. There is no doubt that the proposal of interventions that are effective and acceptable to the community is the primary objective of the RAR. An action plan describes the activities suitable for responding to the situation at hand. These are not restricted to the establishment of new measures, but also include the refinement of existing services and policies, or the termination of ineffective programs and activities. Elaboration of an action plan relies on a skillfully moderated debate with the RAR team, sponsors, potential donors and key decision makers, such as the government. RAR provides a structure for operationalizing each key finding, including delineating general responses, identifying possible interventions, determining the relevance and effectiveness of such interventions as well as their feasibility and possible obstacles. The success of the RAR will be assessed on whether effective interventions have been put in place as a result . The report may act as an important advocacy tool for gaining support and funding for activities. It is not necessary to wait for the final report before implementing interventions. Interventions should be developed and implemented as soon as adequate information is obtained from the RAR to inform an appropriate response.

Evaluation enables the government and the community to assess how interventions are working and whether they are worthwhile. Evaluation, especially impact analysis for program evaluation is a circular process of assessment informing intervention implementation, with monitoring and evaluation refining the assessment and further development of interventions.

The principles to developing rapid and effective responses can be applied to many public problems including assessment, innovation and pragmatism, application of a hierarchical approach, developing multi-level and integrated strategies, facilitating behavior change, changing service delivery, changing the setting, public perceptions and attitudes and the structural environment, and community participation. Types of intervention may include provision of information, distribution of materials, education, training and skills development, community-based activities, organisational and environmental development, regulatory activities and changes in the law, and treatment of the problem at hand.

The assessment of the consequences of a program can be made at the:

- Individual level (individual behaviors, activities and situations),

- Community level (how community norms effect or exacerbate social consequences for individuals and populations), and

- Structural level (how policy, law and the environment influence social consequences, what impact do local and national policies have on the social consequences for particular problems, health and risk behaviors or population groups).

The assessment of the intervention provides an overall description of the types, extent and nature of current interventions and finally is summarized in an action plan.

An integral and indispensable part of RAR is evaluation of the program.

Evaluation and impact analysis is the systematic application of social research procedures for assessing the design, implementation, and utility of interventions.

Examples of using RAR in population studies

A rapid assessment and response adaptation guide on HIV and men who have sex with men has been prepared. In an adaptation guide for work with men who have sex with men guidelines are offered on how to conduct a Rapid Assessment and Response (RAR) focusing on lifestyles, behaviors and HIV/AIDS concerns. The guideline outlines a series of simple and practical activities that may be used to explore the circumstances, experiences and needs of men who have sex with men across a variety of settings. It is designed to be used either in conjunction with the WHO Rapid Assessment and Response Technical Guide (TG-RAR) or as an independent resource. This manual offers guidelines on carrying out an RAR with men who have sex with men. Specific guidance is offered on understanding HIV/AIDS prevention among men who have sex with men, planning of an RAR on HIV/AIDS and men who have sex with men, community participation and advocacy, training for RAR staff and volunteers, conducting of an initial rapid assessment, identification of methods appropriate for an RAR, analysis of RAR research findings, development of an action plan, and strategies for monitoring and evaluation (Boyce et al., 2004).

A rapid assessment and response adaptation guide has been prepared for work with especially vulnerable young people. All over the world, young people find themselves vulnerable to HIV infection because they lack the knowledge, skills and resources to protect themselves and their partners against infection. However, some young people are especially disadvantaged because of poverty, gender, sexuality and other factors. They include young migrants and refugees, young people involved in sex work, young people who inject drugs and young men who have sex with men. Many such young people have much poorer access to information and services, are more likely to engage in activities that place them at risk of HIV infection and have fewer resources to manage the impact of HIV/AIDS in their lives and communities. These especially vulnerable young people are diverse. Programs and interventions developed for one group do not necessarily address the needs of another apparently similar population. Past history and present context may differ. Understanding the specific individual and societal factors that influence young people's risk of and vulnerability to HIV infection and the settings in which infection is most likely to occur is crucial in developing local responses. All too often, assessment of these factors has been far from timely and does not fit well with the actions that follow. Moreover, programs and interventions have often been developed not in partnership with affected groups but by outside agencies using what they consider to be best practice in a particular domain. Experience shows that locally developed responses are generally more effective in addressing health issues such as HIV/AIDS, especially when young people themselves are integrally involved in the process. Rapid assessment and response (RAR) is an approach that has been developed to assess complex health issues and behavior within a short time frame. Based on the data collected, it offers a means for responding quickly with appropriate program measures and interventions (Malcolm et al., 2004).

For improving sexual and reproductive health services for especially vulnerable young people: a rapid assessment and response tool (RAR) has been prepared. This provides a draft for field testing on how to improve sexual and reproductive health services for vulnerable young people. It gives guidelines on a rapid assessment and response tool for use in action research. The tool answers basic questions about the development, planning and implementation of an action research. Also it outlines the different instruments for collecting and using information. These include focus group discussions, individual interviews, and self-evaluation questionnaires targeting the youth, youth workers, service provider, parents, guardians, and different health facilities (Lowry, 1998).

For developing strategies for dealing with HIV/AIDS in the former Soviet Union RAR has been used. HIV is spreading with increasing speed among injecting drug users (IDUs) in many parts of the world. A process has been used in the Russian Federation to prevent or control massive HIV epidemics among IDUs. The training program was based on the rapid assessment and response (RAR) guide on injecting drug use developed by the WHO Program on Substance Abuse. Overall, the program stimulated collaboration between health agencies at the city and regional level; health and law enforcement and other administrative structures at these levels; Ministry of Health structures at the federal level; other governmental structures and non-governmental organisations; and international agencies. The combination of RAR methods with the training program appeared an effective approach in assisting countries in Eastern Europe to respond to HIV among IDUs. Similar processes were implemented in Ukraine, Central Asian countries, Romania, India, Nepal, Indonesia and other Asian countries (Burrows, 2000).

Impact analysis as a feedback for program evaluation and communication assessment

Impact is the extent to which a program causes change in the desired direction in the target population: does the project produces desired changes over and above what would have occurred without the intervention? The essence of the analysis of the efficacy of a treatment or program is a comparison of what did appear after implementing the program with what would have appeared had the program not been implemented. Although what would have appeared remains forever in the darkness of the unfulfilled, and this is termed often as the counterfactual, a series of scientific methods may result in evaluative conclusions.

Evaluations are divided into formative and summative evaluations. Summative evaluations consider the effect caused on the outcome of interest, i.e. it reports on the fulfillment of the final objective, and this is often expressed with a p-value of a significance test. Formative evaluations concern not only the final outcome or the final objective, but also regard to the subobjectives, i.e. partial objectives that are needed to reach the final objective. For example it was observed that a bird population in an ecological niche was decreasing continuously. A program was undertaken to prevent the bird from extinction. Several factors affected the bird's survival, i.e. the amount of food, presence of other birds, parasites, agricultural activity that destroyed nests etc. At the end of the program the final goal was not reached in that the bird population did not start increasing, but decrease had slowed down and some elements of the program had already been fulfilled successfully. This and several other examples can be expressed with the concept and tools of summative and formative evaluation within the framework of impact analysis.

Three major types of evaluation designs are experimental, quasi-experimental and ex post facto. Experiments are characterized by that the locus of decision about which treatment a given subject selection will have is centralised. Mode of selection can be random selection – survey), random allocation (quasy-experiment) or other types. Quasy-experiments are between experiments and ex post facto designs. Quasy experiments are experiments with relatively limited control over the design characteristics. In quasi-experiments the intervention group is compared with a comparison or control group who did not receive the intervention. Comparison groups include: people who applied and were eligible to join the project but who were not admitted, communities without the intervention.

Ex post facto designs have also been named as correlational, historical, passive observation, and these are characterized by a very little or no control over the explanatory variables. Explanatory variables are those with which one may explain certain events, i.e. variables to explain.

The following notation will be introduced for describing various types of impact analysis designs in a formal way:

A: autonomous selection of elements (selection of sample elements or subjects are independent of their characteristic features)

C: centralised locus, i.e. the locus of decision regarding which treatment a given subject will have is centralised

R: randomization (randomized method of selection, i.e. the sample is randomly taken as in sample surveys or is randomly allocated as in quasy-experiments. In the latter case randomization sense is the chance assignment of groups to experimental or control conditions

T: Time of event (program, campaign)

E: Experimental group (experimental group is a group of people who receive the intervention)

C: Control group (control group is a group of people who do not receive the intervention)

Y: Parameter examined, e.g. behavior, number of birds or votes etc.

X: other influential or concomitant variables, i.e. demographic characteristics etc.

A control group is a group of people who do not receive the intervention. An experimental group is a group of people who receive the intervention. In before and after studies the same people are compared before and after they received the intervention.

1.1. One-shot case study

T   Y

1.2. Ex post facto design

Simple conclusion from a few observations.

2.1. Elementary quasy-experimental before-after design

Measurement before and after program or campaign. There is no control group. No statistical control variables e.g. demographic characteristics are available.

$$ACY_1.\ T.\ Y_2$$

2.2. Elementary quasy-experimental comparative posttest design

$$\frac{CE:T..Y_E}{A:....Y_C}$$

Similar to 2.1 but there are statistical control variables

3.1. Quasy-experimental comparative change design

$$\frac{CECY_1.\ T.\ Y_2}{CECY_1..\ Y_2}$$

Measurement before and after program or campaign, control group is used, control variables e.g. demographic characteristics are available

3.2. Quasy-experimental interrupted time series design

$$ACY_1.\ T.\ Y_{2..n}$$

Several measurements before and after program or campaign, no control group, no control variables

3.3. Quasy-experimental comparative time series design

Several measurements before and after program or campaign, control group exists, no control variables

4.1. Criterion population design (fortified design)

Similar to 3.1, but the comparative reference group is not sample based but is fortified e.g. with census data

4.2. Subobjective design

T   S   Y

After program or campaign fulfillment of subobjectives then objectives are examined, and this generates a strong basis for the subjective assessment of causality rather than by provision of a statistical basis for that assessment.

5.1. R-comparative posttest design, true experimental design

$$\frac{R\;.\;.\;T\;.\;.\;Y_E}{R\;.\;.\;.\;.\;.\;Y_C}$$

The simplest traditional experimental design. Randomization (random allocation) is used, experimental and control group is the same at the beginning, and after T interventions comparison of the two or more groups are made by the Y output parameter

5.2. R-comparative change design

This experimental design is similar to 5.1, but there is more opportunity for detailed statistical

$$\frac{R\,X_E\,.\,T\,Y_E}{R\,X_C\,-\,-\,-\,Y_C}$$

analysis by control variables.

<u>Validity and reliability</u>

All these designs are subject to threats to internal validity in various ways and measures. Validity is the amount of confidence that the research is accurate or reflective of the situation under investigation. Validity means that we measure what we intend to. Internal validity refers to conclusions regarding the subjects, time and context of the implemented research. A threat to internal validity is an objection that the design employed allows the causal link between program, campaign or treatment and outcome to remain uncertain. In other words in this case the design is weak in some way and does not enable one to have confidence in one's conclusion about what the program did accomplish regarding the subjects, time and content observed. External validity, on the other hand, refers to the generalizability of the research results. A threat to external validity is a problem that casts doubt on the extent to which the results of the evaluation as conducted would be repeated with the same program at a different time or place, or with different subjects, or with other indicators of the main variables. Confidence can be improved through triangulation, i.e. cross-checking information, comparing information collected by different methods and from different data sources. Assessing various types of validity of existing data may be helpful in using information.

Types of validity

- **Content validity:** concepts and methods are theoretical defined and underpinned
- **Face validity** : what measured on the surface is the same as needed
- **Internal validity:** research is suitable for determining causal relationships
- **External or criterion validity:** research results are in line with results of other examinations
- **Predictive validity:** present research results also have a predictive feature
- **Concurrent validity:** old and new methods convey the same or similar results
- **Construct validity:** two groups are well separated by a given variable and this can be proved statistically

Threats to internal validity:

- Events (history) – there is a problem if no control group is available
    - External events – this refers to just one kind of history, i.e. the threat that some outside occurrence, not a property of the program, the study, or the subjects has intervened to affect outcome scores
    - Testing – effect of the research, this refers to the pretest and the possibility that scores on the posttest may be different from what they otherwise would have been, not because of the treatment, but because the subject were subjected to previous measurement, i.e. the pretest
    - Maturation – internal evolution, selective change of the sample
    - Regression – cyclic or episodic change of the sample
    - Attrition – selective diminishing of the sample size
- Selection bias – there is a problem if there are no control variables
    - Difference of experimental and control group at the beginning of the study
    - Nonrandom selection of groups (biases, lack of representativeness)
- Contamination – the treatment is not administered properly, because the treatment group is contaminated with members of the control group or vice versa
- Recall bias – insufficient memory concerning old events.

Reliability

A study has high reliability if another team conducting the same study would generate similar data and arrive at similar conclusions. A measurement is reliable if similar results would be received after repeating the research or measurement

Types of reliability

- **Stability or test-pretest reliability** (similar results at repeated measurements)
- **Equivalence or alternate-form reliability** (split-halves method, repeated measurements)
- **Homogeneity or internal consistency**
- Interobserver or interrater reliability
- Intraobserver or intrarater reliability

The importance of the possible role of communication programs has been proved in an impact analysis of decentralisation in Zimbabwe from a local perspective. Although decentralisation has been on the Government of Zimbabwe's agenda since the early 1980s and there have been several structural reforms, little effective power has been decentralised. Zimbabwe's various decentralisation efforts and effects including fiscal decentralisation, sectoral decentralisation, local political and institutional structures and local economic development and poverty reduction has been analysed. Analyses of their impact in Binga District, which is one of the poorest parts of the country resulted in a number of conclusions drawn from this experience. Firstly, decentralisation is part of a wider process of national political and economic change and cannot be planned independently; moreover, decentralisation for the `wrong' reasons can be worse than no decentralisation at all and, if the political environment is not `right', the problems of decentralisation can be exacerbated by external funding agencies. Secondly, decentralisation must be accompanied by capacity building, and the capacity of local institutions depends to a significant extent on the individuals involved. Thirdly, decentralisation must be seen as a `learning process'; consequently, despite the relatively little effective decentralisation to date, those involved have learnt valuable lessons, and in this communication programs may be crucial (Conyers, 2003).

The importance and role of communication programs has been proved in an impact analysis on the relationship between gender and HIV/AIDS. The impact of gender on HIV/AIDS is an important dimension in understanding the evolution of the epidemic. How have gender inequality and discrimination against women affected the course of the HIV epidemic? Biological, social and cultural determinants put women and adolescent girls at greater risk of HIV infection than men. Violence against women or the threat of violence often increases women's vulnerability to HIV/AIDS. An analysis of the impact of gender on HIV/AIDS demonstrates the importance of integrating gender into HIV programming and finding ways to strengthen women by implementing policies and programs that increase their access to education and information. Women's empowerment is vital to reversing the epidemic. Communication programs may have the beneficial effects (Turmen, 2003).

The importance and role of communication programs, decentralisation on the political organisation, and improving sexual and reproductive health services in Ghana has been revealed by impact analysis. Qualitative research and interviews with key informants have been conducted from the Ministry of Health, donors, NGOs, regional and district health management teams, local government and community leaders. Within a national reproductive health policy framework, previously disparate family planning, maternal and child health, STI and HIV/AIDS programs had become more integrated, and donors have pooled or co-ordinated their funding. Some decision-making about resource allocation was meant to happen at district and regional level but in practice, this remained centrally controlled, which might be a necessary safeguard for sexual and reproductive health services. Earmarked donor funds ensured a regular supply of contraceptives and STI drugs. However, paying for these was problematic at local level. Sexual and reproductive health staff made-up a large proportion of primary health care staff, but especially in rural areas they experienced poor working conditions, and there was high turnover and vacancies. District and sub-district level links were working well in this new system, but clarity was still needed on how different national sexual and reproductive health bodies relate to each other and to regional and district health authorities. The development of formal mechanisms for priority setting and advocacy at local levels with proper communication programs could help to secure benefits for sexual and reproductive health care (Mayhew, 2003)

The importance and role of communication programs has been revealed in an impact analysis on newborn and maternal health policies. Evidence on the impact of maternal and newborn health interventions in less-developed countries has been collected, and compelling support for using research as a tool for identifying the most effective measures for saving maternal and newborn lives offered. World Health Organisation (WHO) and Save the Children's Saving Newborn Lives (SNL) initiative supported a global review of the impact of community-based interventions during the antenatal, intrapartum, and postpartum periods on perinatal and neonatal health status outcomes. The results provide a solid foundation for policies, communication programs, and research studies related to maternal and newborn health, emphasizing the new findings, while recommending an integrated approach to safe motherhood and newborn health (Bhutta et al., 2003).

The importance and role of communication programs has been revealed in an impact analysis on children's residence patterns and educational attainment in rural South Africa. Using data collected by the Agincourt Health and Population Program in a rural sub-district of South Africa's Northern Province, the residential arrangements of a population, and analyses the impact of these arrangements on children's educational attainment has been made. Children with co-resident parents generally have higher levels of schooling than those who have one or no co-resident parents. However, having a father who is away from home as a migrant appears to benefit older children whereas, for girls aged 11 to 15, having a mother who is a migrant lowers educational attainment. Children who live in households headed by Mozambican refugees have lower levels of schooling than those who live in non-refugee households. Living in a household headed by a woman is not associated with lower levels of education and, for some age-sex groups, appears to be an advantage. Proper communication programs may improve the situation (Townsend et al., 2002).

Impact analysis revealed the importance of communication programs in a serious problem that affect women's health. The Global Health Council released a report that provides a first-ever country-by-country global analysis of the impact of unintended pregnancies on maternal deaths in developing countries. The report, "Promises to Keep: The Toll of Unintended Pregnancies on Women's Lives in the Developing World," details more than 300 million unintended pregnancies and the deaths of nearly 700,000 women between 1995 and 2000. Supported by a grant from the David and Lucile Packard Foundation, the Global Health Council conducted the comprehensive analysis as a statistical measure for assessing progress on pledges to reform and fund reproductive health services made at the 1994 International Conference on Population and Development (ICPD). It was at that conference that 179 nations made a commitment to fully support the reproductive health needs of the world's women (Mackin, 2002).

A serious communication problem has been revealed by impact analysis of various factors, especially the AIDS epidemic on household food security in Malawi. AIDS is one of the factors that threaten household food security in rural Malawi. Interviews with respondents from a random sample of 65 rural Malawi households suggested that the threat of AIDS to household food security lied in its impact on social immunity, the collective resistance against problems. Social immunity was rooted in social capital endowments, the reciprocity and redistribution opportunities embedded in networks of interpersonal ties. Favorable social capital endowments engendered significant sharing of labor, food, income, and time among households, and mitigated the negative effect of AIDS on the food security of any specific household. However, when the spread of AIDS reached an epidemic threshold, it made illness and death so extensive that ties in the extended family networks got fractured, social capital endowments became unfavorable, reciprocity and redistribution were undermined, social immunity was weakened, and food security got compromised. Results of this research suggested that, as of 1996, there were signs that the epidemic was approaching threshold levels in rural Malawi. The results also suggested that the analysis of the impact of AIDS and initiatives aimed at controlling that impact should not just be undertaken at the household level but, more importantly, at the extended family level (Mtika, 2001).

Clinical trials

Clinical trials are important tools for assessing various drugs that can be used for improving health and quality of life, and controlling population growth. An example of such a method is the examination of the effect of drotaverine hydrochloride in acute colicky pain caused by renal and ureteric stones (Romics et al, 2003). Objective of the study was to assess the spasmolytic effect of drotaverine hydrochloride in colicky pain caused by renal and ureteric stones. In a placebo-controlled, multicentric, multinational, randomized, double-blind study changes in the intensity of pain were recorded using a visual analogue scale (VAS), a four-grade (five points) pain intensity (PI) scale and a pain-relief scale. The primary endpoint was the evaluation of the antispasmodic effect of drotaverine during a 3-h study period, to confirm that drotaverine abolished or significantly decreased the intensity of pain in renal colic. The painkilling effect was defined as a decrease by at least half in the PI scale, or a ≥ 40 percent decrease in the VAS 40 min after either the first or the second injection of 80 mg drotaverine or placebo (if necessary the dose could be repeated once). In all, 140 patients were enrolled but 38 withdrew, leaving 102 patients for analysis (48 drotaverine, 54 placebo; mean age 42.5 years, S.D. 11.25, and 41.7, S.D. 10.79). Drotaverine was effective in 79 percent of patients and placebo in only 46 percent ($P < 0.001$). There were no serious adverse effects. There were 20 minor side-effects in the drotaverine and four in the placebo group; none of the patients required treatment. The most frequent side-effects were a transitory decrease in blood pressure, vertigo, nausea or vomiting. Intravenous drotaverine provides effective pain relief in more than two-thirds of patients with renal colic, with no serious side-effects.

The effects of antiplasmodial, antibacterial, antimycotic, antiviral and contraceptive drugs are tested similarly.

Quality of life measurements

An important indicator of health status is the quality of life (QoL). A reason of the growing interest about QoL is to give an explanation to the high mortality rates in some countries such as Hungary, for example. An example of QoL analysis was made in Hungary where an assessment of social and health inequalities and quality of life measurements has been made in population-based Hungarian samples by using the EuroQol 5D instrument (Molnár, 2001; Szende, Molnár, 2000, Szende, Molnár, 2001) with a comparison to some UK data. Methods of data analysis included the use of loglinear models, CHAID analysis and the GLM. There were no marked difference between the pooled Hungarian and the UK data in terms of quality of life. However, despite the superficial similarities between the pooled Hungarian and the UK data in terms of quality of life, detailed analysis revealed that although in the "young" (-59) age group there was no marked difference between the pooled Hungarian and the UK data concerning the proportion of people who gave the answer "not any problem", this changed with the older ages in favor of the UK, where 37 percent while in the pooled Hungarian sample only 31 percent of the respondents gave this answer. This was in accord with that life expectancy at birth was also much higher in the UK than in the Hungarian sample but, of course, quality of life by its very nature represented more (and less) than life expectancy. Furthermore, in both age groups -59 and 60- one could see in the Hungarian sample a relatively large proportion of people who had both moderate pain or discomfort *and* anxiety or depression as compared to the UK. However, there was a gap between "subjective" assessment of quality of life and "objectively" measured health characteristics such as mortality or morbidity among males in Hungary, which was a major problem to be addressed by adequate health policy.

Statistical research methods

In statistics, radical statisticians believe that statistics can be used to support radical campaigns for progressive social change. Statistics should inform, not drive policies. Social problems should not be disguised by technical language. A group of researchers and statisticians, who are committed to helping build a more free, democratic and egalitarian society shared a common concern about the political implications of their work and an awareness of the actual and potential misuse of statistics (Radstats).

Exploratory Data Analysis

Exploratory Data Analysis (EDA) is a robust data analytic technique to easily understand and interpret data and it employs a variety of techniques, mostly graphical, especially to maximize insight into a data set, uncover underlying structure, extract important variables, detect outliers and anomalies, test underlying assumptions, and develop parsimonious models. EDA is not a set of techniques but, rather, a philosophy on how data analysis should be carried out. EDA is not identical to statistical graphics although the two terms are used almost interchangeably. Statistical graphics is a collection of techniques, all graphically based and all focusing on one data characterization aspect. EDA encompasses a larger venue; EDA is an approach to data analysis that postpones the usual assumptions about what kind of model the data follow with a more direct approach of allowing the data itself to reveal its underlying structure and model. EDA philosophy is about how to dissect a data set; what and how to look for, and to interpret the data. Most EDA techniques are graphical in nature with a few quantitative techniques. The reason for the heavy reliance on graphics is that by its very nature the main role of EDA is to explore, and graphics gives the analysts power to do so, letting the data to reveal its structural secrets, and being always ready to gain some new, often unsuspected, insight into the data. In combination with the pattern-recognition, graphics provides a good way to do this.

The particular graphical techniques employed in EDA are often quite simple, consisting of various techniques of stem-an-leaf plots, histograms, dotplots, boxplots, pie charts, bar charts, scatterplots, lineplots, normal probability plots. It also relies heavily on simulations and computer-intensive statistical methods.

Boxplots, more precisely the box-whiskers plots, among other techniques, are frequently used and are especially useful tools of exploratory data analysis. Boxplots are defined in terms of the median and hinges of a collection of numbers. The hinges are the 25th and 75th percentiles of a variable. The median is the 50th percentile. The box in a boxplot extends from the low hinge to the high hinge. The horizontal line is the median. The whiskers extend from the box to the highest data value not above

high hinge+1,5 x (high hinge – low hinge)

and from the box to the lowest data value not below

low hinge – 1,5 x (high hinge – low hinge).

Any data value beyond these limit is generally plotted with a circle unless it exceeds either

high hinge + 3,0 x (high hinge – low hinge)

or

low hinge – 3,0 x (high hinge – low hinge)

in which case it is plotted with a starburst.

The often shaded intervals for comparing medians are placed symmetrically around the median at

Median ± 1.58 x (high hinge – low hinge)./√n.

Simple Correlation and Regression

The basic conceptual approach underlying correlation coefficients is the development of a standardized measure of association between variables. For two variables (X and Y). The correlation coefficient, is the product of the deviations of each variable from its mean, i.e.,

$(X_i - \bar{X}) (Y_i - \bar{Y})$ for each observation i. For observations in the first and third quadrants, this product will be positive; for observations in the second and fourth quadrant, this product will be negative. If we sum these products over all observations, a positive sum indicates that the observations tend to fall in the first and third quadrants, while a negative sum indicates that they are more heavily weighted toward the second and fourth quadrants.

Thus, the sign corresponds to the direction of any relationship: a positive sign indicates that larger values of Y tend to be associated with larger values of X; a negative sign indicates that smaller values of Y are associated with larger values of X.

The signs tell the direction of association but say nothing about the strength of the relationship.

Regression and analysis of variance

Regression and analysis of variance are probably the most frequently applied of statistical analyses. Regression and analysis of variance are used extensively in many areas of research. The reason for the frequency of regression and analysis of variance (ANOVA) applications is their suitability for many different types of study design. Regression and ANOVA procedures are applicable to experimental, quasy-experimental and non-experimental data. Regression allows examination of the relationships between predictor variables and a response or dependent variable, and enables values on one variable to be predicted from the values of other variables. ANOVA places no restriction on the number of groups or conditions that may be compared, while factorial ANOVA allows examination of the influence of two or more independent variables or factors on a dependent variable.

Analysis of covariance (ANCOVA) is most frequently used to refer to the statistical technique that combines regression and ANOVA. ANCOVA now is applied frequently in quasi-experimental research. Unlike experimental research, the topics investigated with quasi-experimental methods are most likely to involve variables that, cannot be controlled directly, mostly for ethical reasons. In these situations the statistical control provided by ANCOVA has value.

General linear model

The general linear model (GLM) concept is that data may be expressed in terms of a model plus some error: data=model+error.

The model in this equation is a representation of our hypotheses about the data. The error component is an explicit recognition that there are other influences on the data. These influences are presumed to be unique for each subject in each experimental condition and include anything and everything not controlled in the experiment, such as chance fluctuations in behavior. The relative size of the model and error components is used to judge how well the model accommodates the data. The model part of the GLM equation constitutes our hypotheses about the data and is expressed in terms of a set of variables.

Regression analysis attempts to explain the dependent variable in terms of a set of independent variables or predictors in the form of a model and a residual component, the error term. Typically, a researcher who applies regression is interested in predicting a quantitative dependent variable from one or more quantitative independent variables, and in determining the relative contribution of each independent variable to the prediction. There is interest in what proportion of the variation in the dependent variable can be attributed to variation in the independent variables. Regression also may employ categorical predictor variables. Since regression is the elementary form of GLM, it is possible to construct regression GLMs equivalent to any ANOVA and ANCOVA GLMs by selecting quantitative variables to act as categorical variables. In practice, one should check the validity of the assumptions inherent in the model in a regression analysis. Residuals are the best estimates of error. Therefore, one can check each assumption graphically by using the residuals versus fitted values plot, the normal plot of residuals, the residuals versus order plot, and the plot of residuals versus other variables.

ANOVA also can be thought of in terms of a model plus error. Here, dependent variable scores constitute the data, the experimental condition constitute the model and the component of the data not accommodated by the model is represented by the error term. Typically, the researcher applying ANOVA is interested in whether the mean dependent variable scores obtained in the experimental conditions differ significantly. This is achieved by determiing how much variation in the dependent variable scores is attributable to differences between the scores obtained in the experimental conditions, and comparing this with the error term, which is attributable to variation in the dependent variable scores in each experimental condition, and there is interest in what proportion of variation in the dependent variable can be attributed to the experimental variables. ANOVA is a particular type of regression analysis that employs quantitative predictors to act as categorical ones.

Regression, ANOVA and ANCOVA are but particular instances of the GLM. The full regression GLM equation that describes the data is $Y_i = \beta_0 + \beta_1 X_i + \varepsilon_i$, where Y_i is the observed score for the ith subject and ε_i is the error term for the same subject. In other words GLM is linear with respect to both its parameters and predictor variables.

In GLM fixed effects, random effects and mixed effect analyses refer to different sampling situations. Fixed effects analyses employ only fixed variables in the GLM model. Random effect analyses consider those experimental conditions employed in to be only a random sample of a population of experimental condition, and so inferences drawn from the study may be applied to the wider population of conditions. Inferences from random effects are generalized more widely than fixed effects inferences.

In practice the most important statistic in the resulting table of a GLM analysis is the p-value. There is a p-value for each term in the model, except for the error term. The p-value for a term tells you whether the effect for that term is significant: If P is less than or equal to the a-level you have selected, then the effect for the term is significant. If P is larger than the a-level you have selected, the effect is not significant. If the effect of a fixed factor is significant, then the level means for the factor are significantly different from each other. If the effect of a random factor is significant, then the variance of the factor is not zero. If the effect of an interaction term is significant, then the effects of each factor are different at different levels of the other factors.

<u>Principal component analysis</u>
Principal component analysis is one of the simplest and frequently used multivariate data analytic method. The object of the analysis is to take p variables
$X_1, X_2, ..., X_p$
And find combinations of these to produce indices
$Z_1, Z_2, ..., Z_p$ that are uncorrelated.
The lack of correlation is a useful property because it means that the indices are measuring different „dimensions" in the data. The dimensions are also ordered so that Z_1 displays the largest amount of variation, Z_2 displays the second largest amount of variation, and so on, i.e.
$var(Z_1) \geq var(Z_2) \geq ...... \geq var(Z_p)$, where $var(Z_i)$ denotes the variance of Z_i in the data set.
The Z_i new variables are called proncipal components.
The Z_i principal components are linear combinations of the X_i variables:
$Z_i = a_{i1} X_i + a_{i2} X_2 + ... + a_{ip} X_p$,
I=1, … p, and p is the number of variables.
When doing principal component analysis it is hoped that the variances of most of the indices virtually negligible. So the variation in the data set can be adequately described by a few Z variables with variables that are not negligible.
It is preferred that let say the first two factors account for 70-80 percent of total variance. The chi-squared statistic is used to test the adequacy of a k-factor model.

Factor analysis
Factor analysis is a statistical technique widely used in the social sciences. Factor analysis consists of a number of statistical techniques the aim of which is to simplify complex sets of data. In exploratory factor analysis the aim is to explore the field, to discover the main dimensions with which the data can be described simply. Factor analysis gives an answer to the following question: what constructs or dimensions could account for the correlations between variables? In confirmatory factor analysis hypothesis tests are also used. The main objection to factor analysis is that there is an infinity of mathematically equivalent solution. While this is true, it is also the case that social scientists have developed powerful methods of choosing the right solution.

Path analysis, factor analysis and structural equation analysis
Path analysis, factor analysis and structural equation analysis are all types of latent variable analysis, i.e. some of the variables are not directly observed. In factor analysis the latent variables are factors. Path diagrams represent a relationship between a number of variables. In a typical path diagram a straight one-headed arrow represents a causal relationship between the variables and a curved double-headed arrow represent a simple correlation between the variables.

Multidimensional scaling
Multidimensional scaling is a technique designed to construct a map showing the relationship between a number of objects, given only a table of distances between them. The map can be in on or more dimensions. It is a fact proved mathematically that it may be possible to construct a map from the distances among various objects. A definition of multidimensional scaling (MDS) is the search for a low dimensional space, usually Euclidean, in which points in the space represent the objects, one point representing one object, and such the distances between the space $\{d_{rs}\}$, match as well as possible the original dissimilarities $\{\delta_{rs}\}$, if we suppose a set of n objects, and there is a measurement δ_{rs} of the dissimilarity between two objects. The techniques used for the search for the space and the associated configuration of points from metric and non-metric multidimensional scaling.

Correspondence analysis
Correspondence analysis represents the rows and columns of a data matrix as points in a space of low dimension, and is particularly used in the analysis of two-dimensional contingency tables. The method has been discovered and rediscovered several times and has gone under several names such as reciprocal averaging, dual scaling etc. In some cases the method can be simply viewed as a metric multidimensional scaling method on the rows and columns of a contingency table or data matrix with non-negative entries.

Linear Dependency Analysis
Linear Dependency Analysis (LDA) is a multivariate data analytic technique used in mathematical-statistics. The essence of LDA is to divide a series of variables into a set of explanatory variables and a set of variables to be explained. Time series data on unemployment and main economic indicators was analysed with multiple linear regression (Longley JW, 1967). However multicollinearity made the analysis difficult, since there were several correlations between the variables which exceeded 0.99 in value. Therefore performing the least-squares estimations were very difficult. In another case an attempt was made to give an explanation of the increase of delinquency in Great Britain with some explanatory variables (Ahamad B, 1967). However, principal component analysis was criticized heavily on similar basis (Walker MA, 1967). With the LDA method the best formulas could be selected from among almost 80000 possible formulas that had the smallest errors (residuals). In an attempt to explain high blood pressure in Hungarian sample of size 1600 LDA provided valuable information about the risk factors of hypertension.

Life table method
The life table method is one of the oldest techniques for measuring mortality and describing the survival of a population. It has been used by demographers, actuaries, and medical researchers in studies of survival, population growth, fertility, migration, length of married life, length of working life etc. The cohort life table describes the survival or mortality from birth to death of a specific cohort of persons who were born at about the same time. The current life table is constructed by applying the age-specific mortality rates of a population in a given period of time to a hypothetical cohort of 100 000 people.

Survival Analysis
Survival analysis is a popular data analysis approach for certain kinds of epidemiologic and other data. Although more than one event may be considered in the same analysis, it can be assumed that only one event is of designated interest. When more than one event is considered, the statistical problem is characterized as a

competing risk problem. The outcome variable is generally the time until an event occurs. By event often death, disease incidence, relapse from remission, recovery (e.g., return to work) or any designated experience of interest is meant that may happen to an individual.
In a survival analysis, it is usually referred to the time variable as survival time, because it gives the time that an individual has "survived" over some follow-up period. It is also typically referred to the event as a failure, because the kind of event of interest usually is death, disease incidence, or some other negative individual experience. However, survival time may be "time to return to work after an elective surgical procedure," in which case failure is a positive event. Most survival analyses must consider a key analytic problem called censoring. In essence, censoring occurs when we have some information about individual survival time, but we don't know the survival time exactly. In survival analysis, interest centers on a group or groups of individuals for each of whom there is defined a point event, often called failure, occurring after a length of time called the failure time. Failure can occur at most once on any individual.

<u>Cluster analysis</u>
Cluster analysis consists of a series of mathematical methods, numbering in the hundreds, that can be used to find out which objects in a set are similar. Objects with similar descriptions are mathematically put into the same cluster. Very often in scientific research the making of classifications is essential. One reason that cluster analysis is so useful is that researchers need to make and revise classifications continually. Methods of hierarchical cluster analysis follow a prescribed set of steps, the main ones being: collect a data matrix whose columns stand for the objects to be cluster-analysed and whose rows are the attributes that describe the objects. Then one may standardize the data matrix. Using the (standardized) data matrix the values of a resemblance coefficient are computed to measure the similarities among all pairs of objects. With a clustering method, based on the values of the resemblance coefficients, a dendrogram is drawn that shows the hierarchy of similarities among all pairs of objects. From the tree-like figure the clusters can be read off. Certain methods of standardizing the data matrix, resemblance coefficients, and clustering methods are standard calculations. For example, the UPGMA clustering method is used quite often in hierarchical cluster analysis. Cluster analysis is easily communicated.

In cluster analysis subjects are named objects and their characteristic features are named attributes. Types of cluster analysis include agglomerative and divisive methods. Agglomerative cluster analysis agglomerates separate objects into one cluster, while divisive cluster analysis divides one object into several clusters. Two types of cluster analysis are hierarchical and non-hierarchical. In hierarchical cluster analysis smaller clusters are generally part of certain larger clusters. In non-hierarchical cluster analysis various clusters may be totally separated.
Frequently used clustering methods include agglomerative hierarchical analysis with the creation of dendrograms, and nonhierarchical K-means cluster analysis for finding „market segments".
Frequently used hierarchical clustering methods are:
UPGMA - unweighted pair-group method using arithmetic averages,
SLINK - single-linkage, and
CLINK - complete-linkage.
Standardization of data can be made for example in the following way:

$$(x_i - \bar{x})/sd$$

$$\bar{x} = \frac{1}{n}\sum_{i=1}^{n} x_i$$

$$sd = \sqrt{\frac{\sum_{i=1}^{n}(x_i - \bar{x})^2}{n-1}}$$

The standardized data matrix will be a matrix without dimensions. Further steps generally involve the calculation of a similarity matrix with various coefficients, such as the Euclidean distance $c=\sqrt{(a^2+b^2)}$, the generalized Euclidean distance $g=\sqrt{(a^2+b^2+c^2+d^2+e^2)}$ etc.
The results will be displayed in a dendrogram or phenogram.
The dendrogram is considered good if the value of the cophenetic correlation coefficient is at least 0,8.

R-analysis refers to the analysis of cases, while Q-analysis to that of the variables. In certain research situations both types of analysis provide valuable information about the data.
The cosine coefficient, Canberra metric coefficient, Bray-Curtis coefficient are further frequently used dissimilarity coefficients with continuous variables.

The Pearson correlation coefficient is a frequently used similarity coefficients with continuous variables.
Other coefficients are as follow:

- Hamman coefficient
- Sorenson coefficient
- Rogers and Tanimoto coefficient
- Sokal and Sneath coefficient
- Russel and Rao coefficient
- Baroni-Urbani and Buser coefficient
- Sokal binary distance coefficient
- Ochiai coefficient
- Phi coefficient.

Resemblance coeffecients may be sensitive to additive or proportional translation of data profiles, which may influence the interpretation of the results

<u>Logistic Regression</u>
The independent variables can be denoted as X_1, X_2 and so on up to X_k where k is the number of variables.
We have a flexible choice for the X's, which can represent any collection of exposure variables, control variables, or even combinations of such variables of interest.
For example, we may have:
X_1 equal to an exposure variable E, X_2 and X_3 equal to control variables C_1 and C_2, respectively, X_4 equal to the product EXC_1, X_5 equal to the product C_1XC_2, X_6 equal to E^2.
Whenever we wish to relate a set of X's to a dependent variable, like D, we are considering a multivariable problem. In the analysis of such a problem, some kind of mathematical model is typically used to deal with the complex relationship among many variables.
Logistic regression is a mathematical modeling approach that can be used to describe the relationship of several X's to a dichotomous dependent variable, such as D.
The logistic function, which describes the mathematical form on which the logistic model is based is:

$$f(z) = \frac{1}{1 + e^{-(\alpha + \sum \beta_i X_i)}}$$

<u>Categorical data analysis</u>
Categorical data consist of frequency counts of observations occurring in the response categories. For categorical variables having only two levels the description of two-way contingency tables odds ratios, differences of proportions, and ratios of proportions are often used. Summary measures of nominal and ordinal association for variables having more than two categories are also available. A bivariate relationship is defined by the joint distribution of the two associated random variables. The joint distribution determines the marginal and conditional distributions. Simplification occurs in a joint distribution when the component random variables are statistically independent.
Let X and Y denote two categorical response variables, X having I levels and Y having J levels. When subjects are classified on both variables, there are IJ possible combinations of classifications. The responses (X, Y) of a subject randomly chosen from some population have a probability distribution over the table. This distribution can be displayed in a rectangular table having I rows the categories of X and J columns for the categories of Y. The cells of table represent the IJ possible outcomes. Their probabilities are $\{\pi_{ij}\}$, where π_{ij} denotes the probability that (X,Y) falls in the cell in row i and column j. A contingency table having I rows and J columns is often referred to as a I by J table, and the probability distribution of $\{\pi_{ij}\}$ is the joint distribution of X and Y. The marginal distributions are the row and column totals obtained by summing the joint probabilities, i.e.
$\pi_{i+} = \Sigma_j \pi_{ij}$ and $\pi_{+j} = \Sigma_i \pi_{ij}$. Testing the independence is made with the chi-squared statistics or the likelihood-ratio statistic:

$$X^2 = \sum_{ij} \frac{(n_{ij} - m_{ij})^2}{m_{ij}}$$

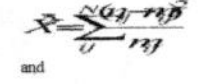

and

$$G^2 = -\log \Lambda = 2 \sum_{ij}^{N} n_{ij} \log(n_{ij}/m_{ij}),$$

where m_{ij} is the expected frequency under the null-hypothesis of independence, and is the likelihood ratio.

<u>Loglinear models</u>
With loglinear models the analysis of multiway contingency tables is easy. In a simple three-dimensional contingency table a saturated hierarchical model is defined as $\ln m_{ijk} = \mu + \lambda_i^A + \lambda_j^B + \lambda_k^C + \lambda_{ij}^{AB} + \lambda_{ik}^{AC} + \lambda_{jk}^{BC} + \lambda_{ijk}^{ABC}$, where m is the model frequency, and the λ parameters are the different one-, two- and three dimensional additive interaction terms. The model fit can be tested with the LR or the chi-squared statistics. The model gives us a picture of the relevant variables and their interactions. Possible models in a three-dimensional table are as follow:
A   B   C   AB   AC   BC   AB, AC   AB, BC   AC, BC   ABC,
where A, B and C are variables of the multidimensional contingency table.

<u>Linear-by-linear association models</u>
Linear-by linear association or interaction models can be fit in two-way and three-way tables.
Within the framework of association models a structure is sought for describing the odds ratios (θ).
For simplicity in a two-way table the following models can be formulated taking into account the row and the column effects. Independence, uniform association model, row effect model, column effect model, row and column effect model. Taking the ideas into a formal way the models can be described with the odds ratios as follow:
Model of independence: $\theta = 1$
Uniform association model: $\theta = x$, where $x \neq 1$
Row-effect model: $\theta_i = x$, where i is a row index
Column effect model: $\theta_j = x$, where j is a column index
Row and column effect model: $\theta_{ij} = x$, where i and j are row and column indices.
In a three dimensional contingency table similar but a bit more complicated models can be formulated and tested in which the layers are also taken into account.

<u>Discriminant analysis</u>
The problem of algorithmic classification arises when an investigator makes measurements on a number of individuals or objects and wishes to classify them either generally, to explore or find existing groups for future analysis or to classify them into one of the several categories, given before the classification, on the basis of the measurements. Methods developed for the first problem are frequently called numerical taxonomy, cluster analysis or unsupervised pattern recognition, while those for the second problem are called discriminant analysis or supervised pattern recognition.
Discriminant analysis consists of a series of methods, conceived to classify people or objects on whom observations are available on different levels of measurements [Stevens 1946], but there are some common features in this respect, that is to construct an accurate prediction rule and to understand the mechanism of prediction.
One approach primarily focuses on discrete discriminant analysis assuming that the variables only have integer number values. Discrete discriminant analysis may be used both in medical decision making and data analysis, when the variables involved in the prediction are categorical (Rudas 1984, 1991; Korom et al. 1990, Molnár 1990, 1991, 1992). It is investigated how these methods work when the prior probabilities, that express our prior knowledge about things to be analysed, are unequal, and the consequences of these circumstances in real life data are ascertained.
Discriminant analysis was introduced by Fisher with an application to a taxonomic problem. He wanted, given an object on whom p measurements, possibly highly correlated, x1, x2, ..., xp had been made, to decide on the basis of the measurements to which of two possible groups the object belonged. Fisher's idea was to substitute for the p measurements on the object, a single measurement, y, defined as a linear compound of them: y=c1*x1+c2*x2+...+cp*xp. If the compounding constants, c1, c2,..., cp were known, each object would then be characterized by a single measurement, y, and the problem of assignment to the proper group greatly simplified. If y were less than a given value, it might be assigned to the first population, while if greater than it to the second one. Finally Fisher's solution led to the relatively easy problem of function maximization. Under the assumption

of multivariate normal probability distribution of the predicting variables in both groups with equal covariance matrices, his solution can also be derived from Bayes theorem.

<u>Discrete discriminant analysis with loglinear modeling</u>
After collecting a 'learning sample' the data are arranged in a multidimensional contingency table to do discrete discriminant analysis. Loglinear models represent a set of ideas about the relationships between categorical variables in terms of generalized independence. Commonly used criteria of model selection are parsimony, simple interpretation and all significant effects (Benedetti and Brown, 1978). Loglinear models are characterized by an interaction structure. For example with three variables A, B and C, the model denoted by AB, BC means, that A and C are conditionally independent in the layers of B. Model fitting is checked by the Pearson's chi-square and the likelihood ratio statistics (Bishop et al. 1977, Upton 1978, Rudas 1982).
Gilbert (Gilbert, 1968), Goldstein and Dillon (Goldstein and Dillon, 1978) have made important theoretical and practical contributions to the application of loglinear models in discriminant analysis. However, as James put it: "The use of loglinear models in categorical classification has not appeared in the literature to any great extent but this is one of the most promising methods and is sure to grow in popularity." (James, 1985, p. 155). The estimated parameters of the loglinear models are typical plug-in estimators in the sense, that the fitted values are plugged in the Bayesian formulas.

<u>Multivariate standardization with loglinear model parameters</u>
A multivariate standardization method was proposed and programmed later on. This method focussed on the marginals of a multiway contingency table. Clogg has proposed a series of more sophisticated standardization methods called purging.
For a simplification of the application of the purging process the variables are considered as compositional (C), group (G) and dependent (D) variables. Members of the compositional, group and dependent variables in this special case for purging.
A general multiplicative model for a three-way table of combined compositional, group and dependent variables is:

$$m_{ijk} = \eta + \tau_i{}^C + \tau_j{}^G + \tau_k{}^D + \tau_{ij}{}^{CG} + \tau_{ik}{}^{CD} + \tau_{jk}{}^{GD} + \tau_{ijk}{}^{CGD},$$

where m is the model frequency, and the τ parameters are the different one-, two- and three dimensional multiplicative interaction terms. When $\tau_{ijk}{}^{CGD} \neq 1$ for at least some (i,j,k) then for example group differences in levels of the dependent variable differ across levels of the compositional variable. When $\tau_{ijk}{}^{CGD} = 1$ for all (i,j,k) then the 2-factor taus measure the partial association between two variables "controlling" for levels of the third variable. A general model for the two-way CG table is:
$$m_{ij+} = \gamma_i{}^C + \gamma_j{}^G + \gamma_{ij}{}^{CG},$$
where the $\gamma_{ij}{}^{CG}$ parameters measure the CG interaction in the marginal CG table, which is called marginal CG interaction, and $\tau_{ij}{}^{CG}$ is called partial CG interaction. When G and D are conditionally independent, given teh levels j of G, then $\gamma_{ij}{}^{CG} = \tau_{ij}{}^{CG}$.
The model-based purging methods are defined as follows.

1. Crude rates
This method is based on observed crude frequencies and is traditionally criticized on the basis of not taking account of the effects of confounding variables on the calculated rates.

2. Partial CG purging
Partial CD purging means that $m^*_{ijk} = m_{ijk} / \tau_{ij}{}^{CG}$, where m^*_{ijk} is the adjusted and m_{ijk} is the observed cell frequency. The m^*_{ijk} estimated cell frequencies depend on all interactions in the model except $\tau_{ij}{}^{CG}$ whose effects has been removed. Partial CG purging will not necessarily preserve group total, in other words m^*_{+j+} need not equal m_{+j+} i.e. they may be slightly different.

3. Partial CG and CGD purging
Partial CD and CGD purging means that $m^*_{ijk} = m_{ijk} / (\tau_{ij}{}^{CG} \, \tau_{ijk}{}^{CGD})$, where $\tau_{ij}{}^{CG}$ and $\tau_{ijk}{}^{CGD}$ are confounding interactions, and the estimated m^*_{ijk} frequencies are freed of these interactions. The use of this purging technique is of crucial importance in the solution of rate-adjustment problems in general.

4. Marginal CG purging
Marginal CG purging means $m^*_{ijk} = m_{ijk} / \gamma_{ij}{}^{CG}$, where $\gamma_{ij}{}^{CG}$ is the marginal interaction in a collapsed table between C and G. Thsi marginal CG purging is related to previously widely used direct standardization methods, when a reference group is also defined.

5. Marginal CG and 3-factor CGD purging
This standardization method is a two-step process to control for both marginal interaction and 3-factor interaction. This means that $m^*_{ijk} = m_{ijk} / \gamma_{ij}^{CG}$, and then $m^{**}_{ijk} = m^*_{ijk} / \tau_{ijk}^{CGD}$, where m^{**}_{ijk} is the frequency obtained in the first step and m^{**}_{ijk} is that obtained in the second step of the calculations.

6. Marginal CG and purging with reference to a standard group
This standardization method is a process to control for marginal interaction with reference to the corresponding group. This method with a standard group leads to the following expression: $m^*_{ijk} = m_{ijk} \tau_{is}^{CG} / \tau_{ij}^{CG}$ where s refers to the standard group.

<u>Computer-intensive methods</u>
Computer-intensive methods comprise a series of methods that can be used both in conventional and non-conventional data analytic situations.
Bootstrap methods use the data to generate more data. This seems similar to a trick used by the fictional Baron Munchausen, who when he found himself at the bottom of a lake got out by pulling himself up by his bootstraps. It turned out that this way a series of statistical problems can be tackled.
A randomization test is a permutation test based on randomization (random assignment) to test a null hypothesis about treatment effects in a randomized experiment. The test is carried out in the following manner. A test statistic is computed for the experimental data, then the data are permuted (divided or rearranged) repeatedly and the test statistic is computed for each of the resulting data permutations. Those data permutations, including the one representing the obtained results, constitute the reference set for determining significance. The proportion of data permutations in the reference set that have test statistic values in general greater than or equal to the value for the experimentally obtained results is the P-value or significance value.
With a Monte-Carlo test the significance of an observed test-statistic is assessed by comparing it with a sample of test statistics obtained by generating random samples using some assumed model. So randomization tests can be considered as special cases in a broader category of Monte-Carlo tests.
An exact test is virtually a special case of the Monte-Carlo method in that the whole probability space is used instead of the sample of it for the calculation of the p-value.
An application example is Monte-Carlo and bootstrap methods for the analysis of multidimensional contingency tables using loglinear models (Molnár et al., 1992). Cross-tabulated data that are not conform with widely accepted requirements concerning the expected cell frequencies in the table or with conventional assumptions on the distributions of some model parameters commonly occur in applied sciences. For example when Holford analysed survival data arranged in a three-dimensional table that was full of random and structural zeros, he fitted proportional hazards (loglinear) models (Holford, 1980). However, sparse contingency tables occur rarely in the literature, because of the warnings that the standard chi-square test of independence can be inaccurate when some expected cell frequencies are less than one count, or 20 percent or more are less than five (Cochran, 1954), although more liberal rules due to Yarnold (Yarnold, 1970) and Fienberg (Fienberg, 1979a) also appeared in the literature. No question, there has been a lingering debate over the reliability of conclusions based on loglinear models in sparse contingency tables and also over the estimation of asymptotic variances of the model parameters with the delta method in indirect models. Monte-Carlo and bootstrap method may help in deciding whether the conclusions based on the asymptotic assumptions on the distributions of the test-statistics are valid, and in estimating the variance of the parameters of the model.

<u>Bootstrap resampling</u>
One of the techniques for assessing variability of the point estimate of a u-term is what is called bootstrapping (Efron, 1979, Efron, 1981). Bootstrapping, again, is a computer intensive resampling method, "which allows estimation of variance and calculation of confidence intervals while making no distributional assumptions bootstrapping is in fact a simulation procedure that 'generates' data from the empirical distribution of the data sample" (Lewis and Orav, 1989, p. 252).
So the basic idea behind bootstrap resampling is that "when the sample contains all of the available information about the population, why not proceed as if the sample is the population for purposes of estimating the sampling distribution of the test statistic?" (Noreen 1989, p. 65). Further contributions were made later asking "if the estimator can take on a continuous range of values, why not use a smoothed version of the empirical density or distribution function?" (Lewis and Orav, 1989, pp. 277-282) that is why not use the distribution function obtained from an accepted loglinear model (P>0.05, let say) to sample from when computing the bootstrap estimate of variance?
One advantage of this method is that it makes us able to graphically display the distribution of every interaction term easily. Certainly, these graphically plotted distributions of the parameters of a loglinear model have never been seen before.

Herewith a natural solution is proposed to compute the bootstrap estimate of confidence intervals for the u-terms. If the loglinear model is saturated, then the sample is drawn repeatedly, with replacement, from the distribution of the observed table. If it is different from the saturated model, then the sample is drawn from a smoothed model distribution, where the model fits well (P>0.05).

Using the former notation let us generate a uniform pseudo-random number between 0 and 1. Now take a ball in hand and set the cell counter i to 1. Each p[i] is then compared with the generated random number in turn. If the generated number is smaller than or equal to p[i], then the cell counter is increased (i:=i+1), otherwise the ball is dropped into T[i]. Then the whole procedure is reiterated with another random number to specify the location of the second ball. After repeating the whole procedure 100 or 1000 times and computing the parameters for every generated table, the probability distributions of the interaction terms are represented on several histograms, and the confidence intervals based on upper and lower 2.5 percentiles together with other statistics are computed.

<u>CHAID analysis</u>
Chi-squared Automatic Interaction Detector (CHAID) is an exploratory statistical data analytic method used to study the relationship between a dependent variable and a series of predictor variables. With CHAID modeling one selects a set of predictors and their interactions that optimally predict the dependent measure. The developed model is a classification tree or answer tree that shows how major types formed from the independent (predictor or splitter) variables differentially predict a criterion or dependent variable.
The dependent variable may be a qualitative (nominal or ordinal) one or a quantitative variable. For qualitative variables, a series of chi-square analyses are conducted between the dependent and predictor variables. For quantitative variables, analysis of variance methods are used where intervals (splits) are determined optimally for the independent variables so as to maximize the ability to explain a dependent measure in terms of variance components.
Reading a CHAID Diagram: CHAID diagrams should be thought of as a tree trunk with progressive splits into smaller and smaller branches. The initial trunk is all of the participants in the study. A series of predictor or explanatory variables are assessed to see if splitting the sample based on these predictors leads to a statistically significant discrimination in the dependent variable. The result at the end of the tree building process is that we have a series of groups that are maximally different from one another on the dependent variable. At each step, statistical tests are made to determine if a significant split can be made. The ultimate result is a series of groups defined by one of more of the predictor variables, that are different from one another in certain variable levels. The tree can be displayed in an orientation from top-to-bottom or left-to-right or right-to-left and that results are identical. Different orientations of the same tree are sometimes useful to highlight different portions of the results.
The CHAID method has certain advantages as a way of looking for patterns in complicated data sets. The level of measurement for the dependent variable and predictor variables can be nominal, ordinal, or interval. The level of measurement for the predictor variables can be nominal, ordinal, or interval. Not all predictor variables need be measured at the same level. Missing values in predictor variables can be treated as a floating category so that partial data can be used whenever possible within the tree. If an appropriately conservative set of statistical criteria are used, the resulting models will primarily emphasize strong results without over-capitalizing on chance. CHAID modeling is essentially a stepwise statistical method and that there is always a potential for too much to be seen in the data even when very conservative statistical criteria are used. Nonetheless, in those cases in which there is not a strong theory in an area that would clearly indicate which variables are, and are not, probably predictors of some dependent measure, CHAID is very useful in identifying major „market segments".

<u>Testing hypotheses with spatial statistical methods</u>
Whittemore-test
Monte-Carlo test of individual data records can be performed with the Whittemore-test (Whittemore, 1987):

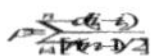

Monte-Carlo simulation of aggregated data records can be performed with the Ohno-test (Ohno, 1979). Clusters may show segregation of poligons. The test-statistic is:

Spatial clustering can be tested with this method, where C is the number of categories, A is the number of near pairs, $N(N-1)/2$ is the number of possible similar pairs, and $n_i(n_i-1)/2$ is the number of all possible similar pairs in category i.

Spatial smoothing

In some cases spatial distribution of data, similarly to the time series, may show oscillations. These oscillations can be eliminated with smoothing of the data. Similar methods can be used for the analysis of spatial data. In the case of spatial smoothing neighbourhood is defined similarly than it is made in temporal data, but the definition referes to the locality instead of time.

Kafadar (1999) used a smoothing method, which was applied in the following figures received with our own computer program on our example data.
Goals of spatial smoothing techniques are:

- Determination of space and event relationship
- Reduce measurement errors
- Eliminate outliers
- Help ascertaining real data patterns
- Minimize the effect of data aggregation bias.

Types of spatial smoothing algorithms
Spatial smoothing algorithms may be linear, e.g. moving averages, local polinomial regression, spatial splines for scale data and empirical Bayesian smoothing methods for binary data, and nonlinear, e.g. Tukey median filter, median polish or the *head-banging* algorithm.
For a general description of these methods let us suppose that we have n observations, and at $x_1, \ldots, x_n$ places there were $y_1, \ldots, y_n$ observations. In some cases the locations are given exactly, in other cases only the *i*th centroid is available. The y_i observation can be modelled with a function, for example with summing $F(x_i)$ plus an error term ε_i.
A good smoothing algorithm probably will have the following characteristics:

- Describe and estimate $F(x_i)$ well,
- Work with linear planes,
- Uneven distributions will not influence is working,
- Will result in smooth result
- Outliers are well identified in residuals but not in smoothed data.

With linear smoothers smoothed data can be described with a linear function of smoothed $\hat{y}_i$ data, where y_i is an observed data at place x_i, and $\hat{y}_i$ is a smoothed data:

$$y_i = \frac{\sum_{j=1}^{n} a_{ij} y_j}{\sum_{j=1}^{n} a_{ij}}$$

Ecological inference

Ecological inference is generally defined as a way of inferring individual behavior from aggregate data. Aggregate data are sometimes also called ecological data since ecologists at the end of the 19th century tried to find a relationship between environment and living organisms by the analysis of these data. Ecological data and ecological inference is frequently related to spatial data and spatial statistical methods. However, many nonspatial aggregate data exist as well. Aggregate data are especially often used in official statistics. Ecological inference is one of the longstanding unresolved problems in quantitative social science, especially in political science, and in many other fields, e.g. epidemiology, marketing research. Ecological inference is required, for example, in political science research when individual survey data are unavailable at precinct level, but they are available in aggregated format, i.e. there is a series of thematic maps. When looking at the beautiful colored thematic maps there is a temptation to make conclusions from the mapped data. For example if on two maps spatial distribution of young people and that of voters of a given party can be seen, then it is probable that a comparison of the two maps is made for finding a spatial correlation between the two features (King, 1997; Adolph et al., 2003).

The conclusions made from mapped data may be controversial, but sample survey data collection may be very expensive or not feasible. In many cases a solution to the ecological problem is required. Some good proposals have been made for such solutions (King, 1997; Adolph et al., 2003; Wakefield, 2004).

While the ecological paradox is related to an unknown relationship between the aggregated marginal and individual marginal data, the so-called Simpson's paradox is related to that between aggregated cross-sectional marginal and individual cross-sectional (layer) data. Categorical data can be displayed in multidimensional contingency tables. With three variables X, Y and Z one can display the distribution of X-Y cell counts at different levels of Z. These tables may be called *partial* tables. One can display the distribution of X-Y cell counts at the total level of Z. This table may be called *marginal* table.

The relationship between X and Y can be characterized by the odds ratio (OR), where $OR=(p_{11}p_{22})/(p_{12}p_{21})$, and p_{ij} (i=1,2; j=1,2) is the corresponding probability in category X=i, Y=j. The problem called Simpson's paradox or amalgamation paradox is that partial tables can show quite different associations than the marginal table. There are different situations when Simpson's paradox may emerge, i.e. a situation when the marginal probability is available, similarly as in the ecological problem, and there is also information about the whole marginal table. This is the case if in a multicentric clinical trial the basic summary data are calculated only, or if in social science official statistics i.e. precinct data are combined with basic cross-tabulated summary of survey data.

A characteristic and sensitive example of Simpson's paradox is that in an aggregated 2 by 2 table a medicine is beneficial while that in the individual centers not, or vice versa.

Another example of Simpson's paradox is about death penalty of individuals convicted of homicide (Agresti, 1970). Radelet (1981). Data can be arranged in a 2x2x2 table according to defendant's race (white or black), victim's race (white or black) and death penalty (yes or no). The data cube can traditionally be analysed from any of the corresponding two-dimensional planes. Since the development of loglinear models, however, this problem can easily be managed (Birch, 1963; Fienberg, 1970; Haberman, 1972; Bishop et al., 1975; Clogg, 1987; Molnár, 1991; Rudas, 1982; 1990; 1992; 1998; 2002; 2005), including computer-intensive methods (Edwards, 1995; Molnár, 1992).

Wakefield concluded that for good ecological inference it is worth to combine aggregate and individual level data (Wakefield, 2004). In other words official statistics and survey data are very useful to combine for finding a more accurate solution to the ecological problem (Wakefield, 2004).

The use of hierarchical modeling in spatial data analysis was extensively investigated by Banerjee (2004). Jackson has developed a software in R called *ecoreg* (Jackson, 2006a) that is suitable for amendment of the inference with traditional methods from aggregate data. Jackson states that individual-level inference from aggregate data alone can be subject to bias due to confounding and other possible errors such as model mis-specification or lack of information, but incorporating individual-level data can reduce these biases (Jackson et al., 2006b). Jackson showed how this can be done by supplementing the aggregate data with small samples of data from individuals within the areas, which directly link exposures and outcomes (Jackson, 2005).

Research for changing family planning attitudes and behavior: men's survey

Representative surveys of men's family planning attitudes and behavior have been taken nationally in 46 countries, most in sub-Saharan Africa, since 1990. Within this set of surveys, repeat surveys about the use of contraceptive methods reported by unmarried and sexually active men of reproductive age between 1993 and 2002 suggest that a growing percentage of men are using contraception, particularly condoms. Nevertheless, in many surveyed countries, mostly in sub-Saharan Africa, a minority of all men report currently using contraception.

Men tend to report higher levels of contraceptive use than women do. This finding suggests that some men use contraception in sexual relations outside marriage.

Among married men of reproductive age, levels of currently contraceptive use, whether modern or traditional, vary widely among 46 surveyed countries. Levels range from 9 percent in Mozambique and Niger to 77 percent in Albania. In only 16 of the surveyed countries do a majority of surveyed men report using any form of contraception. In 32 of 46 countries most married men who use contraception rely on modern methods, particularly oral contraceptives (Ocs), male condoms, injectables, and female sterilization. Reported use of male sterilization is highest in Nepal, at 7 percent. In all other surveyed countries 2 percent or less of men report using male sterilization.

In 14 countries men's use of the two traditional methods i.e. periodic abstinence and withdrawal, is as high or higher than use of modern methods. Eleven of these 14 are in sub-Saharan Africa, and the others are Albania, Bolivia, and Romania. Among 16 countries with repeat surveys of men since 1990, current contraceptive use among married men increased in 12, largely reflecting increases in modern method use. However, only in Burkina Faso, Cameroon, and Tanzania was the increase at least 10 percentage points. In Tanzania the increase in contraceptive use was due to increased use of modern methods, mainly condoms and injectables, while in Burkina Faso and Cameroon it largely reflected greater use of periodic abstinence. Levels of contraceptive use decreased in four countries.

Among 36 countries with data on unmarried sexually active men of reproductive age, levels of current contraceptive use range from 11 percent in Albania to 89 percent in Kazakhstan. In every surveyed country except Albania, more men report use of modern methods, primarily condoms, than of traditional methods.

In 15 countries at least 40 percent of unmarried sexually active men report currently using condoms, and as many as 64 percent in Jamaica and 72 percent in Kazakhstan. Condom use appears to have increased in eight of nine countries with more than one survey since 1990.

Condom use was much higher among unmarried sexually active men than married men. In 29 of the 36 countries with data on both unmarried and married men, current contraceptive use is greater among unmarried sexually active men than among married men, often substantially greater. In all 36 countries levels of condom use are higher among unmarried sexually active men than married men. In 27 of the 36 countries, unmarried sexually active men are at least five times as likely as married men to report condom use.

Many married people resist using condoms with their spouses, according to studies in Africa, because people associate condoms with being unfaithful, and so they fear that their spouses will mistrust them if they want to use condoms. Unmarried men are more likely than married men to use condoms because they want to protect against HIV!AIDS and other sexually transmitted infections (STIs) as well as against pregnancy.

Men and women differed in reported contraceptive use. In surveys men tend to overreport contraceptive use, and women to underreport it, particularly condom use. In societies that associate family planning with modernity, men may overreport contraceptive use to avoid appearing traditional. Men also may tell survey takers that they use contraception in order to be perceived as good caretakers, especially if they think that the interviewers are associated with a family planning program. Conversely, some married women may hesitate to report condom use, particularly in cultures that do not encourage open discussion about sexuality or where condoms are associated with extramarital sex.

Nevertheless, researchers tend to agree that women give more accurate responses than men to survey questions about contraceptive use. Most contraceptive methods are female-controlled, and thus women are more likely to know about their actual use. Some women use OCs, IUDs, and injectables without their partners' knowledge. Also, women usually are more motivated than men to know if they are being protected against pregnancy because they, not men, face the risk of unintended pregnancy.

In 41 of 46 surveyed countries, married men reported higher levels of current contraceptive use than married women. Differences are particularly great in sub-Saharan Africa. In 15 of 25 sub-Saharan countries surveyed, married men's reports of contraceptive use are at least 10 percentage points higher than married women's, and as much as 27 percentage points higher in Burkina Faso.

In 24 of 36 countries with surveys of both unmarried sexually active men and women, more unmarried sexually active men than unmarried sexually active women report current contraceptive use. However, the differences are smaller than differences between married men and women.

Much of the difference between men's and women's reports about contraception is due to differences in condom use. In 42 of 46 countries with surveys of married men-all except Albania, Bolivia, Egypt and Morocco-married men report higher levels of condom use than married women do. Also, in 36 of 46 countries more married men than married women report depending on periodic abstinence and, in 19 countries, on withdrawal.

One reason that married men report more condom use than married women is that some married men use condoms in sexual relations outside marriage, while few married women are presumed to have sex outside marriage. Some men are in polygynous marriages, particularly in sub-Saharan Africa. In the Demographic and Health Surveys (DHS), respondents can report current use of only one contraceptive method; the questionnaire for the men's surveys does not ask about contraceptive use with each wife or sex partner. Therefore men may report use of a particular contraceptive method but may in fact use two or more methods, depending on the partner. In a recent analysis of DHS data, differences in contraceptive use between polygynous and monogamous couples were not statistically significant when the husband in a polygynous marriage reported use of a method that agreed with the reports of any of his wives.

In 2000, countries were given the option of using a new DHS questionnaire in which men are asked about use of contraception at last sexual intercourse for up to three partners during the past 12 months, for example in Haiti and Rwanda. In the Reproductive Health Surveys (RHS) men have been asked this question since the mid-1990s, in addition to questions about current use.

Discrepancies in reported contraceptive use between men and women persist even between monogamous husbands and wives who are faithful to each other. Several reasons may account for these continued discrepancies. For example, one partner may be unaware that the other partner has stopped using a method, or one partner may be using contraception without the other's knowledge. Partners may have different judgments as to what qualifies as "current" contraceptive use, or they may have different understandings of what constitutes a certain contraceptive method, for example, one partner may define periodic abstinence as sporadic abstinence during the postpartum period or during a woman's menses while the other defines it accurately as deliberate abstinence during a woman's fertile period. Furthermore, respondents may give socially expected responses, either overstating or concealing contraceptive practice depending on the context.

With various statistical methods, including multivariate methods and population segmentation methods it can be proved that married men differ in their levels of current contraceptive use according to their demographic and socioeconomic characteristics, including educational attainment, urban or rural residence, age, and number of children born. Such differences resemble the differences in contraceptive use among groups of women, with some exceptions.

Education affects contraceptive use. The more schooling that men have, the more likely they are to use contraception. In all 46 countries surveyed since 1990 except Mauritania, married men's contraceptive use consistently increases with their level of education.

In all surveyed countries except Rwanda, contraceptive use is consistently higher among married men in urban areas than in rural areas. In 10 of 46 countries contraceptive use among married men in urban areas is at least 20 percentage points higher than among rural men. The smallest differences are in the Dominican Republic, Jamaica, and Rwanda, where married men in rural areas are almost as likely as men in urban areas to use contraception.

Among married men the use of contraception generally peaks between ages 30 and 49. Among married women contraceptive use peaks in a more narrow age range-between the ages of 30 and 39.

In general, as among married women, married men without any children are less likely to use contraception than men who have children. But the patterns among men are not as clear as among married women. In 34 of 45 countries surveyed, the level of contraceptive use is highest among men who have two or three children. In over half of surveyed countries at least 30 percent of married men with four or more children report using contraception.

Some nonusers say they intend to use contraception in the future. In 32 of 43 surveyed countries, at least 30 percent of such men say they intend to use contraception in the future. The percentage varies widely among surveyed countries, from 12 percent in Mauritania and Senegal to over 60 percent in Bangladesh, Cape Verde, Malawi, Nepal, Uganda, Zambia, and Zimbabwe.

Most men who say they do not intend to use contraception explain that they want to have more children or that their wives are at little risk of pregnancy, either because they or their wives are infertile or because their wives are postmenopausal. In 21 of 41 countries (17 in sub-Saharan Africa, and the Dominican Republic, Mauritania, Morocco, and Pakistan) the main reason that men give this answer is wanting more children. In 14 countries, most outside sub-Saharan Africa, the main reason is that their partners are unlikely to become pregnant.

Another main reason that men report is opposition to family planning itself, either for religious reasons or other reasons. Also, in sub-Saharan Africa and a few countries elsewhere, some men say they do not intend to use contraception because they know little about it or where to obtain it. Men are less likely than women to mention concerns about health or side effects of contraceptive methods as an important reason to avoid using family planning.

Men are more likely than women to have heard of at least one contraceptive method-most often the condom-surveys show. Men's awareness of female contraceptive methods, however, is almost always lower than that of women's. Men also are more likely than women to be exposed to radio and television messages about family planning and are about as likely as women to approve of family planning messages in the mass media. While most married men approve of family planning, they are less likely to approve than married women in the same country.

Married couples increasingly are discussing family planning, surveys find. Communication between partners about childbearing and family planning is closely linked to successful contraceptive use. Still, many wives do not know or misperceive their husbands' attitudes toward family planning. Overall, more married men are likely to approve of family planning than women think.

In the 21 countries outside sub-Saharan Africa with men's surveys, levels of contraceptive awareness among both married men and women approach 100 percent for at least one method-except in Belize, Bolivia, Mauritania, and Pakistan, where levels for men range between 61 percent and 89 percent, and for women, between 71 percent and 92 percent. In 23 of the 25 countries in sub-Saharan Africa with men's surveys, more married men than women have heard of at least one contraceptive method. However, men are almost always less aware than women of female contraceptive methods, including OCs, IUDs, and injectables.

Concerning mass media communication, and radio and TV family planning messages it was concluded from the research results that messages reach most men. Messages broadcast in the mass media are a key source of family planning information for men. Exposure to family planning messages on radio and television, as well as exposure to the mass media in general, can increase use of contraception and help change reproductive preferences. In over half of the 40 countries with data, at least half of men have heard family planning messages in the mass media, either radio, television, or both. Surveys find that family planning messages on radio and television reach more men than women.

Most men approve of family planning messages in the mass media. In 30 of the 31 countries with data, more than half of men consider family planning messages acceptable in the mass media. Chad is the exception. In the Dominican Republic, Gabon, Kenya, Malawi, Morocco, Nicaragua, Peru, Uganda, and Zimbabwe, over 90 percent find family planning messages acceptable. In general, married men and women report similar levels of approval of family planning messages in the mass media.

The reach of family planning messages through the mass media appears to have grown in recent years, based on limited survey data. Among the eight countries with trend data on men's exposure to family planning messages, the percentage of married men who said they had heard about family planning on radio or TV was higher in the more recent survey in all but Zimbabwe.

Discussion of family planning within the family is important to contraceptive use. Husbands and wives who discuss family planning together are more likely to use contraception effectively and to have fewer children. Surveys ask married men and women whether they discussed the practice of family planning with their partners in the preceding year and, if so, how often they discussed it-whether once or twice, or more often.6

In 23 of 35 countries with survey data, at least half of married men say they discussed family planning with their wives within the past year. Still, the percentage varies widely, from about 25 percent in Cape Verde and Senegal to over 75 percent in Bangladesh, Bolivia, Kenya, Malawi, Nicaragua, Peru, and Zimbabwe. In 24 countries-most in sub-Saharan Africa-most men who discussed family planning did so more than twice within the preceding year.

The percentage of married men who discussed family planning with their wives increased in 9 of 12 countries with more than one men's survey since 1990. In general, similar proportions of married men and women report discussing family planning. Among 33 countries with data on both men and women, the difference between men's and women's responses exceeds 10 percentage points in only 9.

Most men seem to approve of family planning. In 32 of 35 countries with data, at least half of married men say they approve of family planning. In eight surveyed countries-Bangladesh, Malawi, Morocco, Nepal, Nicaragua, Peru, Rwanda, and Zimbabwe-over 90 percent of married men approve. Nevertheless, in 24 of the 34 countries with data on both men and women, more married women than men approve of family planning. Differences between men and women in approval of family planning vary widely among countries.

Women often misperceive men's attitudes. In order for a husband and wife to agree on the use of family planning, couples not only must discuss the topic but also accurately perceive each other's attitudes. Surveys show that, overall, men are more likely to approve of family planning than women believe. In 33 of 34 countries surveyed, all except Kazakhstan, the percentage of married men who say they approve of family planning is much greater than the percentage of married women who say their husbands approve. Differences vary from 4 percentage points in Turkey to 39 points in Burkina Faso.

In 19 countries at least one woman in every five says she does not know whether her husband approves of family planning. Women who do not know whether their husbands approve of family planning, or who believe that their husbands disapprove, are much less likely to use contraception than those who believe that their husbands approve.

Particularly in sub-Saharan Africa, most married men surveyed say they want more children. Men are more likely than women to want additional children, and on average they want to have a larger number of children than women do. Survey findings on these reproductive intentions can help programs make short-term forecasts of fertility and future demand for family planning.

Fewer men than women want to stop having children. Surveys ask men whether they want to have another child. Among surveyed countries the percentage of married men who want to stop having children altogether, including those who are sterilized or whose wives are sterilized, ranges from under 5 percent in Chad and Niger to about 70 percent in Bolivia and Brazil. The percentage of married men who want to stop having children increased between surveys in 9 of 13 countries with repeat surveys since 1990. Only in Malawi and Zambia, however, was the increase at least 10 percentage points.

In 26 of 43 countries, 24 in sub-Saharan Africa, more married men want to continue having children than want to stop having children. Similarly, in 25 of these 43 countries more women want to continue having children than to stop having children.

In 34 of the 43 countries, however, fewer men than women want to stop having children. In Guinea, Jamaica, Mali, Mauritania, Nepal, Romania, Senegal, and Uganda, the gap between men's and women's responses is at least 10 percentage points. In the remaining nine countries where more married women than married men want to stop childbearing, the differences between men's and women's responses are less than five percentage points.

Men want larger families than women do. Surveys also ask men with children: If you could go back to the time you did not have any children and could choose exactly the number of children to have in your whole life, how many would that be? Men without children are asked a similar question: If you could choose exactly the number of children to have in your whole life, how many would that be? Responses to these questions provide data on men's desired, or ideal family size.

Among 41 countries surveyed since 1990, married men's desired family size ranges from an average of as few as 2.4 children in Bangladesh to as many as 12.3 in Niger and 15.1 in Chad. In all surveyed sub-Saharan countries except Cape Verde, and as well as in Mauritania, Morocco, and Pakistan, married men want an average of more than four children.

Married men's desired family size fell in 11 of 17 countries with more than one survey since 1990. In Benin, Cameroon, and Ghana, men's average desired family size declined substantially-by as much as 2.5 children in Cameroon between 1991 and 1998. In the other six countries desired family size remained the same or increased slightly between surveys.

In 21 of 41 surveyed countries with data on desired family size among both men and women, married men on average want at least 0.5 more children than married women want. In 9 of 25 countries in sub-Saharan Africa, married men want at least two children more than do married women, and as many as 6.6 more in Chad. Outside sub-Saharan Africa the differences are much smaller.

As might be expected, polygynous husbands have larger ideal family sizes, and more children than monogamous husbands in the same country. Polygyny is particularly prevalent in West Africa, probably accounting for some of the large differences in desired family size between married men and women in West African countries surveyed, because a surveyed man can be married to multiple wives whereas a woman can be married to only one husband.

Nevertheless, even among monogamous couples married men want more children than married women do. The greatest differences in family size preferences among both monogamous and polygynous men occur in surveyed West African countries. Many African men may become polygynous to have the larger families that they want.

Recent surveys report on the sexual experience of young men, ages 15 through 24, and on their knowledge and use of contraception. Most data on young men come from DHS and RHS. Not all surveys in the DHS and RHS programs have asked young men about their sexual activity, however. In addition, six countries-Costa Rica, the Dominican Republic, Jamaica, Mozambique, Romania, and Zimbabwe-have conducted special surveys of young men specifically to obtain detailed information on their reproductive behavior and knowledge. These six Young Adult Reproductive Health Surveys (YARHS) are part of the RHS program.

In most surveyed countries half of young men have their first sexual experience before age 18. The median age at first marriage is between 23 and 30, surveys find. The percentage of unmarried youth who are currently sexually active varies widely from one country to another. In many countries substantial percentages of young men are sexually active before marriage. Unmarried sexually active young men are more likely than married men of the same age to use contraception, especially condoms, which can help protect against both pregnancy and most STIs, including HIV/AIDS, when used consistently and correctly. Nevertheless, many unmarried sexually active young men do not use any protection.

The DHS asks young men whether they have ever had sex before marriage. The RHS and YARHS classify young men as having premarital sex if their age at first sex is less than their age at first marriage. Surveys also ask young unmarried men if they are currently sexually active-by asking those who are sexually active whether they have had sex in the four weeks before the survey.

In 16 of 41 countries with survey data, at least half of adolescent men ages 15 to 19 have had sex before marriage. In 36 of the 41 countries at least half of men ages 20 to 24 have had sex before marriage. These percentages vary widely by country.

In 17 of 38 countries surveyed, at least one unmarried adolescent man in every five reported having had sex in the four weeks before the survey. In 9 of the 38 countries, however, less than one unmarried adolescent man in every ten said he had sex recently. Levels of recent sexual activity are higher among unmarried men ages 20 to 24 than among unmarried adolescents ages 15 to 19.

Young men are more likely than young women to begin sex before marriage. In 37 of 41 countries with survey data on both men and women, more adolescent men ages 15 to 19 than women of the same ages report having had premarital sex.

Similarly, in all 41 countries surveyed, higher percentages of men ages 20 to 24 than women of the same ages report having had premarital sex. Young unmarried men in most countries, in both age groups, also are more likely than young unmarried women to be sexually active currently.

Young unmarried men face years of potential risk to HIV/AIDS. In most surveyed countries about half of unmarried men are potentially exposed to the risks of HIV/AIDS and other STIs for at least five years. Sexually active unmarried young men and women are at substantial potential risk because they tend to engage in risky sexual practices, is, the age by which half of men in a particular age group including having multiple sex partners.

The length of time between sexual debut and first marriage provides a measure of the period in which young men are potentially most exposed to risk. Men's surveys provide information on the difference between the medial age at first sexual intercourse, i.e. the age by which half of men in a particular age group became sexually active, and the median age at first marriage, i.e. the age by which half of men first married or entered into a legal, consensual, or similar union. People are still at risk after marriage, if they continue to engage in risky sexual behavior. Young who get infected before marriage can transmit the infection to their spouses after marriage too.

First intercourse typically occurs before age 18. In 38 countries surveyed since 1990, among men aged 25-29 the median age at first sexual intercourse ranges from 15.5 years in Honduras to 21.3 years in Ethiopia. In 22 of 38 countries the median age at first sex is below 18. United Nations analysis of survey data for men aged 220-24 indicates that the more education young men have, the more likely they start sex before age 18. In contrast, young women of the same age group with more education are less likely to begin sexual activity before age 18.

First marriage typically is at age 23 or older. Among 41 countries with survey data, the median age at first marriage among men aged 25-29 varies from age 20 in Nepal to age 30 in Senegal. In 29 of the 41 countries about half of such men had first married by the time they reached an age between 23 and 30. The gap between sexual debut and marriage typically is over five years.

Unmarried young men most likely use contraceptives in age group 20-24. In contrast, married men aged 20-24 have the lowest level of contraceptive use. In 15 of 32 countries with sufficient survey data, less than half of sexually active unmarried adolescent men currently use condoms or any other form of contraception. In this group levels of contraceptive use vary from 13 percent in El Salvador to 93 percent in Kazakhstan.

Levels of current contraceptive use are usually higher among sexually active unmarried men aged 20-24 than among those aged 15-19. In 13 of 34 countries, less than half of unmarried men aged 20-24 currently use contraception.
Unmarried young men who do use contraception rely mostly on condoms. In 18 of 29 countries with sufficient data, at least one-third of unmarried sexually active adolescent men currently use condoms, and as many as 80 percent in Kazakhstand. In 21 of 31 surveyed countries with sufficient data for unmarried sexually active men aged 20-24, at least one-third currently use condoms.

Other young men surveyed say they use the traditional contraceptive methods of periodic abstinence and withdrawal. However, these are usually not as effective as condoms in preventing pregnancy, and provide little or no protection against HIV/AIDS or other STIs. In most countries less than 20 percent of unmarried men aged 15-24 currently use traditional methods.

Examples of evidence-based successful communication programs that changed attitudes and behavior in demographic processes

Malaria

One of the largest public health problem on earth is malaria. It is, however, no longer a major public health concern in developed countries. However, quite recently malaria killed 1-3 million people annually, mostly children under the age of five in sub-Saharan Africa. In 1998, the WHO launched the Roll Back Malaria (RBM) drive to halve malaria mortality by 2010. The Italians successfully confronted malaria and eradicated it between the late 19th and mid 20th centuries. The Italians employed education and applied socio-political will; however, ecological and socio-economic conditions in sub-Saharan Africa are more hospitable to the disease. RBM strategies consider the Italian experience while awaiting a major scientific breakthrough necessary to achieve success.

Malaria rendered the Pontine marshlands just south of. Rome completely uninhabitable. Roman legions were so keenly aware of malaria's danger to their ranks that they avoided potential military campsites where it might flourish. The name of the disease is even derived from the Italian expression mal'aria, meaning "bad air," which describes the swampy wastelands where the disease was most often found in Europe. In the mid-seventeenth century, the Pope's physician recognized the anti-malarial properties of the bark of the Peruvian Cinchona and encouraged its widespread distribution. Quinine, later identified as the critical component of the bark, would remain the most effective anti-malarial drug for the next three centuries.

Though the Englishman Ronald Ross was awarded the Noble Prize in 1902 for his discovery in 1898 of the malaria transmission cycle, the Italian trio of Battista Grassi, Amico Bignami, and Giuseppe Bastianelli proved the parasite-vector-host transmission cycle in humans within months of Ross's breakthrough.

Due to the Italian anti-malaria campaign malaria in Italy was eradicated almost a half century ago, the Italian anti-malaria campaign does have relevance to present-day efforts to bring malaria under control in sub-Saharan Africa, where success is much more difficult to reach despite of the WHO's Roll Back Malaria campaign.

Malaria was a killer on the Italian peninsula right up until the mid-twentieth century. It is estimated that before control efforts began in Italy, between 300,000 and 2 million Italians were infected and 10-20 thousand died of malaria every year. The effects on the economy were devastating. Two million hectares of fertile land and millions of hours of worker productivity were lost due to malaria. Through the early 20th century, Italian farm workers lived in the equivalent of a feudal system, impoverished, malnourished, illiterate, and nearly homeless. The Rockefeller Foundation sent American public health expert Lewis Hackett to Italy in 1924 to monitor its malaria problem. After visiting the Roman Compagna, Hackett noted: The mode of life is as primitive as anything I have seen in the tropics one would have to go back to Cro-Magnon days for a parallel. The poor had only one option to combat the seasonal malarial epidemics that were so deadly: escape to more hospitable environs, namely to the north of Italy or more likely to North America. Between 1880 and 1930 nearly 10 million Italians immigrated to countries outside of Europe. Soon after Italy became a unified nation in 1861 the government started to seriously confront the malaria burden. The wide-ranging anti-malarial and health legislation passed by the Italian parliament in the late 19th and early 20th century was meant to attack the disease on all fronts. Parliament passed laws to provide free malaria prophylactic treatment to all citizens, and a system referred to as bonification was instituted. This initially referred to the reclamation and resettlement of malaria-infested areas, through swamp drainage, larvicides, and insecticides. It progressed to the construction of complex irrigation and damn systems and the federal acquisition of large tracts of undeveloped private land for division and redistribution to small property-less farmers. Eventually bonification meant an all-encompassing mode of malaria control, which not only included attacking the malaria parasite through quinine distribution to all citizens, and eliminating the mosquito vector through land reclamation and cultivation and pyrethroid insecticide spraying, but it also entailed the betterment of the citizens themselves.

From the point of communication programs it is important to note that years after Ross and the Italian group had proven the bite of the Anopheles mosquito as the route responsible for transmission, uneducated peasants still attributed malaria to breathing swamp air, drinking swamp water, or eating blackberries. Many were afraid to take the quinine prophylaxis because they feared it was a government conspiracy to poison them and spread the disease. One particularly archaic home treatment was to place malarial infants in hot ovens to rid them of their fevers. Parliamentary laws aimed at dispelling misconceptions, construction of a health infrastructure and improved living conditions for the poor. Schools taught sanitary lessons, distributed quinine, and checked for early symptoms of malaria. In addition to international centers of malaria research and training in Rome, regional malaria stations were set up all over Italy to conduct research and to monitor and coordinate treatment efforts with local physicians and healthcare personnel. The Italian drive met with obstacles and setbacks. The extremely powerful oligarchy of wealthy aristocratic landowners in the south adamantly resisted any change in the status quo. The two world wars resulted in neglect and destruction of many previous land reclamation reforms. Retreating Nazi forces, in a form of biological warfare, deliberately created conditions aimed at fostering malaria epidemics among local populations and Allied forces. Bomb craters filled with rainwater created ideal environments for mosquito vectors to breed. However, the Allied introduction of DDT coupled with postwar reconstruction rid Italy of its last major outposts of malaria, and by the 1950s, the disease was all but eradicated on the peninsula. Malaria's impact on Italian history is fascinating, but its importance lies in its application to current global public health concerns. Malaria remains on a rampage in the tropical regions of the world, especially in sub-Saharan Africa. It is among the greatest causes of mortality in children under 5 years and ranks only with AIDS and tuberculosis in overall mortality of communicable diseases. Although progress has been made, the disease still kills 1-3 million people every year; 90 percent of these people live in sub-Saharan Africa. The Italian experience demonstrates that with enough impetus, resources, and motivation, malaria can be defeated. But can the Italian experiment be applied to sub-Saharan Africa? Deeper analysis is needed for demanding public health issues in the sub-Saharan region of Africa.

Unlike Italy, malaria is not confined to just the swamps or coasts in sub-Saharan Africa. It is almost everywhere, in the forests, cities, savannas, and hills. The tropical climate of sub-Saharan Africa supports survival of mosquito vectors and malaria transmission throughout the year. In Italy there were four major vectors of malaria, two of which had identical behavior. All of the Italian vectors had well defined biting and breeding habits, were endophilic (preferring to rest indoors), and were effective malaria transmitters only between spring and fall. During intense malaria outbreaks, Italians in the affected areas abandoned the land often not to return; the main reason why so much land was left uncultivated. Along the Tyrrhenian coast where large estates had developed, seasonal workers would descend from the interior Appennini Mountains to cultivate the land just as the transmission period was beginning. This type of economy and demographic movement brought about epidemic malaria, which marked a distinct mode of transmission in comparison to most of sub-Saharan Africa, where malaria is endemic. In an endemic area the average person receives at least 100 malaria-infected mosquito bites per year, and the disease is transmittable year-round. Without the protection of screens or insecticide-treated bed nets, many areas of rural West Africa are hyperendemic, potentially recording average biting rates of up to 150-175 bites per person per night and an estimated 35,000 infective bites per person per year.

In sub-Saharan Africa there are 11 main vectors and at least eight or nine others of regional or seasonal importance. Anopheles gambiae is the most lethal and widespread vector species of malaria in sub-Saharan Africa, and it usually carries the Plasmodium falciparum parasite. It is believed that Anopheles gambiae developed its extremely anthropophilic biting behavior in the Afrotropical rain forest with the onset of the agricultural revolution and slash and burn technique. As societies in Africa began to practice deforestation for agriculture and settlement, they easily became Anopheles gambiae's most reliable source of blood as human development produced expanding breeding sites in puddles and ditches. Human populations increased and migrated to new areas, and Anopheles gambiae followed them. The Plasmodium falciparum parasite, because of its high lethality in human hosts, probably evolved relatively recently in genetic evolutionary terms, about 5-10,000 years ago. Its' survival is dependent upon the high biting rates of Anopheles gambiae and its' further transmission and replication from one host to another before killing the host. Wherever man is in sub-Saharan African, Anopheles gambiae and Plasmodium falciparum are nearby, making the vicious gambiae-falciparum-human equilibrium seemingly impossible to break. Indoor insecticide spraying was a very effective tool of the anti-malaria campaign in Italy because the main vectors rested indoors. When a house was sprayed the mosquito vectors were forced to remain outside at night, their most active biting time. In the Italian night, mosquitoes could not easily find human hosts, nor survive the cooler temperatures. The life cycles of Plasmodium falciparum and Plasmodium vivax, the two most prevalent malaria strains in Italy, are interrupted in the mosquito when ambient temperature drops below 18 0 C and 160 C, respectively, temperatures within range of Italian spring, autumn, or even summer night. Indoor insecticide spraying in sub-Saharan Africa is less effective because mosquito vectors there are not necessarily house dwelling, and have built up resistance to DDT and other insecticides. Moreover, the nocturnal temperature of Africa is warm enough to support both mosquito and parasite survival outside. The diverse behavior of African malaria vectors makes it impossible to concentrate on specific breeding areas, as was done so successfully in Italy's interior wetlands and coastal plains. African malaria simply leaves no safe haven for people to take refuge, which contributes to the widespread and somewhat fatalistic perception by many people there that malaria cannot be solved but is simply another burden to bear. Southern Italy's delay in eradicating malaria before the introduction of DDT may parallel the future of the poor and remote regions of sub-Saharan Africa, specifically those places incapable of delivering treatment rapidly to their people. That a measles vaccine exists and yet almost as many children die in Africa from measles as malaria demonstrates that science can only go so far. Even with the best intentions and optimal

administration, RBM may not be capable of addressing such basic challenges as the unavailability of sterile needles to vaccinate. And just as in many parts of southern Italy, sub-Saharan Africa may have to wait for both a greatly improved health infrastructure and the introduction of a revolutionary breakthrough from the lab bench such as genetically modified mosquitoes or oral or transdermal vaccines.

While the Italian strategies cannot be applied to present-day sub-Saharan Africa, the Italian experience proves that malaria and poverty are so interwoven that in order to defeat either plight, they must be attacked simultaneously. The concomitant HIV epidemic has a multifaceted impact on malaria and also contributes to economic and societal disarray, amplifying the need for coordinated strategies. Both scientific progress and socio-economic development are needed in the fight against malaria. Quinine distribution and DDT were equally as important as improved living conditions and swamp drainage in defeating Italian malaria. The sociopolitical and ecological conditions in sub-Saharan Africa may be more challenging than they were in Italy. However, greater resources exist today to deal with the more formidable task. Roll Back Malaria and other health drives such as the Multilateral Initiative on Malaria, and the Global Fund to Fight AIDS, Tuberculosis, and Malaria have been launched. The World Bank, the International Monetary Fund, many nations, and philanthropic organisations have devoted billions of dollars to the cause. Media, public, and government pressure have mounted on pharmaceutical companies to research and develop affordable drugs and vaccines for previously neglected diseases. The genomes of Anopheles gambiae and Plasmodium falciparum have been sequenced. Victory remains far off, but the problem has been defined (Amorosa et al., 2005).

A special issue is that if malaria would be eradicated from the sub-Saharan region of Africa, population growth would speed up further in the overpopulated and fast-growing societies. So successful communication and management programs may have adverse effects or can be the source of newly emerging problems that should be solved.

Iron deficiency

There is consensus that a communications component is crucial to the success of iron supplementation and fortification programs. However, in many instances, we have not applied what we know about successful advocacy and program communications to iron programs. Communication must playa larger and more central role in iron programs to overcome several common shortcomings and allow the use of new commitments and investments in iron programming to optimum advantage. One shortcoming is that iron program communication has been driven primarily by the supply side of the supply-demand continuum. That is, technical information has been given without thought for what people want to know or do. To overcome this, the communication component, which should be responsive to the consumer perspective, must be considered at program inception, not enlisted late in the program cycle as a remedy when interventions fail to reach their targets. Another shortcoming is the lack of program focus on behavior. Because the "technology" of iron, a supplement, or fortified or specific local food must be combined with appropriate consumer behavior, it is not enough to promote the technology. The appropriate use of technology must be ensured, and this requires precise and strategically crafted communications. A small number of projects from countries as diverse as Indonesia, Egypt, Nicaragua and Peru offer examples of successful communications efforts and strategies for adaptation by other countries.

Communication, the strategic and creative use of communication, is central to making the technological advances in successful program stories. Communication affects the entire program. One of the roles for communication is advocacy, telling of our successes, inciting further global interest in action. Another role for communication in program work is to bring to life consumer demand by helping people take action, making programs work more actively. Consumer demand is a key lesson that many programs have trouble applying. Major program waste comes from assuming that making supply available will lead to appropriate use.

When communication is used to its fullest, allowing demand to drive supply, there are five key lessons that must be applied to achieve success.

The first is to implement communication and communicators at the beginning of a program. We should not think of communication in terms of products (fliers, posters, videos) : rather as a process to create and satisfy demand. A professional or team familiar with communication planning, strategy and management is required, not just a designer to draw the poster.

The second lesson is to understand thoroughly the intended beneficiaries or participants of the program through doing the research. Communicators should be able to provide insights from intended participants related to their actual perceptions and practices, and their resistances to and motivations for new ideas, concepts and practices. When done well, the participant's circumstances and needs are analysed in the context of social or epidemiologic profile of the situation. This analysis allows the pros and cons of various strategies to be examined to ensure that the needs of the consumers are met, efficaciously and efficiently.

The third lesson is to use communication strategically. Communication is not about numbers of materials or broadcasts. It is about reaching people and moving them to action. Strategy will depend upon the specific culture, on the goals of the program and on the solutions available. For communication to succeed, the strategy must combine the art and the science of communication. The art is the creative element, i.e. the expression of an idea, a symbol or an action that captures attention because it is meaningful and memorable. The science is the definition of technical content, the efficient and strategic use of media, the development of an educational video or a print material to prompt action or change.

The fourth and fifth lessons also relate to strategy, but to the communication per se, rather than the process. The fourth lesson is to ensure that the communication is precise. A textbook of information belies the lack of strategy. When you see or hear a communication, you should know who is being addressed, precisely what is being communicated and what, precisely. a person should do with the information. There should be evidence that the communication will be delivered at a time and a place relevant to the information and action.

The fifth lesson is that communication must resolve resistances and build on assets, i.e. people's existing knowledge and practices. When you look at a communication, don't check to see if all of the scientific information is correct, but ask yourself the following questions. Is the problem being addressed clear? What is the resistance or barrier being removed so that the problem can be solved? Is the communication convincingly addressing the barrier to action? Resistance resolution should be evaluated, not just the facts about the issue in focus, for example iron or anemia in the case of targeting iron deficiency as an example.

For communication to do its job for iron programs, these five lessons have been and must be applied. Otherwise the call for better education and more consumer participation will not be realized. During the application of these lessons to programs points the following questions should be answered and the communication programs managed accordingly.

Is communication a consideration from the beginning? Alliances must occur at the beginning of program design with local communication experts, whether in public or private agencies. Professionals are available in most countries.

Have we done the audience research? For example there is excellent qualitative and quantitative research related to perceptions and practices, particularly in the area of iron supplementation for women. Although much of this research is country specific, in some cases, there have been enough studies that findings can be generalized and methods certainly can be shared among all programs.

Examples of results from research concerning iron deficiency and replacement:

- Almost all women but those experiencing extreme nausea are willing to take iron pills.

- Women want to know what to do about side effects

- Women, especially pregnant women, need to be reassured that iron pills are not medicine.

- Remembering to take the pill is a problem.

- Tea drinking behavior can be modified.

- Heme iron and vitamin C food intake are entirely dependent on availability, but if available, they will be consumed.

With this knowledge in hand before, not after, program design, appropriate steps can be taken to adjust to consumer needs. Although country-specific work may be required, some findings can be generalized and used by others. Also, there is clear guidance that should be made more widely available to programs to help streamline the process of participant research.

Are we using communication strategically to promote the global iron agenda? The answer is no, but there are plans to remedy the situation. One proposal for future advocacy action calls for the development of activities on two fronts, i.e., globally, and within specific sectors, with information tailored for each.

Concerted efforts on networking, creating advocates, mobilizing sources, and also on materials development and dissemination are proposed. Putting this plan into action would optimize many dormant commitments.

Are we using communications strategically within programs? Looking at the sum of all programs, the answer would undoubtedly be no. But, there are programs in which communications have been used strategically, the communication was precise, resistances were resolved and assets used convincingly.

Concerning iron deficiency and iron supply key program factors in ensuring the effect of communications on compliance included the following:

1. Individual counseling. With counseling, almost all women, ($\geq$80 percent) were willing to take iron tablets.

2. Training in interpersonal communications. In exit interviews, 98 percent of women respondents served by personnel trained in counseling skills said that would follow the advice offered vs. only 32 percent of women who were counseled by people who had not been trained.

3. Addressing the common danger points for dropping out of supplementation programs. Research and program experience indicated there were key times for action to address side effect to urge continuation of pill taking.

4. Finding a way to remind women to take pills every day.

The take-home message from the success of the program communication highlighted here was that it was not information about anemia, iron or blood that was important, but rather creation of demand by specifically addressing concerns and problems of women that were articulated during research.

For iron supplementation programs for women, a communication strategy framework existed that was not complicated or costly to implement, that had been tested and that was available to minimize investments in pills and their distribution.

Another area with recent success in iron communications was adolescent programs, both school and non-school based proms.

Also, critical to supplementation efforts with adolescents seemed to be the addition of education on diet improvement.

As with communication programs to support iron supplementation for women, communication strategies and programs for adolescent school children do not have to be complex. The strategy must include information for parents and students about the supplement (why, when, where), offered through community channels such as school, meetings and possibly through local mass media, answers to fears, if they exist, about the supplement; and discussion of the supplementation in the context of overall dietary improvement. Adolescents should be given tools as part of the communication to improve dietary practices and to become a medium for dietary change in the home.

In conclusion, a successful supplementation program incorporates implementation and strategic use of communication plans from program inception. Effective use of communication strategies will bring vitality to supplements programs resulting in advocacy and behavior changes (Griffiths, 2002).

The dreaded Poliovirus causes serious paralysis in children. However, Poliovirus eradication effort added new weapon to its armory. The leaders of the global program to eradicate poliovirus are reintroducing an old tool to fight the disease: an oral polio vaccine designed specifically to protect against the most pervasive strain of poliovirus, known as type 1. The only vaccine used in the 16- year eradication campaign targets three strains of the virus. The new monovalent oral polio vaccine (mOPV)-a version of which was used extensively before the adoption of trivalent OPV in the 1960s- offers "more wallop per punch". The program is coordinated by the World Health Organisation (WHO). It is not a silver bullet, caution officials at WHO and the U.S. CDControl and Prevention. Program officials stress that mOPV will augment, not replace, the well-honed strategy of immunizing every child under age 5 where polio remains a threat with several doses of trivalent OPV each year. But if mOPV works as hoped, it may be what it takes to tip the scale" says David Heymann, who heads WHO's eradication effort (Roberts, 2005).

A Brazilian HIV/AIDS success story is about the use of anti-retroviral drugs (ARVs) that in developing countries have in the past focused on the limitations caused by the high cost of the drugs and by the lack of health system capacity to adequately deliver and make use of them. An additional concern has been the risk of increasing resistance to ARVs if there were widespread inappropriate administration and lack of monitoring. Lately, however, there have been stronger calls for scaling up access to ARVs with less attention paid to these concerns and limitations. The experience of Brazil has often been mentioned in this context. One prominent feature of Brazil's HIV/acquired immunodeficiency syndrome (AIDS) program - universal access to ARVs - plus epidemiological data indicating that the spread of the disease has been brought under control, have resulted in the program often being hailed as a success story (Oliveira-Cruz et al., 2004).

Another success story is about avoiding HIV infection through a prevention communication campaign. In the global fight against the spread of HIV/AIDS, there are few happy stories to tell. Thailand may be one. Asia looks to Thailand's AIDS success story. Asian health workers train at Thai university after nation cuts HIV rate by 83 percent. Its nationwide prevention campaign, launched in the early 1990s, has dramatically cut the spread of the disease. As a result, the number of people testing positive for HIV, the virus linked to AIDS, fell last year to 23,676, down 83 percent from a peak in 1991 of 142,819 according to the Thai government. Thailand's success in averting an epidemic on the scale of the most afflicted African nations has won international praise - particularly its promotion of 100 percent condom use in its sex industry, and the involvement of Buddhist monks. Keen to share its experience, Thailand is emerging as a learning center for developing countries in Asia, where AIDS is spreading rapidly. At Thailand's Chiang Mai University, training courses for AIDS prevention have attracted healthcare workers from around the region, including most recently from Afghanistan, East Timor, and Sri Lanka. "We need condom promotion at a district level. Now we have zero percent condom use in our country," says Shiafiqullah Shahim, a member of Afghanistan's Ministry of Health. "We also have large numbers of drug users sharing needles." Experts say countries at risk of an AIDS epidemic can adopt Thailand's lessons of early intervention and pragmatic policies for illicit activities. In Afghanistan's case, which has only recorded 15 cases of HIV this year, this would involve targeting intravenous drug users and refugees, and screening unsafe blood supplies. What may prove harder to transplant is Thailand's other strength in battling AIDS: grass-roots community activism. That factor was brought home to Chiang Mai's latest batch of students on a field trip to Phrao, a rural province that, since 1992, has recorded over 800 HIV/AIDS cases among its 50,000 population. Hospital officials in Phrao explained how their workload has eased as patients take on more responsibility for their own care and support. This has translated into better monitoring of drug regimes and fewer patients being hospitalized. Another key to success has been removing prejudices about those afflicted by the epidemic - prejudices that fuel ignorance of the disease among people who think it only happens to others. Chaiban Veeratsak, a former soldier who contracted HIV in the mid-1980s, recalls how the food he brought to local festivals would sit untouched as people avoided him. He says the stigma attached to the disease has fallen away over the past four years as HIV-positive residents have invited local leaders to come to meetings of their self-help group. Group members support each other and gain local visibility through small businesses. Mr. Veeratsak and his wife, who is also HIV-positive, cook food and sell it from their home. Others in their self-help community, which now number 130, grow pesticide-free crops to sell at the hospital and on local markets. "Without community self-help groups like ours, we would still face discrimination," he says. Stigmas persist in Asia. Such attitudes are an exception in most Asian countries, where AIDS sufferers are often shunned. Former US President Bill Clinton attracted attention in China at a recent AIDS conference when he embraced a young AIDS patient in front of television cameras - something that few Asian leaders are prepared to do publicly. "Societies with lots of stigma don't lend themselves to an open dialogue about AIDS. It's not enough to give people information, there needs to be open discussion and people living with AIDS must participate," says Hakan Bjorkman, deputy representative to Thailand for the United Nations Development Program, which supports the Chiang Mai training courses. For conflict-torn countries like East Timor, Afghanistan, and Sri Lanka, AIDS often takes a back seat to more pressing needs, including other infectious diseases like malaria and tuberculosis. But experts warn that HIV/AIDS can breed fast and thrives on ignorance and social discrimination. In East Timor, only a handful of people have tested positive for HIV, but healthcare workers say poor monitoring and the widespread stigma is probably masking the true picture. "People don't know who is infected, but they are scared. Of course, if they hear that HIV-positive people are being treated at a clinic, they would run away from that clinic," says Rui Carvahlo, a HIV/AIDS field worker in East Timor. As well as community networks, Thailand has also nurtured faith-based responses to HIV/AIDS that proponents say could also be applied elsewhere in Asia. Initial reluctance by clergy to take a stance on a disease seen as sinful has softened in recent years, prodded by high-profile monks who have opened hospices for abandoned AIDS patients. In northern Thailand, Buddhist monks have begun running frank AIDS-education programs in local schools, as well as offering support and counseling to HIV-positive people. One of those is Somya Uthejan, whose husband died after passing the disease to her. She lauds the involvement of monks in her self-help collective. "We live like an extended family in the community and now members of the family are able to understand and support us because monks are respected in the community," she tells her visitors (Montlake, 2003).

A success story is the use of ABC approach in communication for the prevention of AIDS. Between the late 1980s and mid- 1990s, at a time when HIV/AIDS was well on its way toward ravaging Sub- Saharan Mrica, Uganda achieved an extraordinary feat. It stopped the spread of HIV/AIDS in its tracks and saw the nation's rate of infection plummet. By now, Uganda's success story has become virtually synonymous with the so-called ABC approach to HIV/AIDS prevention, for Abstain, Be faithful, use Condoms. And, indeed, it is clear that some combination of important changes in all three of these sexual behaviors contributed both to Uganda's extraordinary reduction in HIV/AIDS rates and to the country's ability to maintain its reduced rates through the second half of the 1990s (Cohen, 2003).

Hailed as a Sub Saharan African success story Uganda's HIV prevalence has declined from a high of 20 percent in 1992 to 6.1 percent in 2001. This decrease has been attributed both to a significant change in sexual behavior, with young Ugandans entering sexual activity later and having fewer non-regular partners, and high level political commitment. Despite this success, HIV is still a major issue with approximately 800,000 Ugandans presently living with HIV/AIDS and 1.7 million children orphaned by the disease. Uganda was the first country to adopt a multi-sectoral approach to HIV, and in 1991 established the Ugandan AIDS Commission to advocate for and co-ordinate multi-sectoral response to HIV and AIDS. However, UAC and line ministries have tended to respond to the call for mainstreaming by focusing on `sensitisation' and condom distribution rather than addressing the issue more systematically at macro and institutional levels. In 2002 the National HIV Partnership Committee was established which brings together representatives from different sectors and stakeholder groups to support co-ordination of activities and strengthen the process of mainstreaming. This structure is seen as a potential mechanism for revitalizing the multi-sectoral response in Uganda (Butcher, 2003).

A success story is about positive changes in breastfeeding. Recent breastfeeding duration trends in Latin America and the Caribbean seems increasing, although rural-urban differentials, differences in educational levels remained. Secondary data analyses were conducted with 23 Demographic and Health Surveys collected between the mid-1980s and mid-1990s. Results indicate that median breastfeeding duration is still greater in rural as compared to urban areas and among less versus more educated women, although these differentials are decreasing with time. In five of the six countries examined for secular trends, breastfeeding duration continues to increase in both rural and urban areas. Breastfeeding duration in urban and rural areas was strongly correlated within countries. Breastfeeding duration improved more among women with the highest and declined among those with the lowest levels of education. Results indicate that breastfeeding duration has increased in Latin America and the Caribbean at a time when the opposite was predicted, given the region's increased urbanization. Breastfeeding protection policies, promotion communication programs may explain part of the increase in breastfeeding duration (Pérez-Escamilla, 2003).

A residency program in Ghana that was developed to train obstetrics and gynecologist specialists for Ghana and the subregion to promote and manage the reproductive health of women and to reduce a high maternal mortality rate. The Carnegie-supported program, begun in 1989, is a 5-year residency in the two medical schools in Ghana, but with one central coordinating office. It has features that equip the graduate resident to practice in her environment. The fourth year of the program is unique: the resident attends a hospital management course for 3 months, goes for a clinical rotation in the United States or United Kingdom for 3 months, and moves to live and work in a rural district hospital for 6 months. The success rate of the Ghanaian residents in the examination of the West African College of Surgeons has been three to four times higher than the overall pass rate. As of October 2002, the program had produced 26 specialists, all of whom are practicing in Ghana. In contrast, of 30 specialists who were trained abroad between 1960 and 1980, only 3 specialist had returned home by the end of the 1980s. The current chairpersons of the two medical schools are graduates of the program. Carnegie financial support for the program came to an end in January 2000, but the Ghana Ministry of Health has increased its support enthusiastically. The program is being sustained. Maternal mortality and morbidity rates are falling slowly in the two teaching hospitals; case fatality rates have been reduced markedly. New residents are entering the program and are progressing to completion. The program has been an unqualified success and merits replication (Klufio et al., 2003).

The Philippine Government addresses the causes and consequences of population growth primarily through the work of two national government agencies, the Department of Health (DOH) and the Commission on Population (POPCOM). The DOH is mandated to implement the National Family Planning Program within the Reproductive Health Framework. It also provides technical and financial assistance to Local Government Units (LGUs) and ensures that sufficient contraceptives are available and distributed in all local public health facilities. Decentralisation, which formally took effect in 1992, propelled the devolution of numerous functions of the national government and placed Local Government Units (LGUs) at the forefront of providing their constituencies with social services, including health and family planning. It also tasked LGUs with the formulation of comprehensive development plans, the implementation of multi-sectoral development programs, and the promotion of community-based population programs and services. Hence, in 1999, the DOH launched the Matching Grant Program (MGP) to provide financial and technical assistance to municipalities and cities to improve their service delivery, particularly in the areas of family planning, maternal and child health, and nutrition. Many of the LGUs participating in the MGP are interested in establishing specific services particularly no-scalpel vasectomy (NSV), IUD, and a new natural family planning method, the standard days method (SDM) but they do not know how to go about it. Concerns were also raised on the cost implications of establishing such services. However, the experience of Bago City in Negros Occidental in promoting and providing NSV showed that it could be done. Other MGP areas like Naga City and Donsol, Sorsogon in the Bicol Region and Kapalong in Davao Norte were also NSV success stories. Promoting IUD services in Pantukan, Compostela Valley and SDM in Lupon and Banaybanay can also be models for setting up these FP services. This module documents the process in setting up NSV services based on the experiences of LGUs that have successfully set them up. It also compiles existing local materials that may be used by interested LGUs in orienting prospective clients (Management Sciences for Health, 2003a).

Consultancy assistance was requested by USAID at the Philippines through the MEDS Project to develop a draft strategy for future USAID support to the Well-family Midwife Clinic (WFMC) franchise network. USAID at the Philippines wished to ensure a smooth transition of the franchise management from John Snow International, Research Triangle International (JSI/RTI) to the Well-family Partnerships Foundation, Inc., that was established to sustain the business and social development operations of the network. A three-person consultancy team assessed the status and adequacy of the current WFMC business franchise system, and its prospects for successfully expanding and sustaining the network during coming years. The many success stories of Well-family (WF) midwives repeatedly demonstrate that a private sector program can work successfully in complementing public sector efforts to meet the demand for quality family planning and maternal child health (FP/MCH) services. One of the greatest achievements of the program is the remarkable transformation of participating midwives from ordinary health care providers to successful entrepreneurs demonstrating confidence, professional status, and earning capacity while making contributions to national safe motherhood and family planning objectives (Ravenholt et al., 2003).

The Philippine Government addresses the causes and consequences of population growth primarily through the work of two national government agencies, the Department of Health (DOH) and the Commission on Population (POPCOM). The DOH is mandated to implement the National Family Planning Program within the Reproductive Health Framework. It also provides technical and financial assistance to Local Government Units (LGUs) and ensures that sufficient contraceptives are available and distributed in all local public health facilities. Decentralisation, which formally took effect in 1992, propelled the devolution of numerous functions of the national government and placed LGUs at the forefront of providing their constituencies with social services that include health and family planning. It also tasked

LGUs with the formulation of comprehensive development plans, the implementation of multi-sectoral development programs and the promotion of community-based population programs and services. Hence, in 1999, the DOH launched the Matching Grant Program (MGP) to provide financial and technical assistance to municipalities and cities to improve their service delivery, particularly in the areas of family planning, maternal and child health, and nutrition. The 1998 NDHS showed that a large number of eligible women (about 20 percent) who do not want any more children are not using any form of contraception. Many of the LGUs participating in the MGP are interested in establishing specific services, particularly for No-Scalpel Vasectomy, IUD, and a new natural method, the Standard Days Method (SDM) but they do not know how to go about it. Concerns were also raised on the cost implication of establishing such services. However, the experience of Bago City in Negros Occidental in promoting and providing NSV showed that it can be done. Other MGP areas like Naga City and Donsol, Sorsogon in the Bicol Region, and Kapalong in Davao Norte are also NSV success stories. Promoting IUD services in Pantukan, Compostela Valley and SDM in Lupon and Banaybanay can also be models for setting up these FP services. The process in setting up these specific FP services based on the experiences of LGUs that have successfully set them up and compiles existing local materials that may be used by other interested LGUs planning to set up similar services (Management Sciences for Health, 2003b).

A remarkable success story has emerged from Egypt, where maternal deaths have reportedly gone down by more than half in the past decade. In 1992-1993, the maternal mortality ratio was 174 per 100,000 live births; in 2000, it was 84 per 100,000 live births. According to Egypt: National Maternal Mortality Study, 2000, this achievement follows this country's sustained efforts to: improve quality of obstetric care; increase access to family planning; educate women and families to seek prompt medical care for problems during pregnancy and labour; and train dayas, i.e. traditional birth attendants to refer women with obstetric complications (Success stories. Improved services in Egypt. Safe Motherhood, 2003a).

In the 1990s, Bolivia had the highest rates of maternal and infant mortality in the Latin American and Caribbean region after Haiti. But when government insurance put skilled care within reach of women and their newborns, the situation began to improve. In 1989, an integrated women's health program was created in Bolivia. This recognized that women were at a profound social disadvantage, and that their health is related to women's role in society. The aim was to improve the quality of life for women and children, and to safeguard their right to life. The new program incorporated family planning services, sex education and obstetric care. Health and sex education materials were revised in cooperation with the National Secretariat for Education. The program also worked with the sub-secretariat for Gender, and PAHO/WHO, in order to prioritize women's health (Success stories. National insurance in Bolivia. Safe Motherhood. 2003b;(30):3.).

Bangladesh has seen one of the developing world's great public health successes, the conversion of the drinking water source for 94 percent of the rural population to 'safe water', in the form of tubewells, with the aim of reducing morbidity and mortality from water-borne disease. Now, that success is being endangered by the discovery that 20 million people may be in great danger and another 20 million in lesser danger of being poisoned by arsenic contamination from tubewell water. Findings from the first national probability sample survey of the rural population and a census of tubewells investigating the social, demographic and epidemiological context of the crisis resulted in several conclusions. The survey covered 3780 households containing 20260 people. The tubewell census covered 9174 tubewells. The article presents data on the respondents' history of drinking tubewell water, knowledge of the arsenic problem, identification of arsenicosis, as well as the impact upon them of the national campaign, the testing of tubewells, and their subsequent sources of water. Eighty-seven per cent of households drank water from ordinary tubewells (at most risk from arsenic poisoning) and 7 percent from deep tubewells. Among males, 47.5 percent had heard that something may be wrong with tubewell water, compared with 39.6 percent of females. A much lower proportion (20.6 percent males, 11.3 percent females) had heard that the water contained poison called arsenic. Only about 1.5 percent of the entire population had stopped using tubewell water. Of survey respondents, 0.5 percent of males and 0.4 percent of females reported symptoms consistent with chronic arsenicosis. Suggestions are made for a more effective program on improved communication campaigns and management of the problem (Caldwell et al., 2003).

On a moonless evening, a group of female and transgendered sex workers wearing identification cards around their necks strolls through a park that abuts a Buddhist temple in downtown Phnom Penh. The dark park has a wide variety of sex for hire. Men seeking men head for the fountain. Straight women sit on the grass with small piles of oranges in front of them, a thinly veiled cover for negotiating a later sexual rendezvous. Men dressed as women, some of whom have breasts from taking steroids, hang out near the restrooms. The people with the identification cards have worked this park themselves many a night, but this evening they have a different mission: Oxfam Hong Kong has hired them to distribute condoms. Like neighboring Thailand, Cambodia has mounted a "100 percent condom program" that, with help from sex workers themselves, aims to persuade everyone selling or paying for sex to use a condom with each encounter. Supported by government and non-governmental organisations, the campaigns have yielded measurable successes. In Cambodia, HIV prevalence among all adults fell from 4 percent in 1999 to 2.6 percent by the end of 2002, by which point the Ministry of Health estimated that a total of 259,000 Cambodians had become infected since the first case surfaced in 1991. A recent study by the Cambodian Ministry of Health projected that without increased condom use and other behavior changes, Cambodia would have had about three times as many HIV infections (Cohen, 2003).

For decades nutritional surveys have been conducted using various definitions, indicators and reference populations to classify child malnutrition. The World Health Organisation (WHO) Global Database on Child Growth and Malnutrition was initiated in 1986 with the objective to collect, standardize, and disseminate child anthropometric data using a standard format. Methods: The database includes population-based surveys that fulfil a set of criteria. Data are checked for validity and consistency and raw data sets are analysed following a standard procedure to obtain comparable results. Prevalences of wasting, stunting, under- and overweight in preschool children are presented using z-scores based on the National Center for Health Statistics (NCHS)/WHO international reference population. New surveys are included on a continuous basis and updates are published bimonthly on the database's web site. Results: To date, the database contains child anthropometric information derived from 846 surveys. With 412 national surveys from 138 countries and 434 sub-national surveys from 155 countries, the database covers 99 percent and 64 percent of the under 5 year olds in developing and developed countries, respectively. This wealth of information enables international comparison of nutritional data, helps identifying populations in need, evaluating nutritional and other public health interventions, monitoring trends in child growth, and raising political awareness of nutritional problems. The 15 years experience of the database can be regarded as a success story of international collaboration in standardizing child growth data. We recommend this model for monitoring other nutritional health conditions that as yet lack comparable data (de Onis et al, 2003).

Population growth

From a historical perspective during the Paleolithic period, 10,000-100,000 people lived on the earth; their number exceeded 1 million at the beginning of the Neolithic period, reached 10 million during the Bronze Age, 100 million at the beginning of the Iron Age, 1 billion at the beginning of the 19th century, and 5.7 billion in 1995. The estimated global population will be 10 billion by the middle of the 21st century and is expected to stabilize at around 10-12 billion subsequently. Increased agricultural production helped bring about greater numbers of humanity and the advancement of society with a developing social hierarchy, although life expectancy was low at 22-28 years. In Europe, the Renaissance gradually evolved into the Industrial Revolution, and a demographic revolution accompanied this process. In some countries, population size increased more than five times. Eventually, mortality and fertility levels decreased and life expectancy increased. In Western civilization, increased individualism, secularization, compulsory school attendance, decreased agricultural population, emancipation of women, increased costs of raising children, and social and economic progress ensued. All this was preceded by 18th century conditions, when, in England, capital accumulation led to wealth on the one side and destitution on the other, giving rise to Malthus's famous theory. However, during the 19th century these social inequalities gradually evened out. After World War II, the question arose of whether the populations of other civilizations (Confucian, Japanese, Islamic, Hindu, Slavic-Orthodox, Latin American, and African) would also undergo a demographic transition and how soon. At any rate, developed country population size, as a percentage of global population, will drop from 22 percent to 13 percent, and that of Africa will increase from 12 percent to 26 percent, during the 21st century (Pavlik, 1995). In such circumstances scientific and mass communication, including various forms of risk communication is necessary, and several examples show the efforts made to meet the expectations to slow down population growth and diminish striking demographic inequalities and problems, first of all the Popline project is such an example.

Population concerns increase for the next century. The population of the world has grown at increasing speed since reaching 1 billion in 1804. Fertility is also declining rapidly, but stabilization is not expected until the numbers reach 11.6 billion around the year 2200. Of the components of this population growth, mortality decline is positive, population momentum is inevitable, wanted fertility reflects social and economic inequities, and coerced motherhood is unacceptable. The huge increases in population will bring new realities which must be addressed to achieve sustainable resource use and prevent environmental degradation while producing adequate food. Population growth has led to voluntary adaptation of human reproduction made possible by contraceptive technology. Because there has been a major worldwide expansion in contraceptive usage, contraceptive safety has become a major concern and the number of contraceptive options has expanded. New technologies are being developed to assure that only healthy babies are born (substituting quality for quantity). Other changes include the consideration of sex as pleasure instead of a duty linked to reproduction and an increase in the size of the elderly population demanding "intergenerational equity." The period of adolescence necessary to achieve socioeconomic maturation will increase while bisexual maturity occurs at an ever earlier age. These changes will ultimately result in an improvement in the status of women who will be freed from reproduction to pursue education and employment. In the 21st century, a second (woman-centered) revolution in contraceptive technology will result in new methods to meet the diverse needs of users, and research must address the biological ramifications of the resulting reduced use of the female reproductive system and a life expectancy while extends well into the postmenopausal period (Fathalla, 1995). This situation needs family planning and communication programs to overcome the difficulties of world demographic problems.

Concerning shifting paradigms and setting goals of population and development The United States and other Western nations advocated already in the 1970s the implementation of programs aimed at controlling the high rates of population growth in resource-poor countries in Africa, Asia, and Latin America. Most leaders from these countries, however, saw this as an inappropriate, imperialist goal to be imposed on their countries, when the real problems were related to poverty. Ten years later, at the second international conference in Mexico City, representatives of the Reagan administration argued that population growth was not a key issue and that, instead, the expansion of free-market systems was the key to development in poor countries. But by that time, many leaders of developing countries had reached the opposite conclusion - namely, that high rates of population growth were indeed hindering both economic and social development. At the meeting, there was also much debate about abortion-related issues, with the U.S. government and the Vatican highlighting an antichoice agenda (Rosenfield et al., 2005).

A special example is urbanisation in Indonesia which is characterised by the high concentration of urban population in a few large cities, notably Jakarta Metropolitan Area

(Jabotabek), which indicates an interurban disparity between Jabotabek and other cities, and between large and smaller cities. It might also reflect an integration of Jabotabek into the global economy. The populations on the outskirts of large cities are growing rapidly, while those in core areas have a very low rate of growth. The small towns and intermediate cities on the outer islands are experiencing higher population growth compared with those in Java, which might suggest that those towns and cities are playing a more significant role in regional development (Firman, 2004).

High fertility rates are not a traditional feature of Indonesian societies but, on the contrary, should be regarded as a recent phenomenon. This is not an entirely new argument, but it has not received adequate attention in the recent discussion of low population growth rates in premodern Southeast Asia. Death rate was assumed to be the most important determinant of the rate of population growth. Other features of Indonesia's premodern fertility pattern have been misrepresented or ignored, particularly the female age at first marriage and the influence of bridewealth payments. Java aside, marriage in Indonesia was probably neither universal nor concluded at an early age before 1850, even though extended families were found in many places outside Java. Extended families, therefore, need not go hand in hand with early and universal marriage (Boomgaard, 2003).

Overpopulated South Asia play a vital role in achieving the global goal of 'Health for All' (HFA). After all, 22 percent of the world's population resides here, as does 40 percent of that living in absolute poverty. In stark contrast, the region's share of the global income is a paltry 1.3 percent. South Asia has a gross national product of US$ 460, as against a whopping US$ 3680 for Latin America and the Caribbean and US$ 480 for sub-Saharan Africa. Not surprisingly the region's health status is just as grim (Mukhopadhyay, 2004).

With every passing year, prospects for population growth in the more developed and less developed countries grow more dissimilar. On this year's Data Sheet, the total fertility rate (TFR) for the more developed countries is a mere 1.5, compared with 3.1 in the less developed countries-3.5 if outlier China's large statistical effect is removed. But the passage of time, as well as the difference in fertility rates, is ensuring that the two types of countries can expect to continue to have different population sizes in the future. The decline in Europe's fertility rates is not a recent phenomenon; those rates have been low for quite some time. As a result, there have been long-term changes to age distributions in Europe, and this "youth dearth" is now taking on a more significant role in the near certainty of population decline. Population Reference Bureau [PRB] (2003 world population, 2003).

A meeting of Asian parliamentarians in Bangkok, Thailand, in December reaffirmed the regional countries' commitment to the implementation of the Program of Action of the 1994 International Conference on Population and Development. The meeting was attended by 89 Parliamentarians from 30 countries. The population of the Asia-Pacific and Central Asian regions stood at 3.52 billion in 1995. In spite of the fact that population growth is slowing down in countries, the regions' population will, in general, continue to increase (Asian parliamentarians commit to ICPD goals, 2003).

Concerning causes of declining sex ratio in Orissa, India, over the last decade, the sex ratio in India has shown a marginal increase, However, the female deficit in the age group 0-4 is a cause of great concern. In Orissa, where women demographically dominated till 1961, the sex ratio is showing a continuous decline and the girl child deficit is alarming. Covering a wide spectrum of socio-cultural practices, this paper explores important causes responsible for female deficit in Orissa (Devi, 2003).

Latin America and the Caribbean (LAC) doubled its population to 322 million from 1950 to 1975 and will double it again by 2015, the latter a somewhat longer period but with greater numerical growth. And by 2050, the region's population is projected by the United Nations to be anywhere from 657 million to 975 million, significant growth by any standard. In terms of world population growth, Latin America and the Caribbean stand in the middle of the demographic picture. LAC growth outstrips its northern neighbors, the United States and Canada, and is expected to have roughly twice North America's population by 2050. In 1950, the two Western Hemisphere regions had about the same population. For the 2000-2050 period, by way of contrast, the southern European population is projected to decline, with Italy and Spain being the most conspicuous losers (Carty, 2003).

With regard to what will happen to Brazilian fertility, there is a need for a historical reconstruction of the various ways in which changes in social roles, purposes, motives and intentions are crucial to understanding the processes and causes of fertility change in Brazil, Although the mid-1960s may be an important turning point towards a generalization and acceleration of the process of decline, it does not represent its onset. Furthermore, the insistence on that the hygienist medical discourse in the middle of the nineteenth century, reinforced by the eugenics movement at the beginning of twentieth century, and the contraceptive revolution in the 1960s was socially absorbed and legitimated by what Brazilians believed it could offer. Through this complex interaction, an interesting set of elements emerges pointing towards a profile of a policy affecting population reproduction that go beyond contemporary neo-malthusian conceptions or measures aimed to control population growth. Also, through the institutional arrangements and interactions, there are relevant indications of how gender systems; labor market practices and aspects of the national legal administrative system have constrained women's reproductive behavior. Women's movement victories since the 1970s, in part encoded in the Brazilian Constitution of 1988, changed the official perspective on family and reproduction. Since then, government and civil society has been instrumental in creating, both legally and in practice, more equality and equity between men and women. However, as the discussions about sterilization practices show, there continues to be an enormous gap between the legal victories and actual life conditions (Goldani, 2004).

Despite the ravages of the parasitic and infectious diseases, HIV/AIDS, malaria and tuberculosis chief among them, that are inflicting untold damage, Africa continues to be the planet's fastest growing continent (Leahy, 2003).

Jordan's annual rate of population growth is among the highest in the world, at 2.3 percent. If this rate continues unabated, Jordan's population, estimated at 5.3 million in 2002, will increase to 8.7 million by 2025. There has been widespread political and cultural acceptance of family planning due to donor-funded activities and the support of the Jordanian government. As a result, contraceptive use increased from 40 percent in 1990 to 56 percent in 2002. A concurrent trend in delayed marriage - related to Jordan's efforts to promote education and literacy for women - also has contributed to a reduction in fertility from 5.6 children per woman in 1990 to 3.6 in 2002. Modern-method use, however, seems to have leveled off at just under 40 percent. There are several factors contributing to this stagnation. The discontinuation rate for oral contraceptives and condoms is high - 68 percent, according to the 1997 Demographic and Health Survey (DHS). While fear of side effects and widespread misconceptions continue to pose barriers to modern-method use, research also points to the need to address more fundamental beliefs and attitudes that inhibit use, including the desire for large families, preference for male children, pressure to have a child within the first year of marriage, and husbands' opposition to family planning (Deloitte Touche Tohmatsu, 2003).

Concerning current issues of poverty, HIV/AIDS, and youth fertility issues have never been of greater importance in South Africa. Fertility is inextricably linked to socio-economic development and reflects the health and well-being of a population. For example, high fertility rates among adolescents have implications not only for population growth, but also for educational achievement of both young mothers and their children, employment, poverty and social welfare, sexual and reproductive health, and even family policy. Further, given that South Africa is one of the few countries in the region (besides Zambia) where abortion is legal, it is an opportune time to explore in greater depth the relationship between fertility (control) preferences of women (and men for that matter), their ability to access safe and appropriate healthcare services, and factors which influence their ability to control the timing of conception and birth (Varga, 2003).

Demographic transition

Current human population is too large. However, in an evolutionary perspective, given human beings' pronatalist biological nature, it will probably take more than just the availability of fertility control technologies to stabilize population growth. Moreover, improvements in the quality of life, such as better nutrition and less disease, are likely to improve fecundity, decrease mortality, and exacerbate the population condition. Economic development may help stabilize population growth and size if it persuades people to have fewer children in exchange for other goods. Current cultural and economic conditions in the areas of the world with high growth rates are very different from those which fueled the demographic transition in Europe. While economic development may solve some population growth problems, such development typically adversely affects the environment. Environmental awareness and cooperative behavior at every level of social and political organisation hopefully can be cultivated among humankind as a prerequisite of truly sustainable development. Education and communication has an important role to play (Harrison, 1995).

Concerning the demographic transition revisited as a global process, with dramatic declines in fertility taking place throughout the world, it is increasingly important to understand the demographic transition as a global process. While this universality was a cornerstone of classic transition theories, for many decades it was largely neglected by experts because fertility in the developing world did not seem to follow the expected pattern. When comparing earlier and more recent transition experiences, important similarities and disparities can be seen. Everywhere mortality decline appears to have played a central role for fertility decline. The differences in the timing of the response of fertility to mortality decline, with very small gaps historically and prolonged ones in more recent transitions, plus the much more rapid decline in vital rates in many developing countries, constitute an important challenge to any general explanation of the process. The specific characteristics of recent transitions have led to decades of higher population growth rates, and promise to give way to much more rapid dynamics of population ageing in many countries. This may limit the ability of newcomers to take full advantage of the demographic transition for the social and economic modernisation of their societies (Reher, 2004).

With regard to the security demographic: population and civil conflict after the cold war, questions emerge. Do the dynamics of human population-rates of growth, age structure, distribution and more- influence when and where warfare will next break out? The findings of this report suggest that the risks of civil conflict (deadly violence between governments and non-state insurgents, or between state factions within territorial boundaries) that are generated by demographic factors may be much more significant than generally recognized, and worthy of more serious consideration by national security policymakers and researchers. Its conclusions - drawn from a review of literature and analyses of data from 180 countries, about half of which experienced civil conflict at some time from 1970 through 2000 - argue that: recent progress along the demographic transition-a population's shift from high to low rates of birth and death-is associated with continuous declines in the vulnerability of nation-states to civil conflict. If this association continues through the 21st century, then a range of policies promoting small, healthy and better educated families and long lives among populations in developing countries seems likely to encourage greater political stability in weak states and to enhance global security in the future (Cincotta et al., 2003).

The analysis of population momentum following a gradual decline in fertility to replacement level provides valuable insights into prospects for future population growth. Work has recently been made in the area by applying a new form of the quadratic hyperstable (QH) model, which relates exponentially changing fertility to the resultant exponentiated quadratic birth sequence. Modeling gradual transitions from an initial stable population to an ultimate stationary population indicates that such declines in fertility increase momentum by a product of two factors. The first factor is a previously noted continuation of stable growth for half the period of decline. The second is a not previously appreciated offsetting factor that reflects the interaction between the decline in fertility, the changing age pattern of fertility, and the changing age composition of the population. Numerical examples using both hypothetical and actual populations demonstrate that for declines of any length, the product of the two factors yields momentum values that closely agree with the results of population projections. The QH model can examine monotonic transitions between any two sets of constant vital rates. As a generalization of the fixed-rate stable model, it has great potential value in numerous areas of demographic analysis (Schoen et al., 2003).

World population was transformed in the 20th century as technological and social changes brought steep declines in birth rates and death rates around the world. The century began with 1.6 billion people and ended with 6.1 billion, mainly because of unprecedented growth after 1960. The momentum created by this population growth will carry us past 7 billion by 2015. Beyond that, the future of world population is less certain. Public discourse on population today tends to flow in one of two directions. One emphasizes the continued growth in the less developed regions, and the economic, social, environmental, and political strains associated with adding a few billion more people in the next 50 years. The other focus centers around the unprecedented low fertility in many countries. About 40 percent of the world's population lives in countries in which couples have so few children that the countries' populations are likely to decline over the long term. These countries, which include China and most of Europe, must grapple with social, economic, environmental, and political challenges associated with ageing and eventually dwindling populations. And, if fertility rates continue to fall around the world, more countries will face this low-fertility predicament (Population Reference Bureau, 2004).

Demographic theory has been largely transformed over the last half-century from grand theory to short-term theory, often endowed with such immediacy as to so limit our vision of the future that even population policymaking is made difficult. Demographic theorists lost their nerve as the globalization of declines in mortality and fertility proceeded much more rapidly than they had anticipated and as the "baby boom" in a number of developed countries quelled expectations of continuing fertility decline. There is a parallel here to the undermining of Malthusian theory by dramatic increases in the nineteenth and twentieth centuries in food production, a phenomenon explained by the Industrial Revolution's effects on agricultural and transport technology. Focusing on the leading countries in the demographic transition far too little attention has been paid to the nature of the economic and related social revolutions of our age and that our theoretical perspectives pay too little attention to ultimate constraints on population growth (Caldwell, 2004). Also the relevance of scientific research, evidence based management and evidence-based communication programs cannot be overemphasized.

Family planning

Communication has played crucial role in a series of family planning programs. In 1991, the Ministry of Health (MOH) conducted focus group discussions, interviews, and participant observations in villages of Dangme West, Bolgatanga, and Berekum Districts in Ghana to determine reasons for low contraceptive use and to assess community capacity to sustain family planning (FP) services. Rumors, misconceptions, exaggeration, and misunderstandings formed a set of obstacles. A 41-year old man believed if a woman does not receive sperm she becomes skinny and, if abstinence lasts for 5 years, she can never conceive. Some frequent rumors were witches would make the contraceptives cause permanent infertility, IUDs go to the heart, and infants are born with an IUD in their hands, This misinformation caused fear and rejection of FP methods. Some men feared that contraceptives would make their partner promiscuous and a hussy. Women who did use contraceptives wanted to keep it a secret for fear of being labeled promiscuous or a prostitute. The other set of obstacle s was limited program accessibility and socially inappropriate setting of FP services in rural areas. Most potential acceptors needed to travel 1-2 hours to go to a FP clinic in major towns. It was rare for anyone in the villages to distribute contraceptives. Those who sometimes distributed contraceptives were community health nurses, drug peddlers, and traditional birth attendants. People said low availability and accessibility were the major reason for low contraceptive usage, and women did not feel they were able to keep their contraceptive use secret at FP clinics. Women were able to discretely buy methods from drug peddlers. The villagers welcomed community-based family planning service delivery, however. They even determined who should be the providers and designed the delivery system. As a result, MOH managers developed a series of interventions to achieve a sustainable delivery system (Ghana.

Ministry of Health. Health Research Unit, 1992). Evidence-based communication programs had to be launched to eliminate obstacles from the carry out of family planning projects.

In family planning programs in Cameroun communication programs also have played crucial role. The people of Cameroon enjoy having large families for reasons of prestige, economics, and psychological contentment. For Cameroon, family planning means spacing births in order to safeguard the health of the mother and child, as well as to ward off sterility. The issue of limiting births has long been considered taboo. However, since the beginning of the 1980s, how Cameroonians perceive population questions has evolved considerably from pronatalism to encouraging the ability to master one s own fertility. It turned out from family planning behavior data collected in Cameroon s 1998 Demographic and Health Survey (DHS) that knowledge of modern contraceptive methods varied by socio-demographic characteristics (Tsafack et al., 1999). Research results made it possible to target messages to appropriate population segments and so develop effective communication programs.

Nuptiality

The perspectives of family-planning service providers in eight sites in China have been ascertained on the provision of sexual and reproductive health services to unmarried young people. Data were drawn from a survey of 1927 family-planning workers and 16 focus group discussions conducted in eight sites in China in 1998-99. Family-planning workers recognized the need to protect the sexual health of unmarried young people and were unambiguous about the need for government agencies to provide information and education on sexual and reproductive health to unmarried young people; however, perceptions about the appropriate age for and content of such education remained conservative. While about 70 percent of family-planning workers were willing to provide contraceptives to unmarried young people, and about 60 percent approved government provision of contraceptive services to unmarried young people, only one quarter agreed that the services could be extended to senior high schools. Family-planning workers in China are ambivalent about the provision of sexual and reproductive health services to unmarried young people, which potentially poses a significant obstacle to the adoption of safe sex behaviors by young people, as well as to the provision of sexual and reproductive health information and services to young unmarried people in China. Training programs for family-planning workers are urgently needed to address this issue (Tu, 2004). Research results made it possible to target messages to appropriate population segments and so develop effective communication programs for improved family-planning work in China to support provision of sexual and reproductive health services to unmarried young people.

Maternity

In low socio-economic settlements of Karachi, Pakistan a qualitative and quantitative study was conducted to explore traditional beliefs and practices, to assess puerperal morbidity, and to understand care-seeking behaviors. Five focus group discussions and 15 in-depth interviews were conducted in July and August 2000. 525 Muslim women, who were 6-8 weeks post-partum, were then interviewed at home. Maternal care was relatively good-more than three-quarters of recent mothers sought antenatal care and more than half delivered in a hospital or maternity home. Counseling to attend post-partum clinics among facility deliveries was 16 percent, of which only 26 percent attended. Practices during the delivery and puerperium, such as massaging the vaginal walls with mustard oil during labor to facilitate delivery and inserting vaginal or rectal herbal pessaries to facilitate `shrinkage of the uterus' or `strengthening of the backbone', were pervasive. The core symptoms that are clinically significant during the puerperium are heavy vaginal bleeding and high fever, since they are potentially fatal symptoms if appropriate and timely care is not sought. About half of the study women (53.3 percent) reported at least one illness symptom, high fever (21.1 percent), heavy vaginal bleeding (13.9 percent), and foul smelling vaginal discharge (9.6 percent). Women did not know the underlying biologic cause of their perceived post-partum morbidity; weakness was frequently mentioned. Women sought care initially from close relatives or traditional healers and if they continued to suffer from their morbidity they finally approached a trained health care (allopathic) provider. The high prevalence of perceived post-partum morbidity shows the demand for post-partum community-based health care programs. Promoting maternal health education and implementing appropriate communication program was suggested that encourages women to seek appropriate and timely care by accessing public or private health services (Fikree, 2004).

In a study, Uganda's Jinja Hospital and the Quality Assurance Project developed and implemented case management maps (CMMs) for two distinct pregnancy-related conditions: pregnancy-induced hypertensive disorders (PIHD) and postpartum hemorrhage (PPH). CMMs are pre-printed forms that serve as job aids to help prompt members of the healthcare team to perform required tasks. At Jinja the tasks on the CMM for PIHD reflected a new protocol of care that hospital staff and management had adopted as part of the development of the CMM. Jinja's CMMs list down the left side of a sheet of paper the tasks providers must accomplish for a particular condition, and they list across the top a timeline (e.g., hourly, daily) when the tasks must be accomplished. The study measured adherence to three care standards and patient outcomes for both intervention conditions during the 12 months before the introduction of each CMM and during the 12 months afterward. The care standards for PIHD were proteinuria on admission, blood pressure three times daily, and propanolol on admission; for PPH they were hemoglobin test on admission, complete blood count daily, and iron and folic acid daily. The sample sizes for PIHD were 36 cases before and 50 after; for PPH they were 20 cases before and 10 after. Before and after measurements were also obtained for a comparison (control) condition, acute pelvic inflammatory disease (PID), for which no CMM was developed. PID was chosen as the control condition in part because it was treated in the gynecological ward, physically separate from the maternity ward where PIHD and PPH were treated. Different staff treated the intervention conditions and the control condition. The PID sample sizes were 37 cases before and 29 after. The results with PIHD were clear. Pooled adherence for all three normal management indicators increased from 22.6 percent to 87.3 percent for PIHD; the difference was highly significant. In contrast, pooled adherence for the PID comparison group rose only slightly from 15.3 percent to 20.7 percent. Patient outcomes also improved for PIHD patients after the CMMs were implemented, but not so dramatically, nor were they statistically significant. In the study sample, fewer cases of pre-eclampsia progressed to eclampsia (11 percent before, 8 percent after), a highly desirable outcome. In addition, fewer stillbirths (38 percent before, 16 percent after) and fewer maternal deaths occurred (5.9 percent before, 4.0 percent after, and 0.7 percent at follow-up a year later). These results are probably due to the new protocol for managing PIHD (including new medications and the CMM) and the process of developing and implementing the protocol and the CMM. Until the relative contribution of the CMM itself and its development process can be assessed, care should be taken in attempting to generalize the result to other settings. The results of the CMM for PPH were not so clear. Average adherence to the three care standards for PPH increased from 27.9 percent to 39.3 percent following the introduction of this CMM; this increase was comparable in magnitude to the increase observed for PID, the control condition. The number of maternal deaths from PPH actually increased, from only one death in the before period to five after. A careful analysis of these deaths did not explain the increase, but it may have been due in part to this CMM's small sample size and in part that staff may have needed more time to gain proficiency in the use of the PPH CMM. We conclude that for PIHD, the development and use of CMMs clearly improved the process of care and perhaps patient outcomes. However, the impact of the PPH CMM on care and outcomes was small at best. Before going to scale, information is needed about which conditions benefit from CMMs and which do not, and about the relative contribution of CMMs separate from the process of developing them (Kerstiëns, 2004). Appropriate communication program could improve quality of maternal care.

The number of women coming to the Safe Abortion Clinic of Maternity Hospital for counseling and abortion services is on the rise in Nepal. After one and a half years of legalisation of abortion, on Mar 18, 2004, a legal abortion service was for the first time launched in Maternity Hospital, the largest obstetric care center in Nepal. Around 500 women have, so far, received the new service. Abortion clinics will operate soon in three other regional hospitals in the country Abortion was illegal in Nepal, under any circumstance, before Sept 26, 2002, when King Gyanendra agreed to a new law. The law allowed termination of pregnancy at 12 weeks for any woman with her consent, at 18 weeks if it resulted from rape or incest, and at any time during pregnancy with the recommendation of an authorised medical practitioner, if the pregnancy posed serious threats to the mental and physical health or life of the woman or if the pregnancy would result in a disabled baby (Dahal, 2004). A research-based communication program could improve maternal health.

The objective was to investigate the relation of diastolic blood pressure in pregnancy with birth weight and perinatal mortality. The design was a Prospective study. The setting was a 15 maternity units in one London health region, 1988-2000. 210,814 first singleton births of babies weighing more than 200 g among mothers with no hypertension before 20 weeks' gestation and without proteinuria, delivering between 24 and 43 weeks' gestation. The main outcome measures were birth weight and perinatal mortality. The mean (SD) birth weight of babies born to mothers with no hypertension before 20 weeks' gestation or proteinuria was 3282 g (545 g) and there were 1335 perinatal deaths, compared with 94 perinatal deaths among women with proteinuria or a history of hypertension. Diastolic blood pressure at booking for antenatal checks was progressively higher from weeks 34 to 40 of gestation. The birth weight of babies being delivered after 34 weeks was highest for highest recorded maternal diastolic blood pressures of between 70 and 80 mm Hg and lower for blood pressures outside this range. Both low and high diastolic blood pressures were associated with statistically significantly higher perinatal mortality. Using a linear quadratic model, 94 of 825 (11.4 percent) perinatal deaths could be attributed to mothers having blood pressure differing from the optimal blood pressure (82.7 mm Hg) predicted by the fitted model. Most of these excess deaths occurred with blood pressures below the optimal value. Both low and high diastolic blood pressures in women during pregnancy are associated with small babies and high perinatal mortality (Steer, 2004). And education and communication program could reduce pregnancy risk.

In a study the objective was to quantify maternal risk associated with multiple cesarean sections (CSs) and determine whether the third CS defines a threshold for increased morbidity. From January 1997 to January 2002, the clinical records of 3191 women who were delivered by CS at our referral maternity center were examined for selected indicators of maternal morbidity. The women were assigned to groups based on number of CSs and the frequency of each indicator was determined. A composite score for each indicator among women grouped by number of consecutive CSs was then derived to compare risk between groups and against the third CS. By all indicators studied, morbidity increased with successive CSs before and through the third CS. However, compared with the third, the risk of major morbidity was significantly increased with the fifth, and much worse at the sixth CS for placenta previa (odds ratio [OR]=3.8, 95 percent confidence interval [CI]=1.9-7.4), placenta accreta (OR=6.1, 95 percent CI=2.0-18.4) and hysterectomy (OR=5.9, 95 percent CI=1.5-24.4). But the third and fourth CSs had the same risk of major morbidity for placenta previa (OR=1.4, 95 percent CI=0.8-2.2), placenta accreta (OR=1.0, 95 percent CI=0.3-2.9) and hysterectomy (OR=0.3, 95 percent CI=0.0-2.7). The third CS does not define a threshold for increased risk to the mother. Instead, overall morbidity rises continually with each successive CS. However, specifically for major morbidity from the triad of placenta previa, placenta accreta and hysterectomy during CS, the fourth CS carries the same risk as the third (Makoha, 2004). A communication program could reduce maternal morbidity, and diminish maternal risk associated with multiple cesarean sections.

Fertility

With dramatic declines in fertility taking place throughout the world, it is increasingly important to understand the demographic transition as a global process. While this universality was a cornerstone of classic transition theories, for many decades it was largely neglected by experts because fertility in the developing world did not seem to follow the expected pattern. When comparing earlier and more recent transition experiences, important similarities and disparities can be seen. Everywhere mortality decline appears to have played a central role for fertility decline. The differences in the timing of the response of fertility to mortality decline, with very small gaps historically and prolonged ones in more recent transitions, plus the much more rapid decline in vital rates in many developing countries, constitute an important challenge to any general explanation of the process. The specific characteristics of recent transitions have led to decades of higher population growth rates, and promise to give way to much more rapid dynamics of population ageing in many countries. This may limit the ability of newcomers to take full advantage of the demographic transition for the social and economic modernisation of their societies. (Reher, 2004). Without evidence-based communication programs the world demographic programs will probably fail.

Following extensive research activity to develop an effective agent to control male fertility, such a product may be available for use within ~5 years. However, little is known concerning contraceptive knowledge, desires and attitudes of men in different countries, and their acceptance of male fertility control (MFC). A survey of >9000 males aged 18-50 years was performed in nine countries on four continents in 2002. The objective was to compare, on a cross-cultural basis, the knowledge, attitudes and acceptability of MFC among men and assess their willingness to use such a method. Between 50 and 83 percent of the male respondents currently use contraceptive methods, and 55-81.5 percent reported that both partners participate in selecting the method of contraception employed. Overall acceptance of hormonal MFC was high (>55 percent), with 28.5-71.4 percent of survey participants of various nationalities expressing the willingness to use such a method. While MFC appears to be well accepted overall, the willingness to use this type of contraception varies widely between differing population groups. The specific characteristics and profile of any MFC product will have to be carefully evaluated to accurately assess its acceptance, both by men and their female partners. To achieve the goal to develop an effective agent to control male fertility proper communication programs are needed (Heinemann, 2005).

In retrospect, the invention of contraceptives was as fundamental for the evolution of humankind as the invention of the wheel; today more than 550 million couples are using contraceptive methods. The large-scale use of contraceptives triggered the most powerful social revolutions of a century in reproductive health and gender equity, and substantially contributed to an unparalleled demographic change, characterized by a rapid ageing of populations. One of the important reasons for population ageing is a significant decline in fertility rates, resulting in gradually changing population structures with fewer and fewer children and more and more elderly persons. The causes underlying these demographic changes are complex and manifold; they reflect major societal changes of historical dimensions. Many of our institutions cater increasingly for a population structure that no longer exists. There is therefore an increasing need for institutional reforms in social security, health care, housing and education. In addition, several surveys conducted in the developed world have indicated an erosion of confidence in our basic institutions, e.g. courts and justice, the Church and Parliament. Where as modern sociologists are concerned about an increase in crime, decrease in trust and depleted social capital, one can also observe an accelerated perception of our global destiny and a re-awakening of the moral impulse with a strong demand for increased transparency in public affairs. Also, various global communities have assumed a growing importance. It can be predicted that international professional communities, such as the European Society of Contraception, will play an increasingly important future role in influencing policies in general and health policies in particular, because of their profound commitment to the improvement of the human condition by the judicious use of new scientific information. For having a working contraceptive project, evidence-based, effective communication programs should be implemented (Diczfalusy, 2002).

Economic pressures, better education, and change of attitudes contribute to the decline in birth rate in Africa. Improved education, urbanization and stronger government programs, including communication programs aided in the reduction of fertility rates in African countries, as well as fear of child mortality. In countries like Kenya, Senegal, Zimbabwe, Ghana and parts of Nigeria, economics have played a major role, particularly in the stagnation and shrinkage of the per capita income, high inflation and increased cost of basic services. In Nigeria, the primary reason for contraceptive use and marriage delay was said to be caused by economic hardship. Traditionally, African families have been large for traditional, political and economic reasons with government refraining from promoting birth control for fear of being accused of betraying the African traditions. In the face of this dilemma, the government then took the initiative to implement programs to reverse the alarming population growth (Buckley, 1998).

A study compared notions of reproduction in Gambia and the West, and analysed 1992 baseline fertility survey data from the North Bank areas of rural Gambia. The sample included 2980 women from 40 villages. The second phase was a multi-round survey in 1993 and 1994 in 8 of the original 40 villages among 270 women who had a pregnancy in the past 3 years. The Western model of fertility assumes a fixed life course and that contraception is a device for exploiting the time limits of fecundability. Gambian models of reproduction rely on a body resource framework that is based on declines in muscles, strength, and blood due to wearing life events. The Gambian fertility model includes more than fecundability in determining a woman's ability to reproduce. Mishaps are destructive of reproductive capital. Mishaps include a heavy workload, overly frequent childbearing, a shortage of blood, or simply being tired. Time and ageing are not predictable forces that work independently of other life events. Reproduction is a potential to be realized without time limits. Fertility in the study sample was a 7.5 children/woman. Birth intervals were around 2.5 years. Contraceptive use was low, and was mostly the pill and Depo-Provera. The rationale for contraception was the desire to protect the health of the children and the mother. Birth interval is regulated. Fertility behaviors change throughout the life cycle. Young women in their 30s spoke about being too old to bear another child. Older women were eager to delay childbearing. Contraceptive use was higher among women who had a miscarriage or stillbirth. A child spacing framework inadequately explained contraceptive behavior (Bledsoe, 1998). The results underlie the need for proper communication programs and the relevance of research.

Hungary's fertility trends over the past 50 years clearly reflect social changes observed during the period. As in most industrialized countries, Hungary has experienced changes associated with women's and children's changing social and familial roles. Changing values, norms, and social and individual preferences have encouraged the trend. However, fertility in Hungary has characteristics particular to the country, such as its cyclical baby booms and baby busts. Hungary also had well-established below replacement fertility rates well before most Western European countries. These low rates, typical of demographic transition, have been constant in Hungary since the end of the 1950s. At the beginning of the 1960s, while most of Western Europe was experiencing a baby boom, Hungary had the lowest overall fertility level in the world. In recent decades, Hungary's government has developed targets and measures to boost domestic fertility. The author presents the main trends and characteristics of Hungarian fertility in sections on long-term trends, the sociopolitical context of fertility, new fertility and marital behaviors, birth limiting, opinions and values on couples and children, and possible population policies. Communication programs may change marital behaviors, opinions and values on couples and children (Kamarás, 2000).

Birth

With regard to policy perspectives on fertility regulation in developing countries surveys show a favorable climate for fertility declines in many developing countries since the peak period of growth in 1965-1970. What are the policy options available to the developing countries to accelerate the pace of the fertility decline which has already commenced, or to ensure that the decline is not slowed down or reversed? Findings from an opinion survey by the United Nations in 1979 of the governments of developing countries are presented in tables that show the governments' perception of current levels of fertility (satisfactory or unsatisfactory); government policies to modify fertility (encourage or discourage it); and policies on access to modern methods of birth control (degree of government for access). Provision of family planning services alone cannot be expected to continue present declining trends in fertility, nor can modernization of any kind automatically produce it. Selected social, health, and economic interventions that interact favorably with family planning services are necessary. Policy perspectives discussed include the importance of social and economic development. Indicators such as infant mortality, literacy, life expectancy, and per capita gross domestic product are more closely related to fertility levels than in family planning programs in statistical studies. Other recommendations considered include: 1) birth control emphasis on limiting births in preference to spacing, and on promoting female methods. 2) fixation of long-term goals in terms of a NNR (Net Reproduction Rate) of 1; and 3) changes in women's status such as in education and employment as the best way to achieve rapid decline in the fertility level. This needs proper communication programs (Srinivasan, 1983).

For improving population strategy an approved US Agency for International Development (USAID) document is available which provides guidance on implementation of the Agency Population Assistance Policy. It is based on recent scientific knowledge and program experience and stresses the priority emphases of the Agency: host country policies; the private sector; institutional development; and technology development and transfer. USAID has 2 basic population policy objectives: to enhance the freedom of individuals in less developed countries (LDCs) to choose voluntarily the number and spacing of their children; and to encourage a rate of population growth consistent with the growth of economic progress and productivity. Service delivery, together with support for related research, are the highest priority population assistance activities. Implementation of AID's population policy involves both: programs in other development sectors which influence parents' desire to space or limit the number of children and enhance their ability to understand and use effectively modern contraceptive methods; and programs to ensure the widespread availability of high quality voluntary family planning services through which couples can regulate their fertility. Social and economic conditions that contribute to high birthrates and a low prevalence of family planning use include high infant mortality; status of women based on low educational and income earning prospects, early age of marriage, and high preference for sons; cultural and social barriers to limiting births; dependency on children for old age security; and institutional barriers to the provision of family planning services. Strategies for each of these areas are outlined. In regard to the institutional barriers to the provision of family planning services, the strategy is to identify the improvements in human and financial resources, delivery infrastructure, and management skills required for a broad range of family planning information and education and communication activities directed at both women and men. In the initial stages of family planning program development, priority should be given to AID strategies that: provide information about the country's demographic situation; build consensus that couples have the right to choose voluntarily the number and spacing of their children; strengthen existing family planning information and service delivery facilities to address unmet needs for services; and provide training opportunities. Priority strategies are to establish awareness and create consensus on the importance of family planning and population issues and to assist existing family planning information and service delivery systems. Priority strategies in the stage of broad program assistance and phase out of external assistance are outlined along with strategies to advance scientific and technological knowledge in support of voluntary family planning programs (McPherson, 1983).

A document on prevention and management of high risk pregnancy was prepared for planners and administrators. Principal risk factors to be considered are listed as socio-biological characteristics of the mother (height, age, parity, interval between pregnancies, socioeconomic factors), diseases affecting the mother (diabetes, toxemia, hypertension, and anemia--one of the principal causes of maternal mortality in developing countries), and previous obstetric history (hemorrhage, Caesarian section, pre- or post-mature delivery.) Duration of maternity leave and allowance are compared for Algeria, France, Ghana, India and Sweden. Hours and pace of work outside the home are often not adapted to suit working pregnant women; stillborn babies are most often born to mothers from the working classes, living in inadequate housing. Women should be allowed to stop work during pregnancy without losing wages. Compulsory antenatal visits and prenatal death rates are compared for 3 countries; in France, there is an average of 4 visits and the death rate is 18/1000; in Sweden, an average of 14 visits, death rate is 11/1000; and in Ghana, 30 percent of pregnancies come to the attention of the medical team, and the death rate is 133/1000. In certain high risk cases, weekly visits may be necessary; the community midwife should advise and inform future mothers about such pregnancies. While home delivery is most suitable for normal pregnancies, identified high risk pregnancies should deliver in a hospital. Out of 25 million low birth weight infants born in the world each year, 22 million come from the 3rd world, especially southeast Asia. It is important to organise long term follow-up for such high risk infants. Before leaving the hospital, mothers should be advised on family planning techniques for birth spacing or birth limiting, which needs proper communication programs (International Children's Centre, 1983).

The importance of sexual and reproductive health within the general concept of health cannot be overstated, and it is important to begin providing children from the earliest age with the knowledge they will need to protect their health. All persons have a right to be informed of the care they will need during their reproductive lives, of optimal reproductive strategies, and of contraceptive methods which will allow them to control their fertility. Specific strategies for fertility control include initiating reproduction when the woman is at least 20 years old, spacing children 2-3 years apart, and terminating reproduction by age 35. Contraceptive methods may be temporary or definitive. Condoms are made of latex in various colors, sizes, and forms, lubricated or not. They are effective when used correctly and consistently, and addition of a spermicide increases their efficacy. They offer some protection against sexually transmitted diseases. The diaphragm is a circle of latex with a semirigid border that must be fitted by a physician or obstetrical nurse. It should be coated with a spermicide before coitus and left in place for 6 hours afterward. Used with a spermicide, the diaphragm offers acceptable protection, but it is not practical where sanitary conditions are poor or privacy is lacking. Spermicides are available in foam, tablets, jellies, creams, and ovules. The manufacturer's instructions must be carefully followed, especially in regard to application in sufficient time to ensure dispersion before ejaculation. Their efficacy is low but increased when they are used in combination with condoms, diaphragms, or vaginal sponges. IUDs may be inert or bioactive. Inert devices may be left in place for several years, but bioactive devices must be replaced when their bioactive substance is used up. IUDs are highly effective. Devices containing copper or progesterone have lower rates of expulsion and cause less bleeding than inert devices. Different formulations of hormonal contraceptives use combinations of synthetic estrogens and progestins to prevent ovulation. Because of their multiple mechanisms of action they are the most effective methods apart from surgical sterilization. Hormonal methods can be administered in the form of pills or injections. They are contraindicated for some women and should be prescribed by a doctor. Rhythm methods based on abstinence during the fertile period indicated by the calendar, basal body temperature, or changes in cervical mucus are difficult to use and have relatively high failure rates. Coitus interruptus and lactation are other measures with high failure rates. Vasectomy and tubal ligation, the most common techniques of male and female surgical sterilization, offer very high efficacy rates. Choice of a method should be based on personal factors such as number and ages of children as well as on health status and medical history. Evidence-based communication programs may help proper use of contrac eptive methods (Monroy, 1983).

A study examined abortion motivation among women. Analysis was based on published findings from 27 countries, an analysis of 3 countries, and representative surveys from 52 countries. Popline, Medline, and Population Index databases, bibliographies, and unpublished sources were also used. Women's desire to postpone or stop childbearing ranged from 39 percent in the Central African Republic to 89 percent in Japan. In 23 countries, women chose abortion for many reasons. In 4 developing Asian countries and 3 developed countries, women commonly desired a postponement or stop to childbearing. In 10 out of 20 countries, 50 percent of women gave birth timing and family size control reasons for abortion. A second key reason was poverty and economic concerns. Being young and unmarried was a key reason in some countries. Risk to maternal health was less important in Latin America and developed countries. African women tended to report socioeconomic reasons, followed by postponement or limiting of births. Asian women favored family size control reasons. Latin American women chose socioeconomic and relationship reasons. Developed countries favored family size control and timing reasons. In 10 countries, education was not associated, age was moderately associated, and marital status was associated with reasons. Married women tended to give socioeconomic and family size control reasons. Unmarried women cited socioeconomic factors and youth or parental objections. In the US, abortion reasons were similar to reasons for stopping childbearing. Research affirms that improved contraceptive practice is an important way to reduce abortion (Bankole, 1998).

Health and medicine

In Africa the fusion of modern and traditional health care is needed for solving the problem of providing primary health care. In sub-Saharan Africa 1 child in 10 dies before its first birthday, and resources are desperately needed in reproductive health. The available resources include modern medical practitioners (doctors and nurses) and alternative medical practitioners (traditional healers, chiropractors, and homeopaths), which resources must be reevaluated to solve the health crisis. In accordance with the World Health Organisation recommendation many governments have tried to integrate traditional medicine into their health systems. The difficulty lies in the psychosocial orientation of traditional medicine compared to physiological, scientific approach advocated by modern medicine. The fusion of these two approaches is evident in post-apartheid South Africa among professional nurses who are also traditional healers and make up about 1 percent of all African nurses. When providing prenatal care, they diagnose through "fortuning" and physically examining the patient, and give herbal medicines and massages. They also take into consideration the women's psychological and emotional conditions in the treatment. They use their clinical training by referring patients to hospitals, and they make sure that patients attend prenatal clinics. They act as a bridge between modern health care and traditional medicine, even though often doctors and nurses harbor negative views about their training as traditional healers, considering them as backyard doctors or witch doctors. Their nursing training assures sterile techniques and good hygiene. Nurses who are also traditional healers are a major underutilized resource in African health services, which must be used to the maximum for the benefit of maternal and child health care, and communication programs are needed to fulfill these goals (Ebey-Tessendorf, 1997).

There remains a critical lack of skilled health professionals in the developing world. Unfortunately, leaving home, family, and work to attend training courses in urban centers large enough to have training facilities or universities is not a viable option for many potential and currently practicing health professionals. As a response, the implementation of distance education programs to widen access to such students has grown steadily in the last two decades. From the University of South Africa to Indira Ghandi Open University (IGNOU) in India, there are now a plethora of preservice and post-graduate programs in health and medicine around the world. The QA Project is studying and implementing cost-effective intervention in international healthcare that improves the quality of healthcare delivery and overall health outcomes. The QA Project believes that education at a distance represents a potentially cost-effective approach for training preservice and inservice health workers in a variety of health topics. A review of the current body of quantitative and qualitative research on the implementation, costs, and effectiveness of distance education for healthcare providers appears on the following pages. Though largely undocumented, an attempt was made to include studies of the use of distance education in developing countries (Knebel, 2001).

Results of the 10-year study of injection drug users infected with HIV has confirmed that women have lower viral load than men, particularly in the first few years after infection. In the study, women initially had three times lower median viral loads than men, but both women and men developed AIDS at the same rate. Sterling explained that this sex difference in initial viral load means that the same viral load measurement does not convey the same risk of AIDS in women and men. Researchers with the Johns Hopkins Schools of Public Health and Medicine note that these results clarify how candidates for antiretroviral therapy should be chosen, suggesting that greater emphasis be placed on CD4+ count than viral load. Moreover, Sterling et al. highlighted the need for further studies of the implications of the sex difference in plasma viral load on initiation of antiretroviral therapy, as well as studies to assess whether there is a viral load cutoff that predicts progression to AIDS. The problem partially can be managed through the implementation of appropriate research and communication programs (Study confirms HIV viral load…, 2001).

In 1993, the book "AIDS: Effective Health Communication in the 90s" noted that AIDS had been reported in more than 152 countries worldwide, a pandemic with epicenters in the US and Africa. Over the years, evidence clearly shows that this number has increased as the scourge of HIV\AIDS has grown in scope for the millions outside the US. This article elaborates on some possible solutions to the HIV/AIDS problem. It argues that the approach to such an issue still needs to focus on the ideal by Sir William Osler that it is much more important to know what sort of patient has the disease than what sort of disease the patient has. In addition, the ideas by Collins Airhihenbuwa and Rafel Obregon, suggesting the incorporation of a perspective that value culture as a central construct that allows for national, regional and local differences in communication, can advance the dialogue so that a critical health literate public can emerge. Moreover, quality communication must enable an environment for community involvement to espouse common values of humankind.

Furthermore, the critical elements that also affect health all require a commitment and understanding to advance health beyond the science sector and combat the HIV/AIDS pandemic through decision-making on policies, expenditures, system design and service availability. Finally, effective communication can lead the advance of medicine and health in this century (Ratzan, 2000).

A prospective study was carried out to determine the association of Acanthois nigricans, hyperinsulinemia, and hormonal levels in female subjects from the United Arab Emirates (UAE). 92 females (age range, 16-65 years) from the Tawam Teaching Hospital of Faculty of Medicine & Health Sciences were recruited. Height, weight, and sitting blood pressure were recorded on 92 female subjects with A. nigricans. Fasting blood samples were obtained for measurements of uric acid, glucose, cholesterol, high-density lipoprotein (HDL)-cholesterol, and triglyceride levels. Serum levels of thyroid-stimulating hormone (TSH), testosterone, luteinizing hormone (LH), follicle-stimulating hormone (FSH), and prolactin were obtained by radioimmunoassay. 92 females with A. nigricans were enrolled in the study. Of the 92 females, 36 subjects were considered to have diabetes mellitus (DM) and 56 were euglycemic subjects. The analysis showed that in cases of family history of DM, HDL-cholesterol (mmol/l) and uric acid (mmol/l) levels were higher. Overall, DM subjects had significantly higher values for hormone levels of TSH, FSH, LH, progesterone, testosterone, cortisol, prolactin, growth hormone, and ferritin. Patients with A. nigricans have a high prevalence of DM and insulin resistance in UAE. Since A. nigricans is rather prevalent in the UAE, identifying this skin lesion can help detect those subjects with a higher risk of DM and hormonal disturbances (Lestringant, 2000).

Minorities

The objectives of a study were to describe the establishment of a community based walk-in outreach genitourinary medicine clinic in south London to target young men under 25 in an area with high rates of sexually transmitted infections (STIs). The outreach clinic was set up within a Brook advisory center, which already had gained the trust of local young people. Epidemiological, clinical, and laboratory data were obtained retrospectively for the first 24 weeks of the service. 134 attendances were recorded, including 94 new and 10 rebook events. The age range of the young men seen was 12-27 years (mean 18.2 years), the patients were mainly from black and ethnic minority groups, and all but one were heterosexual. Most men had heard about the clinic by ``word of mouth," recommendation by Brook staff or through clinic promotional material. Condoms were used more frequently with non-regular sexual partners than with regular partners. The uptake of screening for gonococcal and chlamydial infections, mostly by urine based molecular techniques, was 98 percent. The uptake for HIV testing in men aged 16 or more was 72 percent. An overall STI prevalence rate of 26 percent was detected in the clinic population, which consisted almost equally of asymptomatic and symptomatic patients. The most prevalent STI was chlamydial infection (12 percent). The young men who attended the outreach clinic were happy to undergo both non-invasive urine based testing for gonorrhoea and chlamydia as well as phlebotomy to test for HIV and syphilis. The 374 clinic approach may prove to be a useful model for further outreach services to combat poor sexual health of young men in inner city areas (Lewis, 2004).

Even though vasectomy is a popular method of contraception in the United States, there is limited information on the characteristics of men choosing vasectomy and why they decide to undergo the procedure. Methods: A nationwide, practice-based survey of 719 men receiving vasectomies was conducted between July 1998 and June 1999. Results: Low-income, minority and less educated men were underrepresented among vasectomy recipients. The majority of men were married or cohabiting (91 percent), non-Hispanic and white (87 percent), and educated beyond high school (81 percent). Only 7 percent of men had annual household incomes of less than $25,000, and fewer than 1 percent paid for the procedure using public funding; 81 percent of respondents paid through private insurance or a health maintenance organisation. Half of men reported choosing vasectomy over a reversible method because it is the most secure means of preventing pregnancy, and 62 percent chose vasectomy over tubal ligation because the procedure is simpler and safer. Doctors and nurses were the most important sources of information about vasectomy (cited by 31 percent of respondents), followed by wives or partners (25 percent) and friends (23 percent). Conclusions: Despite the diversity of the U.S. population, vasectomy recipients are a homogeneous group. By identifying users of vasectomy and underserved groups, our findings should assist service providers and program managers in planning strategies to reduce the large difference in levels of vasectomy use among men of different races, ethnicities and income groups (Barone et al., 2004).

More than eighty health professionals and representatives from migrant organisations came together in September 2002 at the 7th European Migrants Meeting in Brussels, to discuss and explore issues around HIV/AIDS care and support interventions for migrants and ethnic minorities in Europe. The meeting showed again the great amount of experience and expertise that is found in community-based organisations, and the broad variety of actions in the field of policies and interventions that are developed by the different actors in the field. The evaluation at the end of the conference showed that all participants were either very satisfied or satisfied with the meeting. In particular the exchange with colleagues from other countries and the acquisition of new ideas were very much appreciated. Many people have contributed to this success of the Migrants Meeting, and I wish to take the opportunity to express my gratitude to them. (Louhenapessy, 2003).

The use of affirmative action has been questioned because it can produce biases in selection that may violate human rights and undermine equal opportunity, excluding people with greater knowledge and skills solely because they do not belong to a minority or disadvantaged group. Although the existence of shortcomings in the implementation of affirmative action has been proven, the arguments partly rest on prejudices and perceptions of the groups involved. Several studies conducted in educational institutions and the workplace conclude that perceptions of affirmative action are more favorable and prejudices against it reduced when preferential selection is applied. On the other hand, the use of hard instruments, such as quotas, generates a negative perception and inflames racial prejudices. (Torres Parodi, 2003).

Gender

In the 1990s, Uruguay underwent a marked process of external opening accompanied by a significant appreciation in the exchange rate, which together significantly altered relative prices and triggered an increase in imports. This resulted in extensive modifications to the production structure and the working of the labor market. Within this context, this paper aims to present a methodological proposal for an approximation to the analysis of the impacts on gender of commercial policies and the expansion of trade and, on the basis of that proposal, to explore the evolution of the situation of women in the Uruguayan labor market in the 1990s, debating some conclusions from a gender-based perspective (Gender analysis of trade policies, 2001).

There is a definite need for an effective and reversible form of male contraception, both for maintaining a stable population in industrial countries and for diminishing population growth in developing countries. It has been agreed upon that contraception is an essential component of reproductive health for men and women (the Weimar Manifesto on Male Contraception). The development of new, effective methods of male contraception has been identified as a high priority by the WHO Task Force on methods of regulation of male fertility. Hormonal male contraception is based on suppression of gondotrophins and substitution of testosterone in order to maintain male sexual function and bone mineralisation and to prevent muscle waist. For complete interruption of spermatogenesis, an adequate suppression of intratesticular testosterone production is needed. Various contraceptive regimens have been developed and tested, including testosterone monotherapy, androgen and progestin combinations, testosterone with GnRH analogs, and selective androgen and progestin receptor modulators. The combination of testosterone with progestogen is currently the most promising approach to hormonal male contraception. Also, several non- hormonal approaches to male contraception are promising and may offer the foundation for developing new male contraceptives. (Weber, 2003).

The Philippine Government addresses the causes and consequences of population growth primarily through the work of two national government agencies, the Department of Health (DOH) and the Commission on Population (POPCOM). The DOH is mandated to implement the National Family Planning Program within the Reproductive Health Framework. It also provides technical and financial assistance to Local Government Units (LGUs) and ensures that sufficient contraceptives are available and distributed in all local public health facilities. Decentralisation, which formally took effect in 1992, propelled the devolution of numerous functions of the national government and placed Local Government Units (LGUs) at the forefront of providing their constituencies with social services, including health and family planning. It also tasked LGUs with the formulation of comprehensive development plans, the implementation of multi-sectoral development programs, and the promotion of community-based population programs and services. Hence, in 1999, the DOH launched the Matching Grant Program (MGP) to provide financial and technical assistance to municipalities and cities to improve their service delivery, particularly in the areas of family planning, maternal and child health, and nutrition. Many of the LGUs participating in the MGP are interested in establishing specific services particularly no-scalpel vasectomy (NSV), IUD, and a new natural family planning method, the standard days method (SDM) but they do not know how to go about it. Concerns were also raised on the cost implications of establishing such services. However, the experience of Bago City in Negros Occidental in promoting and providing NSV showed that it could be done. Other MGP areas like Naga City and Donsol, Sorsogon in the Bicol Region and Kapalong in Davao Norte were also NSV success stories. Promoting IUD services in Pantukan, Compostela Valley and SDM in Lupon and Banaybanay can also be models for setting up these FP services. This module documents the process in setting up NSV services based on the experiences of LGUs that have successfully set them up. It also compiles existing local materials that may be used by interested LGUs in orienting prospective clients. (Management Sciences for Health, 2003).

Religion

Respiratory illness continues to be a leading cause of pediatric morbidity and mortality in Indonesia. The Indonesian government is moving towards a more managed care-based approach as it reforms its health care system following the 1997 financial crisis. In order to better design contractual relationships between the payor and different providers, there needs to be a better understanding of the patterns and predictors of health services utilization for respiratory illness. This study uses the Indonesia Demographic and Health Survey to study the determinants of private, public and non-formal provider utilization for respiratory illness. Multinomial logistic regression models for predicting use were constructed using the Andersen Behavioral Model as the conceptual framework. The findings indicate that age, household size, maternal education, religion, the asset index, location and illness severity play a role in determining use of private, public or non-formal providers. The results indicate that from a policy perspective, the Indonesian government needs be inclusive rather than exclusive in the choice of providers that are contracted by the managed care plans, in order to safeguard the health of the under-five population. (Thind, 2005).

It was called a "national dialogue", but to western eyes it was a strange kind of conversation. From June 13th-15th, in Medina, Saudi Arabian women and men discussed how women's lives could be improved. The women, however, were invisible to the men, except on a television screen. From kindergarten to university to the few professions they are permitted to pursue, as well as in restaurants and banks and in other public places, the female half of Saudi Arabia's population is kept strictly apart. Women are not allowed to drive a car, sail a boat or fly a plane, or to appear outdoors with hair, wrists or ankles exposed, or to travel without permission from a male guardian. A wife who angers her husband risks being "hanged"; that is, suspended in legal limbo, often penniless and trapped indoors, until such time as he deigns to grant a divorce. And then she will lose custody of her children. The 19 recommendations that went to Crown Prince Abdullah on June 15th would change matters somewhat, if they are ever enacted. Participants asked for special courts to deal with women's issues, more women's sections in existing courts, and a public-transport system for them. They wanted more education, more jobs and more voluntary organisations dealing with women's issues. Amid much vague good feeling, the phrase that recurred was "more awareness"-not just of women's rights, but of women as human beings (Arab women, 2004).

The plight of millions of HIV-infected individuals without access to antiretroviral (ARV) medications constitutes an enormous problem. Religious values can influence policymakers in public and personal health issues. This article posits that Jewish religious law mandates the broadest possible access to ARV medications for HIV-infected individuals, and argues that wealthy countries must assist poorer ones to facilitate access. (Spira, 2004).

Poverty

The people of Haiti have long been overwhelmed by health problems related to rapid population growth, poverty, poor diet, and emerging diseases. Since 1995, Management Sciences for Health (MSH) has led the implementation of the USAID-funded Haiti Health Systems 2004 Project (HS2004), working to improve the Haitian population's access to high-quality health services while building systems that can be sustained by Haiti's own technical and financial resources in the future. In Haiti, MSH is working with a network of approximately 30 local, service-delivery non-governmental organisations (NGOs) to implement the HS2004 project. The broad project goal of providing efficient and high-quality primary health care services to the people of Haiti is being met through these organisations. All have an established mission to provide services, and all have engaged in a process to improve efficiency and impact of services (Pollock, 2003).

Concerning rapid growth that continues in poor countries, while growth has slowed substantially in the past decade, over the next 50 years little change is expected in the 1.2 billion current population of more developed regions. But the new forecast estimates that less developed regions, where total population totaled 4.9 billion in 2000, will increase to 7.7 billion in 2050. In fact, the number of people in Burkina Faso, Mali, Niger, Somalia, Uganda and Yemen, where annual growth is expected to surpass 2.5 percent over the next half century most probably will quadruple. (Fornos, 2003).

Migration

Three scenarios of spatial distribution of human population in China are developed in the years 2010 and 2020, respectively by means of the method of surface modeling of population distribution (SMPD). Each one of the SMPD scenarios is defined as a plausible alternative future under particular assumptions of elevation, water system, net primary productivity (NPP), urbanization, transport infrastructure development, and population growth. The SMPD scenarios show that if population could freely migrate within the whole China, the balanced ratios of population in the western region, the middle region and the eastern region to total population in the whole China would be 16 percent, 33 percent and 52 percent, respectively (Yue, 2005). Research results could be used for developing effective communication programs for population control.

Mortality

During the previous decades the mortality rates of most colonies had fallen significantly because of administrative public health interventions. Nevertheless, there was general surprise when evidence began to accumulate in the late 1940s and 1950s that mortality was falling rapidly and population growth rates rising in most of the developing world. The United Nations devoted a Population Bulletin to the matter, including a WHO report on the decline of specific causes of death. Stolnitz, in a 1965 analysis of the situation in Latin America, Asia and Africa, concluded: "it now seems that economic misery as such is no longer an effective barrier to a vast surge in survival opportunities in the underdeveloped world." This was the situation until Samuel Preston published his elegant and easily understood paper (in 1975), which is reproduced here. His scatter diagram of relations between life expectancy at birth (hereafter "life expectancy") and national income per head for nations in the 1900s, 1930s, and 1960s remains one of the most memorable illustrations in the population sciences. That diagram and its accompanying text showed that, at any given level of real per capita income, life expectancy rose substantially in the first three decades of the twentieth century and to an even greater extent in the next three decades. Thus, with a gross national income per capita in 1963 (henceforth "income") of US$ 500, life expectancy was typically 50 years in the 1900s,

58 years in the 1930s, and 69 years in the 1960s. Furthermore, the greatest gains were increasingly concentrated at the very beginning of economic development. As average incomes rose from near zero to US$ 200, the proportion of increased life expectancy gained compared with that achieved in the richest societies was around 70 percent in the 1930s and 87 percent in the 1960s (Caldwell, 2003).

Examples of communication programs in which research played important role

There is consensus that a communications component is crucial to the success of iron supplementation and fortification programs. However, in many instances, we have not applied what we know about successful advocacy and program communications to iron programs. Communication must play a larger and more central role in iron programs to overcome several common shortcomings and allow the use of new commitments and investments in iron programming to optimum advantage. One shortcoming is that iron program communication has been driven primarily by the supply side of the supply-demand continuum. That is, technical information has been given without thought for what people want to know or do. To overcome this, the communication component, which should be responsive to the consumer perspective, must be considered at program inception, not enlisted late in the program cycle as a remedy when interventions fail to reach their targets. Another shortcoming is the lack of program focus on behavior. Because the "technology" of iron, a supplement, or fortified or specific local food must be combined with appropriate consumer behavior, it is not enough to promote the technology. The appropriate use of technology must be ensured, and this requires precise and strategically crafted communications. A small number of projects from countries as diverse as Indonesia, Egypt, Nicaragua and Peru offer examples of successful communications efforts and strategies for adaptation by other countries (Griffiths, 2002).

The media plays a unique role within society either to denounce or to perpetuate the bias and moral judgments against people with HIV/AIDS. Sometimes journalists can underestimate how influential their portrayal of HIV/AIDS is in shaping people's attitudes, especially when society fails to distinguish between people and the disease they suffer from; when denial is so pervasive that the infected are ostracized by their families. In addition, reporters, editors and producers constantly grapple with ways to find fresh angles to discuss HIV, and ensure their viewers and readers remain engaged by a topic that never appears to grow old. To address these and other key topics concerning the media and its treatment of HIV/AIDS, the World

Bank organised a distance-learning course from June to November 2002 that simultaneously brought together journalists and HIV/AIDS project managers from Tanzania, Uganda, Zambia, Nigeria and Malawi. The course, entitled Fighting the HIV/AIDS Pandemic through Information and Strategic Communication, recognizes the role that successful communication campaigns can play in increasing understanding of the disease and promoting life-saving behaviors. Each program stream consisted of eight video-conferenced modules, which were followed up through in-country work (Spadacini, 2003).

A document, entitled How to Talk About Abortion, is a guide that stimulates ideas on how to approach the abortion debate. It is designed for people who already have a public voice or who are beginning to develop their own public voice. It presents information and arguments to use if one is given the opportunity to stand up in front of people or to appear in the media and talk about abortion. The guide is based on the experience of Catholics For A Free Choice working in many countries as an organisation of Catholics who believe abortion can be morally correct and who have a distinct perspective on ethical issues, values, and social justice. The guide is subdivided into the following: strategies for successful communication; women's perspectives about abortion; personhood and rights of a fetus; role of community values and culture; and the standpoint of Roman Catholic Church on abortion. The last part of the guide presents a range of difficult questions and assertions that one may hear about abortion (Kissling, 2000).

A technical manual for health care providers concerns caring for women with circumcision. It provides a background on the central thesis. An introduction is given to female circumcision (FC) and female genital mutilation (FGM). Then the prevalence of the practice and its sociocultural characteristics is presented. Then a definition of female circumcision is given together with WHO s classification of it, records types of FC/FGM, and the functional anatomy of the female external genitals, with a list of terminology. Then why FC/FGM is performed is discussed and who performs it. Maps of African communities practicing FC/FGM and of the largest African-born populations in the US are shown. A table on the prevalence, rates, and types of FC/FGM is displayed. Also included statistics on African immigrants in the US and other Western countries and the characteristics of this population. Then the health care needs of circumcised women are described, beginning with medical and gynecological care, continuing with obstetrical care, and concluding with health care needs of circumcised children and adolescents. Then psychological and sociocultural issues are considered. Information on successful communication tools for interacting with circumcised women is given. Reviews are shown on legal issues surrounding female circumcision. The legal status of FC/FGM in the US, along with the state laws concerning it and the reasons why these laws were passed, is explained (Toubia, 1999).

Family planning (FP) health communication has evolved from its emphasis on IEC (information, education, communication), in which top-down sender-focused messages (such as "a small family is a happy family) achieved only limited behavior change, to a new emphasis on the receiver. The new term "behavior change communication (BCC)" reflects this shift, and the BCC strategy recognizes that the intended audience contains active receivers of messages who act only on messages received from trusted sources and perceived as advantageous. The next step is "behavior change intervention," which also recognizes the affect of social policies and economics on an individual's ability to sustain behavior change. Leading theorists have shown how behavior change is a process involving various stages and key factors. Thus, successful communication strategies consider behavioral objectives, audience segmentation, messages appropriateness for each audience, sources, formats, and timing. Values also dictate the approaches and goals of a health communication campaign and can, for example, lead to a shift in emphasis from controlling individuals to helping them make fully informed choices. Value changes lead to new language; thus, the old passive term "FP acceptor" is being replaced with references to "FP users, adopters, and clients" (Murphy, 1998).

In Latin America in the 1970s, groups that sought social change considered a new form of sex education important because it could address a range of socioeconomic and political issues. The guiding principles of this new approach were 1) avoiding top-down directives; 2) using a democratic, participatory process; 3) being comprehensive; 4) covering ethics and values; 5) viewing sex education as a tool for social change; and 6) acknowledging the positive aspects of human sexuality. Despite political difficulties, successful sex education programs were facilitated by family planning programs and national population policies; women's and feminist movements; gay rights movements; expertise, experience, and experts; and government commitment. Then HIV/AIDS linked sex with death and strengthened taboos while increasing the urgency for sexuality education. In Colombia, national policies are helping build a progressive sexuality education program for all citizens from birth through adulthood. Mexico has achieved significant accomplishments without a national policy because non-governmental organisations have mainstreamed the issue in the media, strong networks have grown from widespread training efforts, and networks have linked programs to government policy. Both countries have developed successful communication strategies. New challenges include finding ways to show sex education works, strengthening the gender approach, ensuring participation of adolescents and children in program development, improving the quality of health care, and reaching underserved populations (Corona, 1998).

A trip report pertains to a consultant visit to Asmara, Eritrea, during May 11-22, 1998, for a 2-week training of trainers course in improving interpersonal communication (IPC) skills. Participants included 25 zonal IEC coordinators and trainers from all of the 6 health zones. This course was part of a 4-part series of courses on national-level capacity building. The course offered the opportunity to test and complete the draft IPC training curriculum. The first week focused on building practical IPC skills. Week 2 was spent on adult learning theory and teaching methods. Trainees had a significant gain in knowledge. Most trainees felt confident about training lower level health workers. Follow-up activities include preparation of a final course guide and visuals and their distribution and speeding up the process of finalizing zonal IEC materials. The skills needed for successful communication pertain to caring, problem solving, and counseling and education. Participants were expected after Week 1 to clarify the differing values among themselves and their communities, identify the basic characteristics of IPC, describe the IPC structure and conduct effective IPC sessions, list and apply the skills in caring and problem solving communication, and use good information gathering skills. Participants should be able to define counseling and use educational materials. Caring communication includes welcoming clients, nonverbal communication, empathizing, and praise and encouragement. Effective problem solving means effective listening, encouraging dialogue, avoiding interruptions, avoiding premature diagnosis, probing, and asking about causes (Dondi, 1998).

A guide is meant to stimulate ideas on how to approach the abortion debate. It is designed for people who already have a public voice or who are beginning to develop their own public voice. The information presented here is by no means complete or comprehensive, but it does suggest arguments that can be used if the opportunity comes to stand up in front of people or to appear in the media and talk about abortion. Included in this guide are a range of difficult questions and assertions, which can be heard about abortion. The very focus of this guide is how to tackle the issue on values, which is most often the heart of every abortion debate. This guide is based on the experiences of CFFC working in many countries as an organisation of Catholics who believe abortion can be a moral action and who have a distinct perspective on ethical issues, values, and social justice (Kissling, 1997).

A volume presents some lessons learned from the use and distribution of "Facts for Life." The book presents easily understandable information about the strategies for giving children a better chance for life, health, and physical and mental development. Knowledge about the world's children that is presented in the book is based on UNICEF information. "Facts for Life" has the active support of 165 leading medical and children's organisations. 12 million copies of the book have been printed and distributed in 213 different languages. This volume evaluates the lessons learned and identifies critical issues so that people do not feel alone in facing some of the same issues. It is assumed that communities can usually define their own problems and agendas. It reinforces the view that the main objective of "Facts for Life" is to communicate about health in a way that brings about positive change in communities. It presents a strategy for communicating "Facts for Life" and practical steps to update or devise a strategy. It synthesizes the experiences of adapting "Facts for Life" for national use and the experiences of monitoring and evaluation. It identifies, for instance, practical issues in working with the mass media and the eight steps to successful communication. It focus on adult learning and interpersonal communication discusses how adults learn best and identifies an approach to training communicators. It discusses child-to-child activities and teacher-with-child activities. It is devoted, respectively, to working with non-governmental organisations, health personnel, religious leaders, and the private sector. Information is so presented on the adaptation of "Facts for Life" messages in the visual arts, drama, and animation. It addresses the issue of cultural sensitivity with regard to sexual health messages. It is also concerned with evaluation tools and methods (McIntyre, 1996).

A paper reports the current state of information dissemination within the Russian health sector and the role of the Internet in meeting the challenges of the health information system. It also describes the Website of the Ministry of Health (MOH), "Medicine for You." This document aims to provide the information necessary for international organisations and private partners to continue the work which Basic Support for Institutionalizing Child Survival (BASICS) has begun. The MOH, in collaboration with the US Agency for International Development and BASICS, identified the Internet as vital to a successful communication program. Between October and December 1996, BASICS and Samovar Internet Consulting worked with computer programmers at "Medicine for You" to establish the Website, which provides information from ministerial decrees to extensive professional articles to bulletins on recent medical developments new to Russia. Furthermore, the Website and on-line database provides immediate access to thousands of medical documents which are approved by the Ministry, official Ministry orders, an up-to-date list of drugs in Moscow pharmacies, new drug information, current medical journal articles, and an official list of the name of drugs. Links to Ministry departments are currently being established and will ensure that more recent data on the health status of the country will appear on the Website. A breakthrough in the dissemination of medical information in Russia, this Website represents the initial step in creating a unified health information system throughout the country (Murdoch, 1996).

A paper reports on the outcome of the survey on communication for development, which aimed for the promotion of attitudinal and behavioral change, enhancement of participation and self-reliance, and improvement of knowledge and skills in developing countries. A total of 39 interviews were conducted after handing out questionnaires. Interviewees unanimously recognized the general importance of communication within development programs. Among the findings was the significance of communication for successful development programs. In addition, broad understanding and knowledge of concept were observed, although misinterpretations and confusion exist. Most development agencies stated their aim of better participation in planning and implementation of their programs; however, political constraints and local power structures have limited these participatory approaches. There was a limited experience of communication for development among interviewees. The implications of these findings for professionals include the need to devote additional resource to communication through program evaluation and produce more competent communication professionals (Fraser, 1994).

Population geographers are involved in contemporary policy issues, the production of quality work, and successful communication of research findings. This article reviewed some contributions population geographers have made to the understanding of the geographic impact of ageing and the consequences of migration. Geographers have come late to the study of ageing and have focused primarily on four main policy issues: fertility decline, housing demography, aged patterns of housing and migration, and government policy. Fertility decline research has highlighted information diffusion theories for fertility decline by researchers such as Zelinsky, Skeldon, and Noin. Changes in attitudes and the removal on constraints has been examined by Woods. Residential mobility studies have been the focus of researchers such as Gober, Moore, and Clark, and Myers. Regional labor markets and the movement of the "baby boom" through the life course have been examined by Miron, Plane and Rogerson, and Clout, who studied the empty nesters and the movement out of suburbia. Private residential housing has increased for the elderly in England and Wales (Hamnett and Mullings), and seasonal migration of Minnesotans results in lost sales revenues and high health and social costs for those too ill to travel (Craig). Geographers have not accomplished a significant thrust into the literature on demographic ageing. Contributions to the transnational and international literature have resulted in internal migration studies by Clout on "counterurbanization" in northwestern industrial Europe, while Fielding, Baltensperger, Marchand and Scott, and Jones have examined the continuing rural-urban migration. The loss of urban population has been associated with inner city problems, the impact of labor supply and market demand, and the revenue and health care consequences in the work of Champion, Gibson, and Champion and Illeris, and Craig. Impacts are felt differently by geographic location, and assorted models have been developed for examining interregional migration. Population movement between countries will be a future major policy issue associated with disparities in development. The benefits and disadvantages of immigration have been examined. Refugee movements have been a neglected area of study (Nash, 1994).

Due almost exclusively to sexual intercourse and perinatal transmission, the number of reported AIDS cases in Zimbabwe has risen rapidly. It is estimated that 500,000-600,000 people may be infected in the population of 10 million. Despite significant information campaigns, misunderstandings persist about AIDS. This paper review the current practice of health education as it has developed within a traditional information giving approach in Zimbabwe and attempts to explain the barriers which have prevented a shift to an approach which is part of a broader policy of health promotion. The current educational strategy must be rethought and will require a widespread training initiative to locate the educator in a social context of AIDS; a shift toward a methodology encouraging a systematic process for obtaining information as a basis of planning; and strategies to enhance successful communication and participation. Planners must acknowledge that the mechanics and resources to effect change in educational practice must be put in place; recognize that education is only part of a health promotion policy; and understand that communities can and should play a role in defining the problem, planning and instituting steps to resolve the problem, and establishing structures to ensure that desired changes are maintained. A framework for a participatory approach to AIDS communication activities is suggested (Laver, 1993).

Successful communication projects show that effective development communication depends on good context, good messages, good channel use, and good audience knowledge. Knowledgeable communication professionals know when and where not to carry out a communication program and when a communication program may be successful based on the context. A communication campaign in Jordan promoting breast feeding within 6 hours of delivery was not successful in private hospitals because they did not promote early initiation of breast feeding. Good communication programs use formative research to develop messages that solve problems of which audiences are aware and build on or respond to current behaviors. In the Philippines, messages about child's age for measles vaccination resulted in improved vaccination coverage rather than those emphasizing the dangers of measles. Precampaign research helps identify what communication channels are the most effective and reach the greatest audience. In Swaziland, face to face communication was 1.5 times more effective than the mass media, but 3 times as many people has access to a radio. So the radio was more effective. Communication programs must know their audience well and be able to track it to determine the successes as well as the failures of the campaign. Even though some professionals have adequate technical knowledge to affect development communication well, the successes of early communication projects do not seem to endure. Sometimes the immediate health benefits justify the communication campaign. Further, limited political will, the fact that the campaign does not match the health educators' routine, and limited skilled health educators are obstacles to institutionalization. The key to sustained communication capacity is patience to stay for the long term. Other needs are a consistent call on budgets and staff, some satisfaction with what has already been accomplished, and translating the successful strategies used in the short term to successful strategies in the long term (Hornik, 1992).

A brochure from Population Services International (PSI) opens with a report from PSI's president, who notes that as a result of its 1991 expansion PSI is now the largest social marketing organisation in the world. Products sold through PSI's programs avert thousands of new HIV infections and are making a major impact on birth spacing and on reduction of maternal and infant mortality and morbidity. PSI depends upon highly successful communication programs and speed to create demand for products and improve quality. PSI's next objectives are to launch condom marketing programs in every country in need, provide significant quantities of birth spacing and family planning products with unparalleled cost efficiency, and demonstrate that millions of children can be saved through the social marketing of essential drugs such as oral rehydration salts and vitamin A. PSI addresses the problem of inadequate resources available to prevent HIV/AIDS, stem population growth, and save children, by developing cost-efficient social marketing of essential health products through the private sector. The brochure details elements and results of PSI social marketing, cost efficiency and performance, and PSI's communication campaigns. The remainder of the brochure is devoted to a description of country programs in Africa (Benin, Burkina Faso, Burundi, Cameroon, the Central African Republic, the Ivory Coast, Ethiopia, Guinea, Kenya, Morocco, Nigeria, South Africa, Zaire, and Zambia); Asia (Bangladesh, India, Malaysia, Pakistan, and the Philippines); and Latin America and the Caribbean (Brazil and Haiti). Attention is then paid to PSI's HIV/AIDS prevention demonstration project in the US, which targets runaways and street kids in Portland, Oregon. The brochure ends with a list of program contributors, directors, staff, representatives, offices, and affiliates (Population Services International, 1992).

A paper presents theories on health education planning, determinants of behavior, health promotion, and developing and implementing behavioral change programs for AIDS prevention and patient education. The theories are based upon research and theory regarding disease prevention, and the care and support of terminally ill patients such as in cases of cancer. It is recommended that health education interventions be well-based in target population research, and be the result of careful planning and evaluation. Behavioral change is not exclusively knowledge-dependent. Accordingly, interventions should focus upon the known determinants of unsafe behaviors, while ongoing research investigates determinants of importance for different risk groups. Health education should be part of more broad health promotion policy, supported overall by successful communications. Communication should stress feasible and effective preventive behaviors at the expense of potentially overpromoted fear campaigns. Moreover, target audiences should be prepared for the negative consequences of new behavior with hopes of minimizing one-time-only behavioral change and relapse. To combat stigmatization of AIDS patients and seropositives, campaigns should create a more positive image of homosexuality, and focus on the right for help and the safety of helping behavior. More research is called for overall, especially in understanding the implementations process for effective AIDS prevention, patient support, and patient care interventions.

Incompatibility with values and norms of decision makers and the public is noted as an obstacle to effective implementation (Kok, 1991).

Sierra Leone's 1974-75 to 1978-79 National Development Plan urged the integration of population planning into socioeconomic planning, the creation of Population Section in the Ministry of Development and Economic Planning, the formation of a National Population Commission, and formulation of a national population policy. However, these steps cannot achieve their intended effect without popular support for population control. People must become convinced that support of the national policy is in their interest and will inprove the quality of their life. This , in turn, requires knowledge and information on the rationales of population policies. Communication, defined as the process through which information is shared, has been successfully utilized in creating awareness of development programs and the adoption of new practices. The use of communication programs to disseminate population policy decisions requires consideration of traditional beliefs and attitudes toward population issues. According to African tradition, a large family is viewed not only as a status symbol but also as a necessity for support in old age. The system of polygamy further pressures women to prove their worth by bearing as many children as possible. Thus, a successful communications strategy must carefully plan the kinds of media to be used, the target audience, the message design, and the content of the message. For example, there is no point in using only printed messages if the target audience is largely illiterate, or in talking to people about the advantages of smaller family size if they are not aware of health programs to reduce infant mortality or alternative sources of old age support. Furthermore, an effective communication strategy should aim to mobilize a 2-way flow of information, as takes place in interpersonal communication. Finally, communications strategy must take into account the relative cost-effectiveness and access to it by the population of the various types of media (Communicating population policy decisions, 1985).

A document presents the conceptual base for the guidelines of communication and seeks to establish the rationale for incorporating effective communication support into agricultural projects, to state the communication problem to be addressed, and to relate communication support to other project components. It concludes with a summary of characteristics of successful communication strategies extracted for the most part from experience gained in the projects. It discusses the rationale for agricultural communication in the context of agricultural development programs and the communication problem to be addressed in improving technology development and transfer programs in agriculture. It then focuses on the following: communication in relation to other program components; communication and communicator functions; communication strategies; characteristics of successful communication strategies; and costs, benefits, and cost effectiveness. The agricultural development and transfer process, which is essential to agricultural development, is presented as an excellent example for including a communication component in agricultural projects. The communication problem to be addressed is that application of communication skills, media, and methodologies often is ad hoc and fragmented, with no operative strategy for their integrated and mutually reinforcing use in effective support of the program. The communication challenge will be to develop viable communication support programs as an integral part of strategies to reorient, remold, and reinforce existing extension systems to increase their coverage, effectiveness, and cost effectiveness. In the context of this paper, the term communication means the transfer of ideas or knowledge in ways that enable the recipient to understand, react to, and act upon the information. In technology transfer programs, the example being used for this discussion, effective communication with and among at least 4 major groups is essential: the farmers, research institutions, extension institutions, and agricultural infrastructure institutions -- public and private. Success in realizing extension's technology transfer objective calls for a high degree of coordination and interaction among the 4 groups as well as integration of communication support into the technology development and support system. In general terms, communication and the communicator should be involved in virtually every phase of program activity. The most important specific functions are developmental investigation, planning and strategy development, production of educational materials, information delivery, evaluation, feedback, coordination, and staff training and support (Ray, 1985).

Jamaica's experience shows how lack of understanding can result in grievous misinterpretation of the communication message. The Ministry of Health initiated a program aimed at reducing the prevalence of childhood malnutrition. 1 aspect of the program was a scheme for changing attitudes and practices related to breastfeeding and infant feeding. Materials and media to be used were slides, booklets, a flannel board and cutouts, and practical demonstrations given by community health workers. The target group was low income mothers attending antenatal and child welfare clinics in 2 parishes of the island. The 1st problem to arise concerned the scripts, which had been written to be read rather than spoken. When they were read aloud to some groups, certain words were not heard correctly.

For example, a word like "rarely," sounded like "really." Thus, the statement could have been heard "A breastfed baby really (rarely) gets diarrhea." Other words were unintelligible to the audience because the script had been prepared without an understanding of local idiom. A thorough background knowledge of the audience being addressed is essential. It is only then that the communicator will be able to respond to the specific behavioral needs of the audience and formulate the most appropriate strategies and approaches for delivering messages. This information needs to be collected early in the program planning process, as was done in a baseline survey undertaken before Jamaica's Nutrition Education Program in 1977. This helped in the selection of themes and in the exact content and wording of the messages and in the choice of media. Messages went beyond recognizing and stating the problems to acknowledging existing behavioral constraints. Health and nutrition programs will continue to fail unless communication is made an integral part of the process of change. Successful communication helps ease the transition between old and new ideas by motivating people to accept change and then giving them the tools and skills to deal with new practices. The best way to learn if people will respond to messages and media at the behavioral level is to listen to them (Okwesa, 1983).

Teenage pregnancy can be linked to inconsistent or lack of contraceptive use. In this study, a model is presented considering contraceptive use as a series of steps including several which are preliminary to the actual method use, and which involve social interaction. Several different causal sequences for this model were tested using the multiple regression technique of path analysis. Support was found for the temporal sequential model as originally presented by Byrne (1982), in which learning about contraceptives is viewed as causally linked to discussing contraceptive use with the partner, which is finally seen as causally linked to actual contraceptive use. An attempt to find a significant relationship between this model of contraceptive effectiveness and the set of social skill and person history variables hypothesized as influencing successful communication about contraceptives, again using the technique of path analysis, was not successful. The social skill and person history variables assessed include positive and rights assertiveness, sex role orientation, emotional orientation to sexuality, factual knowledge of birth control, past sexual experience, and gender. Supplemental analysis show these insignificant results may be due to a low level of power among the variables in the study and a low effect size; i.e., a lack of difference among subjects in the phenomena measured in the population, especially in performance on the dependent measures assessing effective communication about contraceptives (Hynes, 1982).

Some key issues in evaluation, communication and learning which might be helpful in determining the potential value of any audiovisual approach are clarified. In this discussion of evaluation of audiovisual methods of medical teaching, focus is on "inputs" - those things which can be controlled, which are indispensable to meaningful communication and learning. A selected, incomplete list of characteristics of potential receivers which determine whether a transmission gets through as a message or is rejected as a noise includes solicited versus unsolicited information, perception, intelligibility, relevance, dissonance tolerance, principles of learning, activity, organising principles, learning range of the student, and feedback. Against this background of some of the basic requirements of effective communication and successful learning, some generalizations can be made regarding audiovisual methods of instruction. The most important generalization is that those approaches and devices which are used and labeled audiovisual methods should not be viewed apart from instruction generally. At times these approaches supplement, complement and even replace more conventional modes of instruction. These approaches allow for amplification of sounds, magnification of images, clarification of relationships and transposition of remote resources to local receivers, but they do not enjoy a special exemption from the rules and conditions necessary for effective communication and learning (Jason, 1968).

Sex education programs that teach only abstinence have little impact on adolescents' behavior, a study in Texas, George Bush's home state, has concluded. The number of adolescents who had had sexual intercourse did not change or increased after they had received abstinence only sex education, according to the report `Abstinence Education Evaluation Phase 5 Technical Report' from the Texas health department. The evaluation was prompted after Henry Waxman, a Democratic senator, and 18 other congressional representatives complained that 11 of the 13 commonly used programs included false and misleading statements. Senate majority leader, Bill First, a surgeon, said on national television that the government should review the sex education programs, but he did not discuss their medical accuracy. Abstinence only sex education has been federally funded in the United States since 1999. And Congress has approved $167m (t'89m; e130m) for abstinence only programs for 2005. More than 100 programs are federally funded, and several million children have received instruction (Tanne, 2005).

Rich countries should increase aid and make it work better for poor people, cancel world debt, and change the rules of world trade so that they favor the interests of the poor. That was the new year's message to Britain's prime minister, Tony Blair, from a coalition of more than 100 UK charities, trades unions, and campaigners, including rock and pop stars. Their Make Poverty History campaign, which was launched on 1 January, came as the tsunami disaster in South East Asia brought harrowing television images of the tragedy directly into the homes of those in the developed world, highlighting the conditions of poorer countries. The coalition, which includes Oxfam, Wateraid, and the World Medical Fund, is calling on Mr. Blair to change the unfair trade rules and high levels of debt that hinder the developing world. It is part of a global call to action, a worldwide movement that will come together at key points during 2005 (Eaton, 2005).

Drawing on the family process literature, child health models, and recent studies of macro-level effects on health, we examine the effects of household structure, resources, care-giving, reproduction, and communication on child nutritional status and infant mortality. Using Demographic and Health Surveys, we analyse the influence of these factors across 42 countries in Latin America, Africa, and Asia. We also consider country-level including nontraditional family structure, level of economic development and expenditures on health care. Our results underscore the importance of family resources, decision-making, and health and feeding practices on child well-being in less developed countries. Although there is cross-national variability, the size of the variability was small relative to the overall effect. The country-level measures had modest effects on infant mortality and child nutritional status (Heaton, 2005).

An exploratory study has been made to examine the social and cultural determinants of the teaching of HIV/AIDS sex education among secondary school teachers in Eastern Nigeria. The research analyses how teachers perceive passing their knowledge of HIV/AIDS prevention measures to their students in the context of their cultural and social norms, which restrict open discussion of sex. This is a qualitative study based on in-depth interviews with 60 teachers drawn from secondary school teachers in Eastern Nigeria, supplemented with five focus group discussions, and content analysis of teachers' lesson preparatory notes. The findings show a high level knowledge of HIV/AIDS preventive measures among teachers. However, teachers are not passing on this knowledge because of cultural and social inhibitions. In addition, teachers have not been receiving adequate training and motivation on information, education and communication for HIV/AIDS sex education. The situation calls for serious policy intervention (Oshi, 2005).

Many studies suggest that aspects of culture be included in human immunodeficiency virus (HIV) education efforts in the United States. Few, however, clearly identify specific strategies that respond to the unique cultural issues of women of color. This article reviews the literature for culturally competent HIV prevention efforts for women of color-Latina, African American, Asian Pacific Islander, and Native American-and synthesizes components that need to be addressed in programs and interventions. Findings suggest that for programs to be culturally competent, both race or ethnicity and gender, along with population-specific, culturally based attitudes, beliefs, and behaviors, must be considered in interpersonal and organisational strategies (Scott, 2005).

The internet is one of a range of health information sources available to adolescents. It is recognised that young people have difficulties accessing traditional health services; in theory, the internet offers them confidential and convenient access to an unprecedented level of information about a diverse range of subjects. This could redress adolescents' state of relative health `information poverty', compared to adults. A paper seeks to explore United Kingdom (UK) and United States (US) adolescents' perceptions and experiences of using the internet to find information about health and medicines, in the context of the other health information sources that are available to them. The study involved a series of 26 single-gender focus groups with 157 English-speaking students aged 11-19 years from the UK and the US. Many students reported that the internet was their primary general information source. Information sources were defined during analysis in terms of previous experience of the source, saliency of the available information, and credibility of the source (defined in terms of expertise, trustworthiness and empathy). Most focus group participants had extensive personal experience with the internet and some information providers therein (notably search engines). Internet health information was regarded generally as salient. Its saliency was increased through active searching and personalisation. Perceived credibility of the internet varied because expertise and trustworthiness were sometimes difficult to determine, and empathy could be facilitated through online communities but the individual could control disclosure. The internet combines positive features of traditional lay and professional, personal and impersonal sources. Although it is unlikely to supplant the role of trusted peers and adults, the internet has found an important place among adolescents' repertory of health information sources (Gray, 2005).

As part of qualitative research for developing a culturally sensitive and developmentally appropriate videotape-based HIV prevention intervention for heterosexual African-American men, six focus groups were conducted with thirty African-American men to determine their perceptions of AIDS as a threat to the African-American community, characteristics of past situations that have placed African Americans at risk for HIV infection, their personal high risk behaviors, and suggestions on how HIV intervention videotapes could be produced to achieve maximum levels of interest among African-American men in HIV training programs. The groups took place at a low-income housing project in Houston, Texas, a major epicenter for HIV/AIDS. Each group was audiotaped, transcribed, and analysed using theme and domain analysis. The results revealed that low-income African-American men perceive HIV/AIDS as a threat to their community and they have placed themselves at risk of HIV infection based on unsafe sex practices, substance abuse, and lack of knowledge. They also cite lack of income to purchase condoms as a barrier to safe sex practice. They believe that HIV training programs should address these risk factors and that videotapes developed for prevention should offer a sensationalized look at the effects of HIV/AIDS on affected persons. They further believe that programs should be held in African-American communities and should include condoms to facilitate reduction of risk behaviors. The results indicate that the respondents taking part in this study believe that HIV and AIDS are continued threats to the African-American community because of sexual risk taking behavior, that is, failure to use condoms. Further, African-American men are having sex without condoms when having sex with women often when they are under the influence of alcohol or other mind-altering substances and they are having sex with men while incarcerated and become infected and once released resume unprotected sexual relations with women. According to the men, substance abuse is an important part of the problem of HIV in the African-American community. This is in keeping with research that shows that drug use, especially crack cocaine, is linked to sexual risk taking among African Americans and to increased likelihood of becoming infected with other sexually transmitted diseases (STDs) including HIV. Thus, interventions for men should address condom use, condom availability, skills for using condoms, eroticizing condoms and substance abuse prevention. Men in the present study also strongly recommended that HIV/AIDS videotaped messages should include footage of the sensational effects of the disease (Essien, 2005).

The effectiveness of an intervention was evaluated designed to increase preventive health care seeking among adolescents. Adolescents and young adults aged 12 to 21 years, recruited from community-based organisations in 2 different communities, were randomized into either a 3-session intervention or a control condition. Outcomes from 3-month follow-up data were estimated using logistic and ordinary least squares regression. Female intervention participants were significantly more likely than female control participants to have scheduled a health care appointment (odds ratio [OR]=3.04), undergone a checkup (OR=2.87), and discussed with friends or family members the importance of undergoing a checkup (OR=4.5). There were no differences between male intervention and male control participants in terms of outcomes. This theory-driven, community-based group intervention significantly increased preventive health care seeking among female adolescents. Further research is needed, however, to identify interventions that will produce successful outcomes among male adolescents (VanDevanter et al., 2005).

Examples of crisis management programs in which research and communication played important role

The September 11 attacks have demonstrated the indivisibility of security in the Euro-Atlantic area. The attacks and the ensuing campaign against terrorism have also brought into focus the importance of Central Asia to Euro-Atlantic security and the need for closer cooperation between the North American Treaty Organisation (NATO) and its Central Asia Partners. An essay notes that the Partnership for Peace offers an extensive menu of security-related activities covering areas such as civil-emergency planning, crisis management, language training, scientific cooperation and the interoperability of armed forces. Two key principles underpin the Partnership for Peace: 1) it is not directed against the interests of a third party; and 2) it does not seek to substitute or duplicate other cooperative initiatives. As such, NATO and its Central Asian Partners have been able to embark on cooperative activities in various areas. Moreover, they are also benefiting from the opportunity to work together in the field of scientific and technological research. In conclusion, efforts to pursue closer partnerships and cooperation through both Partnership for Peace Program and the Euro-Atlantic Partnership Council have been of benefit to all (Yavuzalp, 2002).

Since the inception of democracy in Venezuela, there has been a pattern of conflict and change marking the system over the years. There has also been extensive debate among scholars concerning the causes of crisis and the significance and viability of reform. In this paper, the authors aim to make theoretical sense of the decay and crisis of democracy in Venezuela. They attempt to capitalize on four perspectives: stress on how contingent historical conditions shape processes and likely outcomes; attention to institution building, rules of the game, and interbranch relations; focus on specific political vehicles, political parties; and concern with civil society as generative of new actors and more democratic rules of the game and the state- society relations. Their argument underscores the need to combine perspectives and to look in detail at the actual capabilities of civil society and social forces. Overall, it is noted that although there can be no doubt about the severity of the crisis of democracy in the country, political management of the crisis has been steady and constitutional norms have been followed (Levine, 1999).

An article summarizes the main issues revealed at a women's roundtable discussion on the Economic, Social, and Political Impacts of the Southeast Asian Financial Crisis. The discussion was organised by the Development Alternatives of Women for the New Era (DAWN) and was held during April 12-14, 1998, in Manila, the Philippines. The aim was to explore the effects of the financial crisis and its management by states and multilateral agencies on women's political, economic, cultural, and social status; and to reach regional understanding of new issues for the women's movement in Asia and to identify areas of advocacy. Participants included women scholars and activists from Southeast, East, and South Asia; Africa; the Caribbean; Latin America; and the Pacific. Participants came from a wide variety of backgrounds. Nine issues were emphasized. For example, some predicted the currency devaluation before July 1997. The financial crisis is linked with globalization. The International Monetary Fund (IMF) is the primary institution for addressing the financial crisis. IMF conditions on inflation rates and budget surpluses are recessionary and government budget oriented. The crisis has exposed cronyism and corruption within capitalism. Patriarchal values have reemerged as Asian values. Women have lost jobs and income, while the cost of living continues to increase. Prostitution has become more acceptable as legitimate work. Women's human rights are not legally protected. State ideology assumes domestic and sex roles. Issues in each region are identified (Kelkar, 1998).

Future of multicultural communication concerning demographic issues

Present communication processes are embedded in a situation which is characterized by a low recognition of diversity, a poor record of education of diversity, and low employment of racial or ethnic minorities and other members of diverse populations. Future communication represents a practice of communication which is culturally sensitive and characterized by communication based on genuine dialogue. This communication focuses on building strong communities within a more human global society. From a social-interpretive view, it is not possible to control the future, otherwise, the principles of emergence, contextuality, and open-endedness of meanings would be invalidated. However, through enacted environments including climate change, green revolution, blue revolution, changes in the living earth, demographic processes, human attention and action do have consequences, enabling individuals to influence and partially predict future conditions. It can be seen from current processes in and forecasts of earth ecosystem crisis and multifaceted demographic crisis that the situation will worsen in many respects within the near future. Managing these processes cry for evidence-based risk management and proper risk communication in a multicultural environment. To achieve these goals the importance of training and education will increase. Several meta-analyses have concluded that cross-cultural and managerial training can improve practitioners' effectiveness in culturally diverse settings. Training for cultural sensitivity, international adjustment, intercultural communication, and valuing diversity are essential to creating personal changes in multicultural settings. A diverse and rapidly expanding variety of approaches to these sorts of training are available, and organisations should assess their needs and select a training modality that suits their conditions.

In future education more emphasis should be on the concepts, values, assumptions, and research methods of all prominent communication theories, including social-interpretivism, and social sciences, further research methods, cultural studies, and communication ethics. Future graduates should be critical thinkers and responsible, literate citizend than to be skilled in any of the task requirements of communication professionals. Effective communication is a key component of managing future demographic processes in a multicultural world. From a social-interpretive, effectiveness always has a moral dimension. If our social knowledge is constituted in our communicative practices, the knowledge is of our making, and we are responsible. Since our knowledge is based on values, then we have incorporated, by implication, what we believe is good and desirable. Therefore our communicative practices have a sound moral dimension. The problem of ethical communication is to identify a standard for responsibility in communication, so that it can be applied across countless actual situations. The central issue for ethical communication is the proper governance of power and conflict, where the standard must be based on equality in the sense that all humans must be considered equal in that they have the right to a life of quality and that their life should succeed. The underlying ethical principle is equality of consideration in the pursuit of fulfillment, such that no party gains at the expense of others. This leads us to solidarity, the norm and fundamental moral virtue in communication, and to act in such a way that one shows solidarity of all parties involved. Thus the standard of solidarity through equal consideration is recognizable only as a communicative behavior, not as a psychological form or state. In ethical communication one must learn the interests of those, involved, they must be sensitive to their equal right to succeed, and construct communication as genuine dialog. Genuine dialog is only possible when parties approach one another with mindfulness. Mindfulness is more than concentration. Mindfulness is an openness to understanding whatever concentration focuses on. Mindfulness is characterized by creation of new categories of understanding, openness to new information, and awareness of multiple perspectives. Mindfulness is that state of mental openness where new cognitive categories are welcome and where readiness to accept new information and perspectives motivates communication. Mindfulness must be learned and practiced as a way of being. The ethical principles in which mindfulness is grounded should be incorporated into organisational policies and corporate philosophy statements. Genuine dialogue with relevant human populations concerning recent and imminent future demographic and environmental processes can only occur when organisational leaders personally demonstrate that they ground their own communication in solidarity and mindfulness. Without total commitment to these principles only partial solutions, if any, will be given to the earth ecosystem crisis and the demographic crisis.

Conclusion

New research methods and inventive evidence based communication programs provide lessons, important tools and assistance to solve, successfully manage major demographic problems of the world.

RAR is used to help make decisions about appropriate interventions for various demographic, social and health issues. Rapid Assessment and Response (RAR) is a technique for the assessment of an issue in a particular study area, including the characteristics of the problem, population groups affected, settings and contexts, demographic, social, health and risk behaviors, and social consequences. RAR is a method to assess and rapidly respond to issues especially in situations where there is scarcity of information and data are needed very quickly. Instead of using the heavy and traditional armament of traditional scientific method RAR uses, among other things the triangulation method, which is a process of collecting and cross-checking information.

Multivariate and computer-intensive statistical methods comprise a series of methods that can be used both in conventional and nonconventional data analytic situations. These methods can be used when the data are scarce, when the distribution of a variable is skewed, when the problem cannot be formulated in a closed format, or even if the sample is nonrandom.

Present and anticipated future demographic processes involve the following observations:
- Demographic problems are increasing and are threatening human quality of life
- New scientific research, multivariate and computer intensive statistical methods are good to find and present the relevant information
- New communication programs are related to ICT and adult education
- These communication programs help in managing world demographic problems
 - Success stories show the effectiveness of research and communication programs in managing major world demographic problems
 - Research and communication based feedback plays a crucial role in managing increasing demographic problems

In management and communication for organising better services feedback is crucial. Even in small-scale projects to perform well, staff members need to know how they are doing compared with expectations for their job. Managers can clarify what is expected by preparing and distributing guidelines and by writing job descriptions and discussing them with staff. Feedback on job performance can come not only from supervisors' evaluations but also from clients' comments and from self- and peer-assessments.

Service providers need to be able to interact and communicate well with their clients, as well as with their supervisors and co-workers. When clients and service providers communicate openly, share information, and ask and answer questions freely, clients are more satisfied and understand and recall information better. Staff members who are able to communicate openly with their supervisors and co-workers can do their jobs better.

Without appropriate feedback management and communication will fail and the project will not be efficient and successful.

In large-scale demographic and communication projects the role and relevance of feedback is crucial. In large-scale projects vast resources are used and thousands or millions of people are affected. In such cases management and communication of the project cannot be made without appropriate feedback based on scientific research.

Feedbacked communication relies heavily on evidence-based strategy.

- New methods of communication such as soap operas, rap music contests, drama, a newsletter, posters and other methods are successfully used for controlling major demographic problems, targeting especially children, adolescents and parents.
- Risk communication is properly used in many cases primarily in relation to global processes. However, risk communication is scarcely used in relation to local processes.

Risk communication has a strong link to communicating in a crisis. Establishing a relationship with the news media is critical. As part of disaster preparedness, governments and humanitarian agencies have or should have a plan of working with news media in crisis situations. In times of conflict and natural disaster, radio and other media can provide survivors with information about the security situation and about where to find shelter, food and water, and health services, including reproductive health care. The broadcast media may well be the only working means of communicating with the public.

Communication concerning demographic issues is related to adult education, which is the practice of teaching and educating adults. Educating adults differs from educating children in several ways. One of the most important differences is that adults have accumulated knowledge and experience which can either add value to a learning experience or hinder it. Another important difference is that adults frequently must apply their knowledge in some practical fashion in order to learn effectively; there must be a goal and a reasonable expectation that the new knowledge will help them further that goal.

Around the wold, conflicts and natural disasters challenge health care providers to meet people's basic needs, including reproductive health care, under the most difficult conditions. Every year armed conflicts and natural disasters kill hundreds of thousands of people and inflict great suffering. Armed conflicts tear societies apart and disrupt people's lives, often for years. Natural disasters devastate whole regions without warning, as the December 2004 Asian tsunami, the August 2005 New Orleans hurricane, and the October 2005 Pakistan earthquake demonstrated. Health care systems, often struggling to meet people's needs in the best of times, can be quickly overwhelmed by the added burden of injury and infectious diseases. At the same time, health systems themselves may be crippled by disaster or conflict. As of 2005 some 45 countries, predominantly in Africa and Asia, faced crises related to armed conflicts or natural disasters. Nearly 40 million people have fled their homes as a result of conflict and now are living as refugees outside their countries or, more often, as displaced people within their own countries. Natural disasters affect millions more. According to the United Nations refugees can formally be distinguished from internally displaced persons, according to whether or not they have crossed an international border. However, this distinction is not necessarily important from the point of risk.

My study proved that impact analysis for program evaluation is a widely used, indispensable method and that these methods should have a much greater emphasis in education. Impact analysis is a must to prove that a project effective and provides value for money.
The study proved that RAR is very rarely used in an expressed format in demographic projects as an evaluation tool. However, certain elements of RAR are applied. This is an inexpensive and still very valuable, very effective tool for collecting and information. Although demographic analysis of data is often based on large population databases, RAR would be a very valuable supplementary tool.

The study proved that among sophisticated statistical methods project evaluators used CHAID analysis very rarely. This is surprising because CHAID is for finding "market segments" and it is useful for targeting certain population groups with special communication packages.
The study proved that the Fishbein-Ajzen communication model proved applicable in many demographic communication projects. An advantage of the application of the Fishbein-Ajzen communication model is that it, instead of focusing on the attitudes, wants to change intention and behavior.

In my view although evaluation is often made, feedback to the participants is not typical. In other words the participative method is not used in demographic projects as it ought to be. As a matter of fact, the participative method is preferred primarily in surveys on peripheral, "alternative" segments of the society. However, the participative nature of demographic projects should strengthened, since it is an invaluable element of democratic communication.

Future communication for solving demographic crisis must represent a practice of communication which is culturally sensitive and characterized by communication based on genuine dialogue. This communication focuses on building strong communities within a more human global society. It can be seen from current processes in and forecasts of earth ecosystem crisis and multifaceted demographic crisis that the situation will worsen in many respects within the near future. Managing these processes cry for evidence-based risk management and proper risk communication in a multicultural environment. To achieve these goals the importance of training and education will increase. In future education more emphasis should be on the concepts, values, assumptions, and research methods of all prominent communication theories, including social-interpretivism, and social sciences, further research methods, cultural studies, and communication ethics. Effective communication is a key component of managing future demographic processes in a multicultural world. From a social-interpretive, effectiveness always has a moral dimension. The underlying ethical principle is equality of consideration in the pursuit of fulfillment, such that no party gains at the expense of others. This leads us to solidarity, the norm and fundamental moral virtue in communication, and to act in such a way that one shows solidarity of all parties involved. In ethical communication one must learn the interests of those, involved, they must be sensitive to their equal right to succeed, and construct communication as genuine dialog. Genuine dialog is only possible when parties approach one another with mindfulness. Mindfulness is characterized by creation of new categories of understanding, openness to new information, and awareness of multiple perspectives. Genuine dialogue with relevant human populations concerning recent and imminent future demographic and environmental processes can only occur when organisational leaders personally demonstrate that they ground their own communication in solidarity and mindfulness. Without total commitment to these principles only partial solutions, if any, will be given to the earth ecosystem crisis and the demographic crisis.

Literatur

@RISK. Advanced risk analysis for spreadsheets. Palisade Corporation. 1997.

Adler JP, Markova EV, Granovszkij JV. Kísérletek tervezése optimális feltételek meghatározására. Műszaki K. Budapest. 1977.

Adolph, C. and G. King, G. With Herron, M.C. and K.W. Shotts. A consensus on Agresti, A. (1990). Categorical data analysis. Wiley 2003.

Aggleton P. Health. Routledge. 1993.

Agresti A. An introduction to categorical data analysis. Wiley. 1996.

Agresti A. Categorical data analysis. Wiley. 1990.

Agresti A. Categorical Data Analysis}, John Wiley and Sons. 1990. New York.

Ahamad B. An analysis of crimes by the method of principal components. Appl. Stat. 1967(16):17-35.

Alexander FE, Ricketts TJ, Williams J, Cartwright RA. Methods of mapping and identifying small clusters of rare diseases with application to geographical epidemiology. Geographical Analysis. 1991(23):158-173.

Alles V, Makea M, Persson L, Seuntjens L. Tools and methods for quality improvement in general practice. STAKES National Research and Development Centre for Welfare and Health. Gummerus Printing Finland. 1998.

Allison PD. Event history analysis. Regression for longitudinal event data. Series: Quantitative applications in the social sciences. A SAGE University Paper 46. 1984.

Allott M, Robb M (eds) Understanding health and social care. An introductory reader. Sage. 1998.

Alsop RJ. The 18 immutable laws of corporate reputation. Creating, protecting, and repairing your most valuable asset. A Wall Street Journal Book. 2004.

Ambrus P, Csépe P, Forrai J. Kommunikáció Egészségügy Cigányság. Új Aranyhíd Kft. Budapest. 2002.

Amorosa LF Jr; Corbellini G, Coluzzi M. Lessons learned from malaria: Italy's past and sub-Sahara's future. Health and Place. 2005(11):67-73.

Anderson JA, Rosenfeld E (eds.). Neurocomputing. Foundations of research. The MIT Press. 1990.

Anderson NH, Titterington DM. Some methods for investigating spatial clustering, with epidemiological applications. Journal of the Royal Statistical Society A 1997(160):87-105.

Anselin L. Local indicators of spatial association-LISA. Geographical Analysis. 1995(27,2):93-115.

AnswerTree 1.0. User's guide. SPSS Inc.1998.

Answer tree. SPSS, Inc., Chicago 1999.

Arab women. Out of the shadows, into the world. Economist. 2004 Jun 17;:[6] p.

Arlington V. Partnership for Child Health Care, Basic Support for Institutionalizing Child Survival [BASICS], 1998. [4], 17, 15 pp. Repor; USAID Contract No. HRN-Q-17-93-00032-00

Armstrong D. Az orvosi szociológia alapjai. Semmelweis K. Budapest. 1995.

Armstrong D. Outline of sociology as applied to medicine. Butterworth Heinemann. 1994.

Ashraf H. Experts gather to discuss water crisis that the world is ignoring. Lancet. 2003 Mar 15;361(9361):935.

Asian Development Bank. ADB loan to Bangladesh for primary health care services. [Manila, Philippines], Asian Development Bank, 1997 Sep 16. [3] p. ADB News Release No. 76/97

Asian parliamentarians commit to ICPD goals. Population 2005: News and Views on Further Implementation of Cairo Program of Action. 2003 Mar-Apr;5(1):12.

Atkinson P, Molesworth A. Geographical analysis of communicable disease data. In Spatial epidemiology: methods and applications. Elliott P, Wakef, JC, Best NG, Briggs DJ (eds). Oxford University Press Inc. New York. 2000: 253-265.

Babbie E. A társadalomtudományi kutatás gyakorlata. Balassi K. Budapest. 1995.

Bachman R. Violence against women. A national crime victimization survey report. NCJ-145325. Washington D.C. 1994.

Bagozzi RP. Principles of marketing research. Blackwell. 1994.

Bailar IIIJC, Eisenberg H, Mantel N. Time between pairs of leukemia cases. Cancer. 1970(25):1301-1303.

Bailey TC. Spatial statistical methods in health. \\http://www.dpi.inpe.br/cursos/ser301/referencias/bailey$_$review.pdf, 2001.

Banerjee S, Carlin BP, Gelfand AE. Hierarchical modeling and analysis for spatial data. Chapman & Hall/CRC. 2004.

Bankole A, Singh S, Haas T. Reasons why women have induced abortions: evidence from 27 countries. International Family Planning Perspectives. 1998 Sep;24(3):117-27, 152.

Baracskai Z. Profi döntések. Nyíregyháza. 1997.

Barbujani G, Calzolari E. Comparison of two statistical techniques for the surveillance of birth defects through a Monte Carlo Simulation. Statistics in Medicine. 1984(3):239-247.

Barone MA, Johnson CH, Luick MA, Teutonico DL, Magnani RJ. Characteristics of men receiving vasectomies in the United States, 1998-1999. Perspectives on Sexual and Reproductive Health. 2004 Jan-Feb;36(1):27-33.

Barrett RE. Using the 1990 U.S. ce3nsus for research. Guides for major social science data bases. Sage. 1994.

Barros DS, Lima LL, Pinheiro MS, Passos MR, Bravo RS. Biological, socioeconomic and cultural aspects of women with vaginal discharge. [Aspectos biológicos, socioeconômicos e culturais de mulheres com corrimento vaginal.] DST -- Jornal Brasileiro de Doenças Sexualmente Transmissíveis. 2003;15(1):4-15.

Barta T, Tóth T. Minőségmenedzsment. Szókratész. 1995.

Bartfai, P., Rudas, T. (1988) Conditionally independent extension of measures. Preprint No 57/1988, Mathematical Institute, Hungarian Academy of Science.

Barton DE, David FN, Merrington M. A criterion for testing contagion in time and space. Ann Hum Genet. 1965(29):97-102.

Barton DE, David FN. Randomization basis for multivariate tests. I. The bivariate case: randomness of n points in a plane. Bull Int Stat Inst. 1962(i39 II):455-67.

Barton DE, David FN. The analyses of chromosome patterns in the normal cell. Ann Hum Genet. 1962(25):323-32.

Batyrshin I, Rudas T. (2000) Invariant clustering procedures based on corrections of similarities. In: Proceedings of the 8th Zittau Fuzzy Colloquium, 302-309, Fachhochschule Zittau.

Batyrshin, I., Rudas, T. (2006) Invariant Hierarchical Clustering Schemes, in: Batyrshin, I., Sheremetov, L., Kacprzyk, J., Zadeh, L. (eds.) Perception Based Data Mining and Decision Making in Economics and Finance. Studies in Fuzziness and Soft Computing, Springer.

Batyshin IZ, Rudas T, Klimova A. (2004) On a general scheme of invariant clustering procedures based on fuzzy similarity relations. In Batyrshin, I., Kacprzyk, J., Sheremetov, L. (eds.) Proceedings of the International Conference on Fuzzy Sets and Soft Computing in Economics and Finance. Instituto Mexicano del Petroleo and Russian Fuzzy Systems Association, 122-129.

Baudrillard J. The consumer society. Myths & structures. Sage. 1998.

Bearden WO, Neteme3yer RG, Mobley MF. Handbook of marketing scales. Multi-item measures for marketing and consumer behavior research. Sage. 1993.

Benedetti, J. K. and M. B. Brown. Strategies for the selection of log-linear models. Biometrics, 1978(34):680-686.

Beral V. Childhood leukemia near nuclear plants in the United Kingdom: the evolution of a systematic approach to studying rare disease in small geographic areas. Am J Epidemiol. 1990(132(1 Suppl)):S63-8.

Béres István - Horányi Ö. (szerk.) Társadalmi kommunikáció. Egyetemi tankönyv. Budapest, Osiris, 2001. http://www.communicatio.hu/konyvek/beres_horanyi_tarsadalmi_kommunikacio/maintartalom.htm

Bergsma W, Rudas T. (1999) On marginal log-linear models. International Conference on Applied Statistics, Preddvor. Abstracts 17, University of Ljubljana.

Bergsma W, Rudas T. (2000) Marginal log-linear parameterizations: applications and potentia pitfalls. In: Collected papers on marginal models, precision of estimation and parameter orthogonality. WORC paper 00.08.04, 23-38, Tilburg University Press.

Bergsma W, Rudas T. (2000) On applications of marginal modeling. Social Science Methodology in the New Millenium. Proceedings of the Fifith International Conference on Logic and Methodology, 418, University of Cologne.

Bergsma W, Rudas T. (2000) Smooth and variation independent marginal parameterizatrions and implications for modeling. In: Collected papers on marginal models, precision of estimation and parameter orthogonality. WORC paper 00.08.04, 1-22, Tilburg University Press.

Bergsma W, Rudas T. (2001) A class of hierarchical models for categorical data. International Meeting of the Psychometric Society, Abstracts 231, Osaka.

Bergsma W, Rudas T. (2001) Characterization, existence and uniqueness of MLEs for marginal models for categorical data. 16th International Workshop on Statistical Modeling, Abstracts, Odense.

Bergsma W, Rudas T. (2002) Marginal models for categorical data. Annals of Statistics, 30, 140-159.

Bergsma W, Rudas T. (2002) Restricting the marginals of contingency tables: potential problems and how can they be avoided. In Mrvar, A., Ferligoj, A. (eds.) Developments in Statistics. Metodoloski Zvezki, 17, 75-86. University of Ljubljana, .

Bergsma W, Rudas T. (2002) Variation independent parameterizations of multivariate categorical distributions. In: Cuadras, C. M., Fortiana, J., Rodriguez-Lallena, J. A. (eds.) Distributions with Given Marginals and Statistical Modeling. Kluwer, 21-27.

Bergsma W, Rudas T. (2003) On conditional and marginal association, Annales de la Faculte des Sciences de Toulouse, (6) 11, 443-454.

Besag J, Newell J. The detection of clusters in rare diseases. Journal of the Royal Statistical Society, Series A. 1991(154):143-155.

Bhutta ZA, Darmstadt GL, Ransom EI, Starrs AM, Tinker A. Research overview. Basing newborn and maternal health policies on evidence. In: Shaping policy for maternal and newborn health: a compendium of case studies, edited by Sandra Crump. Baltimore, Maryland, JHPIEGO, 2003 Oct. :5-12.

Biemer PP, Groves RM, Lyberg LE, Mathiowetz NA, Sudman S (eds). Measurement errors in surveys.Wiley. 1991.

Bihari, Z. Magyarország új éghajlati térképei. Élet és Tudomány. 2000(6).

Biondini ME, Mielke PW, Berry KJ. Data-dependent permutation techniques for the analysis of ecological data. Vegetatio. 1986(75):161-168.

Birch, M.W. Maximum likelihood in three-way contingency tables. J. Roy. Statist. Soc. B 1963(25):220-233.

Bishop, YMM., Fienberg SE, Holland PW. Discrete multivariate analysis: theory and practice., 2nd ed.M.I.T. Press, Cambridge, Mass. 1977.

Bithell JF. The choice of test for detecting raised disease risk near a point source. Statistics in Medicine. 1995(14):2309-2322.

Black TR. Evaluation social science research. An introduction. Sage. 1993.

Bledsoe C, Banja F, Hill AG. Reproductive mishaps and Western contraception: an African challenge to fertility theory. POPULATION AND DEVELOPMENT REVIEW. 1998 Mar;24(1):15-57.

Bodor Sz, Bodor Sz Ifj, Czakó I, Méreg G. Trendvonalak az egészségügyben. Belső ellenőrzés elméleti és gyakorlati kérdései az egészségügyben. Budapest. 2006. October 14.

Boomgaard P. Bridewealth and birth control: low fertility in the Indonesian Archipelago, 1500 - 1900.

Bornemisza E, Rudas T. (1990) The DISTAN package for discrete statistical analysis in: Gladitz, Troitzsch (eds.) Computer Aided Sociological Research - CASOR 89, 155-162, Akademie Verlag, Berlin.

Bourdieu P, Wacquant LJD. An invitation to reflexive sociology. Blackwell. 1992.

Bourdieu P. The logic of practice. Polity Press. Blackwell. 1992.

Box GEP, Hunter WG, Hunter JS. Statistics for experimenters. An introduction to design, data analysis, and model building. Wiley. 1978.

Boyce P, Aggleton P, Malcolm A. Rapid assessment and response adaptation guide on HIV and men who have sex with men. Geneva, Switzerland, World Health Organisation [WHO], Department of HIV / AIDS, 2004. 61 p. WHO/HIV/2004.14

Böcken J, Butzlaff M, Esche A (eds.) Reforming the health sector. Results of international research. Bertelsmann Foundation Publishers. Gütersloh. 2001.

Breslow NE, Day NE, Davis W. Statistical methods in cancer research. Volume 1 - The analysis of case-control studies. IARC. Lyon. 1980.

Breslow NE, Day NE. Statistical methods in cancer research. Volume II - The design and analysis of cohort studies. IARC. Lyon. 1987.

Brugger W. Filozófiai lexikon. Szent István Társulat. Budapest. 2005.

Buckley S. Birthrates declining in much of Africa; economic pressures, better education, changing attitudes help explain trend. WASHINGTON POST. 1998 Apr 27;:A11.

Bullas S. Managing hospital quality and cost. Using patient-based information. Longman. 1994.

Burrows D. Strategies for dealing with HIV / AIDS in the former Soviet Union. DEVELOPMENT BULLETIN. 2000 Jun;(52):49-51.

Burrows D, Rhodes T, Trautmann F, Bijl M, Stimson GV. Responding to HIV infection associated with drug injecting in Eastern Europe. Harm reduction digest 3. Drug and Alcohol Review. 1998;17:453-463.

Butcher K. Lessons learned from mainstreaming HIV into the poverty eradication action plan in Uganda. DfID Uganda. "Mainstreaming HIV means adapting core business to cope with the realities of HIV and AIDS". London, England, John Snow International Research and Training (UK), 2003(10):15.

Caldwell BK, Caldwell JC, Mitra SN; Smith W. Tubewells and arsenic in Bangladesh: challenging a public health success story. International Journal of Population Geography. 2003;9(1):23-38.

Caldwell JC, Schinndlmayr T. Historical population estimates: Unravelling the consensus. Population and Development Review. 2002(2):183-204.

Caldwell JC. Mortality in relation to economic development. Bulletin of the World Health Organisation. 2003 Nov;81(11):831-832.

Caldwell JC. Fertility control in the classical world: was there an ancient fertility transition? Journal of Population Research. 2004 May;:[25] p.

Caldwell JC. Demographic theory: a long view. Population and Development Review. 2004 Jun;30(2):297-316.

Carlin BP, Louis TA. Bayes and empirical Bayes methods for data analysis. 2nd ed. Chapman & Hall/CRC. 2000.

Carter J. Database design and programming with Access, SQL and Visual Basic. McGraw-Hill. 2000.

Carty WP. A path for balanced population growth? Washington, D.C., Population Reference Bureau [PRB], 2003 Apr. [2] p.

Center for Reproductive Law and Policy. The criminal process and abortion prosecutions in El Salvador. [Procesos penales y juicios sobre el aborto en El Salvador.] In: Persecuted. Political process and abortion legislation in El Salvador: a human rights analysis, [compiled by] Center for Reproductive Law and Policy. New York, New York, Center for Reproductive Law and Policy, 2001. :43-53.

Chambers JM, Cleveland WS, Kleiner B, Tukey PA. Graphical methods for data analysis. Wadsworth & Brooks/Cole. 1983.

Chang ML. Growing pains: cross-national variation in sex segregation in sixteen developing countries. American Sociological Review. 2004 Feb;69(1):114-137.

Chatfield C, Collins AJ. Introduction to multivariate analysis. Chapman & Hall/CRC. 1995.

Chatfield C. The analysis of time series. An introduction. 4th ed. Chapman & Hall. 1994.

Chow SL. Statistical significance. Rationale, validity and utility. Sage. 1996.

Cincotta RP, Engelman R, Anastasion D. The security demographic: population and civil conflict after the cold war. Washington, D.C., Population Action International [PAI], 2003. 101 p.

Citro CF, Hanushek EA. Improving information for social policy decisions. The uses of microsimulation modeling. Review and recommendations. Volume 1. National Research Council. National Academy Press. Washington, D.C. 1991.

Clarke J, Cochrane A, McLaughlin E. Managing social policy. Sage. 1995.

Cliff AD, Ord JK. Spatial processes. Pion. 1981:63-65.

Clogg CC, Eliason SR. Some common problems in loglinear analysis. Sociol. Methods Res. 1987(15):4-44.

Clogg CC, Matthews S, Rudas T. (1995) Analysis of model misfit, structure and local structure in contingency tables using latent class concepts and graphical displays. Conference on Visualization of Categorical Data, Koln, Volume of Abstracts, 7.

Clogg CC, Rudas T, Matthews S. (1997) Analysis of model misfit, structure, and local structure in contingency tables using graphical displays based on the mixture index of fit, in Blasius J, Greenacre M. (eds.) Visualization of Categorical Data. Academic Press. 1997:425-439

Clogg CC, Rudas T, Xi L. A new index of structure for the analysis of models for mobility tables and other cross-classifications. in: P. Marsden (ed.) Sociological Methodology. Blackwell, Oxford. 1995:197-222.

Clogg CC, Rudas T. A new index of structure in mobility tables and related kinds of cross classification, including a general fit index for contingency table models. Sociological Abstracts. 1994(7):59.

Clogg CC, Shihadeh ES. Statistical models for ordinal variables. Advanced Quantitative Techniques in the Social Sciences Series 4. Sage. 1994.

Clogg CC. Some models for the analysis of association in multiway cross-classifications having ordered categories. JASA 1982(77,380):803-815.

Cochran, W. G. (1954). Some methods for strengthening the common chi-square tests. Biometrics. 1954(10):417-451.

Cochrane WG, Cox GM. Experimental designs. 2nd ed. Wiley. 1957.

Cohen J. Two hard-hit countries offer rare success stories: Thailand and Cambodia. Science. 2003 Sep 19;301:1658-1662.

Cohen SA. Beyond slogans: lessons from Uganda's experience with ABC and HIV / AIDS. Guttmacher Report on Public Policy. 2003(12):1-3.

Coles C. Environment. The growing water crisis. Futurist. 2003 Sep-Oct;37(5):10.

Communicating population policy decisions--issues and strategies. Popleone. 1985 Jan;1(2):16-9.

Contraceptive coverage: a 10-year retrospective. Guttmacher Report on Public Policy. 2004 Jun;7(2):[10] p.

Conyers D. Decentralisation in Zimbabwe: a local perspective. Public Administration and Development. 2003;23(1):115-124.

Corder JK, Wolbrecht C. Using prior information to aid ecological inference: a Bayesian approach. In Ecological Inference: New Methodological Strategies (eds. King G, Rosen O and Tanner M). Cambridge: Cambridge University Press, 2004

Corona E. Sex education in Latin America: from Utopia to compromise. In: Report from the Meeting on Changing Communication Strategies for Reproductive Health and Rights, December 10-11, 1997, Washington, D.C., [compiled by] Working Group on Reproductive Health and Family Planning. [New York, New York], Population Council, Health and Development Policy Project, [1998]. :26-9.

Cox DR and Oakes D. Analysis of survival data. Chapman & Hall. 1994.

Cox TF and Cox MAA. Multidimensional scaling. Chapman & Hall. 1994.

Crowder MJ, Kimber AC, Smith RL, Sweeting TJ. Statistical analysis of reliability data. Chapman & Hall. 1995.

Cséfalvay Z. A modern társadalomföldrajz kézikönyve. MTA-OTKA, IKVA K. Budapest. 1994.

Csepeli Gy, Lengyel Zs, Rudas T, Rajkay A, Molcsotár H. (1984) A feltételezett befolyásolás hatása a személyészlelésre. Magyar Pszichológiai Szemle 1984(5):382-389.

Cserháti I, Dobosi E, Molnár Zs. Regionális fejlettség és tőkevonzási képesség. Területi Statisztika. 2003:15-32.

Csikós E, Karsai G (szerk.) Folyamat és kaland. Tanulmányok Whitehead filozófiájáról. Veszprémi Humán Tudományokért Alapítvány. Veszprém. 2005.

Csiszár I, Tusnady G, Ispany M., Verdes E, Michaletzky Gy, Rudas, T. Divergence minimization under prior inequality constraints. Proceedings of the IEEE International Symposium on Information Theory, 21. Washington, DC. 2001.

Curry MR. Digital places. Living with Geographic Information Technologies. Routledge. 1998.

Cuzick J, Edwards R. Spatial clustering for inhomogeneous populations. Journal of the Royal Statistical Society, Series B}. 1990(52):73-104.

Czeizel A., Sankaranarayanan K., Losonci A., Rudas T., Keresztes M. The load of genetic and partially genetic diseases in man II. Some selected common multifactorial diseases: estimates of population prevalence and of detriment in terms of years lost and impaired life. Mutation Research. 1988(196):259-292.

Dahal K. Legal abortion in Nepal and women in prison. Lancet. 2004 Jun 5;363(9424):1905.

Dale MRT, Dixon P, Fortin M, Legendre P, Myers D, Rosenberg MS. Conceptual and mathematical relationships among methods for spatial analysis. Ecography. 2002(25):558-577.

Dalgaard P. Introductory statistics with R. Springer. 2002.

Dalgaards P. Introductory Statistics with R. Springer-Verlag. 2002. Copenhagen, Denmark.

David FN, Barton DE. Two space-time interaction tests for epidemicity. 1966(20):44-48.

Davidson AC and Hinkley DV. Bootstrap methods and their application.Cambridge University Press. 1997.

Dayhoff J. Neural network architectures. An introduction. International Thomson Computer Press. 1996.

de Castro LD. The future of bioethics -- a bioethics for the future? JOURNAL OF REPRODUCTIVE HEALTH, RIGHTS AND ETHICS. 1999;4-5:1-10.

Deloitte Touche Tohmatsu. Commercial Market Strategies. Jordan: an integrated approach to increasing use of modern family planning methods. Washington, D.C., Deloitte Touche Tohmatsu, Commercial Market Strategies, 2003 Oct. [6] p. Country Profil; USAID Contract No. HRN-C-00-98-00039-00

De Mooij M. Global marketing and advertising. Understanding cultural paradoxes. Sage. 1998.

Deming WE, Stephan FF. On a least squares adjustment of a sampled frequency table when the expected marginal totals are known. Ann Math Statist. 1940(11):427-444.

de Onis M, Blossner M. The World Health Organisation Global Database on Child Growth and Malnutrition: methodology and applications. International Journal of Epidemiology. 2003;32:518-526.

Development and the environment. World Development Report 1992. World Development Indicators. World Bank. Oxford University Press. 1992.

Devi K. Causes of declining sex ratio in Orissa: an analysis. Journal of Family Welfare. 2003 Jun;49(1):43-49.

Diczfalusy E. Contraception and society. European Journal of Contraception and Reproductive Health Care. 2002 Dec 1;7(4):199-209.

Diggle PJ, Chetwynd AD, Haggkvist R, Morris SE. Second-order analysis of space-time clustering. 1995(Statist Meth Med Res. 1995(4):124-136.

Diggle PJ, Chetwynd AG. Second-order analysis of spatial clustering for inhomogeneous populations. Biometrics. 1991(47):1155-1163.

Diggle PJ, Chetwynd AG. Second-order analysis of spatial clustering for inhomogeneous populations. Biometrics. 1991(47):1155-1163.

Diggle PJ, Rowlingson BS. A Conditional Approach to Point Process Modeling of Elevated Risk. JRSSA 1994(157, Part 3):433-440.

Diggle PJ. A point process modeling approach to raised incidence of a rare phenomenon in the vicinity of a prespecified point. Journal of the Royal Statistical Society. 1990(153):349-362.

Diggle PJ. Statistical analysis of spatial point patterns. Arnold. 2003:1-159.

Dobosi E. A komplex regionális fejlettség matematikai-statisztikai elemzése. Területi Statisztika. 2003(6;43;1):15-33.

Dobosi E. A regionális elemzések módszertani kérdései. Esettanulmány: Magyarország kistérségi fejlettségének elemzése. Gazdaságelemző és Informatikai Intézet. Budapest. 2001(2):3-53.

Dobosi E. A regionális elemzések módszertani kérdései. Esettanulmány: Magyarország kistérségi fejlettségének elemzése. Gazdaságelemző és Informatikai Intézet. Budapest. 2003(1):3-107.

Dollett D. Modeling binary data. Chapman & Hall. 1996.

Dondi N. Training of trainers course in interpersonal communication, Casa degli Italiano, Asmara, May 11-22, 1998.

Doti JL, Adibi E. The Practice of Econometrics. Quantitative Micro Software. Irvine, California. 1998.

Doti, JL, Adibi, E. The practice of econometrics. With Eviews. Quantitative Micro Software. USA. 1998.

Dow MM, Cheverud JM. Comparison of distance matrices in studies of population structure and genetic microdifferentiation: quadratic assignment. American J of Physical Anthropology. 1985(68):367-373.

Drozdenko RG, Drake PD. Optimal database marketing. Strategy, development and data mining. Sage. 2002.

Durkheim E. Az öngyilkosság. Közgazdasági és Jogi Könyvkiadó. 1982. Budapest.

Dutka S, Frankel LR. Misuses and abuses of statistical techniques in market research surveys. Chance: New directions for statistics and computing. Springer. 1996:18-24.

Dyson T. On the future of human fertility in India. In: Expert Group Meeting on Completing the Fertility Transition, New York, 11-14 March 2002, [compiled by] United Nations. Department of Economic and Social Affairs. Population Division. New York, New York, United Nations, Department of Economic and Social Affairs, Population Division, 2004. :392-408.

Eaton L. Charities and rock stars join forces to tackle world poverty. BMJ. British Medical Journal. 2005 Jan 8;330:59.

Ebey-Tessendorf KL, Cunningham PW. Africa: in search of solutions. WORLD HEALTH. 1997 Mar-Apr;50(2):20-1.

Ederer F, Myers MH, Mantel N. A statistical problem in space and time: do leukemia cases come in clusters? Biometrika. 1964(20):626-638.

Edwards D. Introduction to graphical modeling. Springer. 1995.

Edwards, D. MIM 2.3. 1995.

Efron B. Computers and the theory of statistics: thinking the unthinkable. SIAM Review 1979(21,4):460-480.

Efron B. Bootstrap methods: Another look at the jackknife. Annals of Statistics 1979(7,1):1-26.

Efron B. Nonparametric estimates of standard error: the jackknife, the bootstrap, and other resampling methods. Biometrika 1981(68):589-599.

Eliason, S. (1990). CDAS. Version 3.50. Pennsylvania State University

Eliason SR. Maximum likelihood estimation. Logic and practice. Series: Quantitative applications in the social sciences. A SAGE University Paper 96. 1993.

Ellis R., Whittington D. Quality assurance in health care. A handbook. Arnold. 1993.

Espino A. Gender analysis of trade policies. [Análisis de género de las políticas comerciales.] In: El género en la economía, edited by Rosalba Todaro and Regina Rodríguez. Santiago, Chile, Isis Internacional, 2001. :111-130. Ediciones de las Mujeres No. 32

Essien EJ, Meshack AF, Peters RJ, Ogungbade GO, Osemene NI. Strategies to prevent HIV transmission among heterosexual African-American men. BMC Public Health. 2005 Jan 7;5:[10] p.

EuroQol EQ-5D user guide.

Evans M, Hastings N, Peacock B. Statistical distributions. 2nd ed. Wiley. 1993.

Evans R, Holman R, Lindsay E. Migration of Implanon: two case reports. Journal of Family Planning and Reproductive Health Care. 2005;31(1):71-72.

Evenson RE. Food and population: D. Gale Johnson and the Green Revolution. Economic Development and Cultural Change. 2004 Apr;52(3):543-569.

Everitt BS, Der G. A handbook of statistical analyses using SAS. Chapman & Hall. 1996.

Fathalla MF. Population concerns for the next century. In: Fertility and sterility: a current overview. Proceedings of the 15th World Congress on Fertility and Sterility, Montpellier, France, 17-22 September 1995, edited by B. Hedon, J. Bringer and P. Mares. New York, New York, Parthenon Publishing Group, 1995. :3-13.

Feeney G, Alam I. New estimates and projections of population growth in Pakistan. Population and Development Review. 2003 Sep;29(3):483.

Feller W. Bevezetés a valószínűségszámításba és alkalmazásaiba. Műszaki K. Budapest. 1978.

Ferge Zs, Lévai K (eds) A jóléti állam. ELTE Szociológiai Intézet Szociálpolitikai Tanszék és T-Twins K. Budapest. 1991.

Fienberg EE. An iterative procedure for estimation in contingency tables. Ann Math Statist. 1970(41):907-917.

Fienberg, S. E. The use of chi-squared statistics for categorical data problems. J Roy Statist Soc B, 1979a(41):54-64.

Fienberg, S. E. The Analysis of Cross-classified Data. The MIT Press, Cambridge, Massachusetts. 1979b.

Fikree FF, Ali T, Durocher JM, Rahbar MH. Health service utilization for perceived postpartum morbidity among poor women living in Karachi. Social Science and Medicine. 2004 Aug;59(4):681-694.

Firman T. Demographic and spatial patterns of Indonesia's recent urbanisation. Population, Space and Place. 2004;10:421-434.

Fink A. The survey handbook. Sage. 1995.

Fleck F. WHO insists it can meet its target for antiretrovirals by 2005. BMJ. British Medical Journal. 2004 Jul 17;329:129.

Flynn D, Kofman E. Women, trade, and migration. Gender and Development. 2004 Jul;12(2):66-72.

Fombrun CJ, van Riel CBM. Game & fortune. How to successful companies build winning reputations. Prentice Hall. 2004.

Fombrun CJ. Reputation. Realizing value from the corporate image. Harvard Business School Press. 1996.

Fornos W. Rapid growth continues in poor countries. POPLINE. 2003 Mar-Apr;25:2-3.

Fraser C. How decision makers see "communication for development". Report of a survey commissioned by the Development Communication Roundtable, financed by UNICEF and WHO. [Unpublished] 1994 Sep. [2], 16 p.

Friedrich W, Asmussen J, Burkhardt N, Molnár DL. Country Policy Paper on Social Protection. (PHARE CONSENSUS Programme). With ISG Sozialforschung, Cologne, Brussels. 1996.

Fisher, R. A. [1936]. The use of multiple measurements in taxonomic problems. Ann Eugenics, 1936(7):179-188.

Fuchs K, Deutz A. Use of variograms to detect critical spatial distances for the Knox's test. Preventive Veterinary Medicine. 2002(54):37-45.

Füstös L, Meszéna G, Simonné MN. A sokváltozós adatelemzés statisztikai módszerei. Akadémiai K. Budapest. 1986.

Gaal, A. ISO 9001:2000 for small business. Implementing process-approach quality management. St. Lucie Press. CRC. 2001.

Gabriel Y., Lang T. The unmanageable consumer. Contemporary consumption and its fragmentations. Sage. 1997.

Gatrell AC, Bailey CT, Diggle PJ, Rowlingson BS. Spatial point pattern analysis and its application in geographical epidemiology. Transactions of the Institute of British Geographers. 1996(NS 21): 256-274.

Gatrell AC, Bailey TC. Interactive spatial data analysis in medical geography. Social Science Medicine. 1996(42):843-855.

Gaynor PE, Kirkpatrick RC. Introduction to time-series modeling and forecasting in businedd and economics. McGraw-Hill. 1994.

Gaynor PE, Kirkpatrick RC. Time-series modeling and foirecasting in business and economics. McGraw-Hill, Inc. 1994. New York.

Geary RC. The contiguity ratio and statistical mapping. Incorp Statist 1954(5):115-145.

Gebhardt F. Spatial cluster test based on triplets of districts. Computers and Geosciences. 2001(27):279-288.

Gebhardt F. Survey on cluster test for spatial area data. GMD. 1998(7). Sankt Augustin.

Gelman A, Carlin JB, Stern HS, Rubin DB. Bayesian data analysis. Chapman & Hall. 1995, 2003.

Gelman AJ, Hill J. Applied regression and multilevel models. In Press. 2006.

Geneva, Switzerland, World Health Organisation [WHO], Department of HIV / AIDS, 2004. 61 p. WHO/HIV/2004.14

Gerőcs L. A Fibonacci-sorozat általánosítása. Scolar K. Budapest. 1998.

Getis A, Ord JK. The analysis of spatial association by use of distance statistics. Geographical Analysis. 1992(24):189-206.

Ghana. Ministry of Health. Health Research Unit. Conception and misconceptions: community views on family planning. Accra, Ghana, Ministry of Health, Health Research Unit, 1992 Aug. vi, 31 p.

Gilbert, E. S. On discriminating using qualitative variables. JASA, 1968(63):1399-1412.

Gilks WR, Richardson S, Spiegelhalter DJ. Markov chain Monte Carlo in practice. Chapman & Hall/CRC. 1998.

Gill J. Generalized linear models. A unified approach. Series: Quantitative applications in the social sciences. A SAGE University Paper 134. 2001.

Glynn A, Wakefield J, Hadcock MS, Richardson TS. Alleviating linear ecological bias and optimal design with subsample data. Manuscript. 2006.

Goer H. Humanizing birth: a global grassroots movement. Birth. 2004 Dec;31(4):308-314.

Goldani AM. What will happen to Brazilian fertility? In: Expert Group Meeting on Completing the Fertility Transition, New York, 11-14 March 2002, [compiled by] United Nations. Department of Economic and

Social Affairs. Population Division. New York, New York, United Nations, Department of Economic and Social Affairs, Population Division, 2004. :358-375.

Goldstein M, Dillon WR. Discrete discriminant analysis. John Wiley & Sons, New York. 1978.

Good P. Permutation tests. A practical guide to resampling methods for testing hypotheses. Springer. 1995.Edgington ES. Randomization tests. 3rd ed. Marcel Dekker, Inc. 1995.

Goodman LA. The multivariate analysis of qualitative data: interaction among multiple classifications. J Amer Statist Assoc. 1970(65):226-256.

Gray NJ, Klein JD, Noyce PR, Sesselberg TS, Cantrill JA. Health information-seeking behavior in adolescence: the place of the internet. Social Science and Medicine. 2005;60:1467-1478.

Griffin G. Reputation management. Capstone Publishing. 2002.

Griffiths M. Communication strategies to optimize commitments and investments in iron programming. Journal of Nutrition. 2002;132:834S-838S.

Gubhaju B; Moriki-Durand Y. Fertility transition in Asia: past experiences and future directions. Asia-Pacific Population Journal. 2003 Sep;18(3):41-68.

Guidelines. Útmutató – klinikai irányelvek összefoglalója. Medition K. 2002.

Guo SF, Wu JL, Qu CY, Yan RY. Physical and sexual abuse of women before, during, and after pregnancy. International Journal of Gynecology and Obstetrics. 2004 Mar;84(3):281-286.

Gupta N, Diallo K, Zum P, Dal Poz MR. Assessing human resources for health: what can be learned from labour force surveys? Human Resources for Health. 2003 Jul 22;1:[24] p.

Gulácsi L. Klinikai kiválóság. Technológiaelemzés az egészségügyben. Springer. 1999.

Haaga J. UN projects slower population growth. Washington, D.C., Population Reference Bureau [PRB], 2003 Mar. [2] p.

Haberman, S. J. Algorithm AS 51. Log-linear fit for contingency tables. Applied Statistics 1972(21):218-224.

Haider SI. ISO 9001:2000. Document development compilance manual. A complete guide and CD-ROM. St. Lucie Press. CRC. 2001.

Hand DJ, Taylor CC. Multivariate analysis of variance and repeated measures. A practical approach for behavioral scientists. Chapman & Pesarin F. Multivariate permutation tests. With application in biostatistics. Wiley. 2001.

Haneuse S, Wakefield J. Ecological inference incorporating spatial dependence. In Ecological Inference: New Methodological Strategies (eds. King G, Rosen O, Tanner M. Cambridge: Cambridge University Press. 2004

Hanushek EA, Jackson JE. Statistical methods for social scientists. Academic Press. New York, San Francisco, London. 1977.

Harrison G. Population and environment--our nature and our fate: an evolutionary perspective. In: Population and the environment: the Linacre Lectures 1993-4, edited by Bryan Cartledge. Oxford, England, Oxford University Press, 1995. :32-47.

Hassad R, Molnár L. Modeling in AIDS/HIV Bio-Behavioral Research – A Multimethod Approach. 2000:281-286. Family Studies Unit, Center for Community Health, University of California, Los Angeles (UCLA), New York, NY, USA, Semmelweis Medical University, Department of Behavioral Sciences, Budapest, Hungary. XIII International AIDS Conference. Durban, South Africa, 9-14 July 2000. Social Science, Rights, Politics, Commitment and Action. Monduzzi Editore, International Proceedings Division

Havranek, Sidak, Novak (eds) COMPSTAT 84, Proceedings in Computational Statistics, Physica Verlag, Wien, 1984:389-394.

Healy MJR. Matrices for statistics. 2nd ed. Clarendon Press, Oxford. 2000.

Heaton TB, Forste R, Hoffmann JP, Flake D. Cross-national variation in family influences on child health. [Variación trans nacional en influencias familiares sobre la salud infantil.] Social Science and Medicine. 2005;60:97-108.

Héjjas, I, CAPRA F. A Modern Fizika a Keleti Bölcselet Tükrében (The TAO of Physics). Buddhista Misszió. 1990. Budapest.

Heinemann K, Saad F, Wiesemes M, White S, Heinemann L. Attitudes toward male fertility control: results of a multinational survey on four continents. Human Reproduction. 2005;20(2):549-556.

Hekáné dr. SZI. Statisztikai alapismeretek. Példatár. KSH. Budapest. 1997.

Helembai K (ed.) Tanulmányok az ápolástudomány köréből. I. A SZOTE Főiskolai Kar Ápolási Tanszék Kiadványa. Szeged. 1997.

Hennekens CH, Buring JE. Mayrent SL. 1987. 1987.

Henry GT. Graphing data. Techniques for display and analysis. Applied Social Research Methods Series. Volume 36. Sage. 1995.

Henry GT. Practical sampling. Applied Social Research Methods Series Volume 21. Sage. 1990.

Hills, M.[1967]. Discrimination and allocation with discrete data. Appl Statist, 16, 237-250.

Hoaglin DC, Mosteller F, Tukey JW. Fundamentals of exploratory analysis of variance. Wiley. 1991.

Hodur J. Water for the future. Focus. 2003 Autumn;18(1):23. http://www.ausaid.gov.auhttp://www.ausaid.gov.au

Holford, T. R. The analysis of rates and of survivorship using log-linear models. Biometrics 1980(36):299-305.

Horányi Ö, Szépe Gy. A jel tudománya. (szerk. Horányi Ö. - Szépe Gy.) Budapest, Gondolat. 1975.

Horányi Ö. A jel tudománya. (A tanulmányokat válogatta és szerkesztette Szépe Györggyel együtt) Budapest, Gondolat. 1975.

Horányi Ö. A kommunikációról. Társadalmi kommunikáció. (szerk. Béres I. - Horányi Ö.) Budapest, Osiris. 1999:22-34.

Horányi Ö. A nyelvről való gondolkodás egyik állomása: Charles Sanders Peirce. Általános Nyelvészeti Tanulmányok XIII. Budapest, Akadémiai, 1981:65-90.

Horányi Ö. A participációról. Színes eszmék nem alszanak... (szerk. Andor J. - Szűcs T. - Terts I.) Pécs, Lingua Franca Csoport, 2001:540-557.

Horányi Ö. A vallások és az európai integráció. (szerk. Horányi Ö.) Budapest, Balassi Könyvkiadó - Magyar Pax Romana Fórum. 1999.

Horányi Ö. Alkalmazott médiakritika. Médiakritika. (szerk. Terestyéni T.) Budapest, Osiris - MTA-ELTE Kommunikációelméleti Kutatócsoport. 1997.

Horányi Ö. Beszélgetés a tudományos intuícióról. (szerk. Horányi Ö.) Természet Világa, 1972(1):33-36, 1972(3):125-128.

Horányi Ö. Bevezetés. Kereszténység és közélet. (szerk. Horányi Ö.) Budapest - Pécs, Vigília Kiadó - Pannónia Könyvek. 1991.

Horányi Ö. Interdiszciplináris kommunikáció. (szerk. Horányi Ö.) Természet Világa, 1974(10):464-498.

Horányi Ö. Kommunikáció 1-2. (szerk. Horányi Ö.) Budapest, Közgazdasági és Jogi Könyvkiadó. 1977-78.

Horányi Ö. Replika Niedermüller Péter "Paradigmák és esélyek avagy a kulturális antropológia lehetőségei Kelet-Európában" című írására. Replika 1994:15-16.

Horn HS. Measurement of overlap in comparative ecological studies. American Naturalist. 1966(100):419-424.

Hornik R. Development communication today: optimism and some concerns. DEVELOPMENT COMMUNICATION REPORT. 1992;(79):1-4.

Hout M. Mobility tables. Series: Quantitative applications in the social sciences. A SAGE University Paper 31. 1983.

Hox JJ. Applied multilevel analysis. TT-Publikaties. Amsterdam. 1994.

Hubert LJ. Combinatorial data analysis: association and partial association. Psychometrika. 1985 (4):449-467.

Hunyadi L, Mundruczó G, Vita L. Statisztikai képletgyűjtemény és táblázatok. 2. Kiadás. Aula K. 1996.

Hurgin JI. Mindennapi döntéseink és a matematika. Műszaki K. Budapest. 1971.

Hyder AA, Nadeem S. Health ethics in Pakistan: a literature review of its present state. Journal of Health, Population and Nutrition. 2001 Mar;19(1):6-11.

Hynes MJ. An investigation of the relationship between sex role orientation, level of assertiveness, affective orientation to sexuality and a model of contraceptive behavior. Ann Arbor, Michigan, University Microfilms International, 1982. 231 p. No. 8302712

Ihaka R, Gentleman R. R: A Language for Data Analysis and Graphics. Journal of Computational and Graphical Statistics. 1996(3):299-314.

Ingelfinger JA et al. Biostatistics in clinical medicine. New York. 1987.

International Children's Centre. Programme of Development of Information on Early Childhood. Prevention and management of high risk pregnancies: a document for planners, administrators. Paris, France, International Children's Centre, Programme of Development of Information on Early Childhood, 1983. 8 p.

Investing in health. World Development Report 1993. World Development Indicators. World Bank. Oxford University Press. 1993.

Irvine CA. Quantitative Micro Software LLC. EVIEWS 4.0 User's Guide}. Quantitative Micro Software LLC. 2000.

Jackson C. Improving ecological inference using individual-level data. Statistics in Medicine. 2005.

Jackson C. Ecological inference with R: the ecoreg package. Version 0.1.1. 2006a.

Jackson C, Best N, Richardson S. Hierarchical related regression for combining aggregate and survey data in studies of socio-economic disease risk factors. To be published. 2006b.

Jackson JE. A user's guide to principal components. Wiley. 1991.

Jacquez GM. A k nearest neighbour test for space-time interaction. Statistics in Medicine. 1996(15):1935-1949.

Jacquez GM. Cuzick and Edwards' test when exact locations are unknown. American Journal of Epidemiology. 1994(140):58-64.

James, M. Classification algorithms. Collins, London. 1985.

Jason H. Evaluation of audiovisual methods of medical teaching. CMAJ: Canadian Medical Association Journal. 1968;98(24):1146-50.

Jefferson T, Demicheli V, Mugford M. Elementary economic evaluation in health care. BMJ Books. 2000.

Jennison C, Turnbull BW. Group sequential methods with applications to clinical trials. Chapman & Hall/CRC. 2000.

JHPIEGO. Shaping policy for maternal and newborn health: a compendium of case studies. Baltimore, Maryland, JHPIEGO, 2003 Oct. [119] p.

Johns Hopkins School of Public Health. Population Information Program [PIP]. Population Communication Services [PCS] Basic processes and principles for population/family planning communication. Baltimore, Maryland, Johns Hopkins University, Population Information Program, Population Communication Services, [1983]. [15] p.

Jongman, RHG, Ter Braak CJF, Van Tongeren OFT. Data analysis and landscape ecology. Cambridge University Press. 1995.

Jordán K. Matematikai statisztika. Athenaeum K. Budapest. 1927.

Józan P. Some features of mortality in postwar Hungary: the third epidemiologic transition. Cahiers de sociologie et de demographie medicales. 1989. Jan-Mar, 29(1), 21-42.

Juutinen S. Mainstreaming in employment projects. Tiny trickles from a flow. Description of an operating model. Stakes. STAKES National Research and Development Centre for Welfare and Health. Finland. 2000.

Juvancz I, Paksy A. Orvosi biometria. Medicina K. Budapest. 1982.

Kabos, S. Térbeli statisztika. TÁRKI Preprint. 1992.

Kabos S, Csillag F. The analysis of spatial association on regular lattice by joint-count statistics without the assumption of first-order homogeneity. Computers and Geosciences. 2002(28):901-910.

Kachigan SK. Multivariate statistical analysis. A conceptual introduction. 2nd ed. Radius Press. New York. 1991.

Kafadar K. Simultaneous smooting and adjusting mortality rates in U.S. counties: melanoma in white females and white males. Statistics in medicine. 1999(18):3167-3188

Kamarás F. Fertility trends in Hungary and influencing factors. [Les tendances de la fecondite en Hongrie et les facteurs qui les influencent.] CAHIERS QUEBECOIS DE DEMOGRAPHIE. 2000 Autumn;29(2):255-85.

Kametas NA, McAuliffe F, Krampl E, Chambers J, Nicolaides KH. Maternal cardiac function during pregnancy at high altitude. [Función cardíaca materna durante el embarazo a gran altitud.] BJOG. an International Journal of Obstetrics and Gynaecology. 2004 Oct;111:1051-1058.

Kane VE, Ward RC, Davis GJ Assessment of linear dependencies in multivariate data. SIAM J Sci Stat Comput. 1985(6,4):1022-1032.

Kaner C, Bach J, Pettichord B. Lessons learned in software testing. A context-driven approach. Wiley. 2002.

Kanji GK, Asher M. 100 methods for Total Quality Management. Sage. 1996.

Kanji GK. Statistical tests. Sage. 1995.

Karlin S, Taylor H. Sztochasztikus folyamatok. Gopndolat5 K. Budapest. 1985.

Kaufmann A. A döntés tudománya. Bevezetés a praxeológiába. KJK. Budapest. 1982.

Kelkar G. Women's roundtable discussion on the economic, social and political impacts of the Southeast Asian financial crisis. GENDER, TECHNOLOGY AND DEVELOPMENT. 1998 Sep-Dec;2(3):463-70.

Kemény S., Deák A. Kísérletek trvezése és értékelése. Műszaki K. Budapest. 2002.

Kemny S, Papp L, Deák A. Statisztikai minőség- (megfelelőség-) szabályozás. Műszaki K. – Magyar Minőség Társaság. Budapest. 2001.

Kemp N, Richardson E. The nursing process & quality care. Arnold. 1994.

Kerezsi K. A védtelen gyermek (Erőszak és elhanyagolás a családban) KJK. Budapest. 1995.

Kerstiëns B, Akii A, Mbona N, Zziwwa A, Edson WN. Improving the management of obstetric emergencies in Uganda through case management maps. Bethesda, Maryland, University Research Company, Quality Assurance Project, 2004 Feb. [35] p. Operations Research Result; USAID Contract No. HRN-C-00-96-90013

Kertész Á. A térinformatika és alkalmazásai. Holnap K. Budapest. 1997.

Kind P. Personal communication. 1999.

King G. A Solution to the Ecological Inference Problem. Reconstructing individual behavior from aggregate data. Princeton University Press. Princeton. 1997.

King G. The future of ecological inference. J Am Statist Ass. 1999(94):352-354.

King, G. EzI v2.20 computer software. 1999.

King PE. Problems of spatial analysis in geographical epidemiology. Social Science Medicine. 1979(13D (4)):249-252)

Kissling F. How to talk about abortion: a guide to successful communications. Working draft. [Unpublished] 1997. [4], v, 78, [50] p.

Kissling F. How to talk about abortion. A guide to successful communications. Washington, D.C., Catholics for a Free Choice, 2000. 42 p.

Kis-Varga A, Rudas T, Czeizel A. (1989) A new approach to the germinal mutation surveillance: a pair-wise evaluation of component elements in unidentified multiple congenital abnormalities. Mutation Research, 238, 87-97.

Klauber MR. Space-time clustering tests for more than two samples. Biometrics. 1975(31):719-726.

Klauber MR. Two sample randomization test for space-time clustering. Biometrics. 1971(27):129-142.

Kleinbaum DG. Logistic regression. A self-learning text. Springer. 1994.

Kleinbaum DG. Survival analysis regression. A self-learning text. Springer. 1996.

Kline P. An easy guide to factor analysis. Routledge. 1997.

Klinger A (ed). Demográfia. CSO. Budapest. 1996.

Klinger A. Differenciális demográfiai közelítések felhasználhatósága: közelítések, módszerek, példák. Demográfia. 2004(47):121-166.

Klinger A. Társadalomstatisztikai Alapismeretek. KSH. Budapest. 1998.

Klufio CA, Kwawukume EZ, Danso KA, Sciarra JJ, Johnson. Ghana postgraduate obstetrics/gynecology collaborative residency training program: The success story and model for Africa. American Journal of Obstetrics and Gynecology. 2003 Sep;189(3):692-696.

Knapp TR. Learning statistics through playing cards. Sage. 1996.

Knebel E. The use and effect of distance education in healthcare: What do we know? Bethesda, Maryland, Center for Human Services, Quality Assurance Project, 2001. 24 p. Operations Research Issue Paper Vol. 2, No. ; USAID Contract No. HRN-C-00-96-90013

Knorr-Held L, Best NG. A shared component model for detecting joint and selective clustering of two diseases. J. Roy. Statist. Soc. A 2001(164):73-85.

Knox EG, Gilman EA. Spatial clustering of childhood cancers in Great Britain. J Epidemiol Community Health. 1996(50(3)):313-9.

Knox EG, Lancashire R. Detection of minimal epidemics. Statistics in Medicine. 1982(1):183-189.

Knox G. Detection of space-time interactions. Applied Statistics. 1964(13):25-30.

Kóbor Gy, Rudas T. (1987) Diszkriminancia analízis kategoriális változókkal, programleírás. TÁRKI Információk, 5, 33-44.Budapest.

Koczor Z. (ed) Bevezetés a minőségügybe. A minőségügy gyakorlati kérdései. Műszaki K. – Magyar Minőség Társaság. 2000.

Kok G. Health education theories and research for AIDS prevention. HYGIE. 1991;10(2):32-9.

Kolosi T, Rudas T. (1988) Empirikus problémamegoldás a szociológiában. OMIKK-TÁRKI, Budapest.

Kommunikáció 1-2. (válogatott tanulmányok 1977-1978). Budapest, Közgazdasági és Jogi Könyvkiadó; második módosított kiadása: Budapest, GeneralPress, 2003.

Kopp M, Skrabski Á. Alkalmazott magatartástudomány. Hét Szabad Művészet Könyvtára. Corvinus K. Budapest. 1995.

Kopp M, Skrabski Á. Magyar lelkiállapot. Hét Szabad Művészet Könyvtára. Végeken K. Budapest. 1995.

Kopp M, Skrabski Á, Szedmák S. Medical significance of confidence, social support, social cohesion and cooperation. J. of Regional Mental Health and Psychosomatics. 1998(4):11.

Korán I. Világmodellek. A Római Klub jelentéseitől az ENSZ kezdeményezéséig. KJK. Budapest. 1980.

Korom M, Molnár DL, Simon P. Discrete Discriminant Analysis. Life Style and Mortality. Paper delivered at the MEDICOMP Conference. Szeged, Hungary. 1990:198-199.

Kotler P, Armstrong G, Saunders J, Wong V. Principles of marketing. The European edition. Prentice Hall. 1996.

Kovách I, Róbert P, Rudas T. (1987) A mobilitás igazi dimenziói. Szociológia 1987/1, 79-100.

Kovách I, Róbert P, Rudas T. (1987) Towards the dimensions of mobility. in: Andorka, Bertalan (eds.) Economy and Society in Hungary, Hungarian Sociological Studies, 3, 153-183. Hungarian Sociological Association, Budapest.

Kovach W. Multivariate Statistical Package. Version 3.1 User's Manual. Kovach Computing Services. Pentraeth, Wales. UK. 1999.

Kozmann Gy. Decision Support, Knowledge Representation and Management (Synopsis), Yearbook of Medical Informatics 2004, pp. 503-505, Schattauer, München, 2004.

Kraemer HC, Thiemann S. How many subjects? Statistical power analysis in research. Sage. 1987.

Krippendorff K. Information theory. Structural models for qualitative data. Series: Quantitative applications in the social sciences. A SAGE University Paper 62. 1986.

Kröpfl B, Peschek W, Schneider E, Schönlieb A. Alkalmazott statisztika. Műszaki K. Budapest. 2000.

Kruskal JB, Wish M. Multidimensional scaling. Series: Quantitative applications in the social sciences. A SAGE University Paper 11. 1978.

Kulldorff M, Nagarwalla N. Spatial disease clusters: detection and inference. Statistics in Medicine. 1995(14):799-810.

Kunene B, Beksinska M, Zondi S, Mthembu N, Mullick S. Involving men in maternity care, South Africa. Durban, South Africa, University of the Witwatersrand, Department of Obstetrics and Gynecology, Reproductive Health Research Unit, 2004 Oct. [57] p. USAID Cooperative Agreement No. HRN-A-00-98-00012-00

Kunzmann P, Burkhard F, Wiedmann F. Atlasz Filozófia. Athenaeum K. Budapest. 1999.

Lábos E. Természetes és mesterséges értelem. Magvető K. Budapest. 1979.

Lanzieri TM, Parise MS, Siqueira MM, Fortaleza BM, Segatto TC. Incidence, clinical features and estimated costs of congenital rubella syndrome after a large rubella outbreak in Recife, Brazil, 1999-2000. [Incidencia, características clínicas y costos estimativos del síndrome de rubéola congénita luego de un gran brote de rubéola en Recife, Brasil, durante 1999-2000.] Pediatric Infectious Disease Journal. 2004 Dec;23(12):1116-1122.

Lane J. Public sector reform. Rationale, trends and problems. Sage. 1997.

Laver S. Relocating practice in AIDS education: from didactics to dialogue. HYGIE. 1993 Jun;12(2):26-30.

Lawson A, Biggeri A, Böhning D, Lesaffre E, Viel J-F, Bertollini R. Disease Mapping and Risk Assessment for Public Health. Wiley. 2002:111-117.

Le ND, Petkau AJ, Rosychuk R. Surveillance of clustering near point sources. Statistics in Medicine. 1996(15):727-740.

Leahy E. Africa remains fastest growing continent. Popline. 2003 Jul-Aug;25:1-2.

Lee ET. Statistical methods for survival data analysis. 2nd ed. Wiley. 1992.

Lee PM. Bayesian statistics: and introduction. Edward Arnold. London, Melbourne, Auckland.. 1994.

Lee, S. K. (1977). On the asymptotic variances of u terms in loglinear models of multidimensional contingency tables. J Amer Statist Assoc 1977(72, 358):412-419.

Leimer, HG, Rudas T. (1988) Contingency tables with prescribed conditional odds ratios or prescribed log-linear parameters. Forschungsberichte zur Stochastik und verwandte Gebiete, Johannes Gutenberg Universitat, Mainz, 88-1.

Leimer, HG, Rudas T. (1989) Conversion between GLIM- and BMDP-type log-linear parameters. GLIM Newsletter 19, 47.

Lemeshow S. Hosmer DW Jr, Klar J, Lwanga SK. Adequacy of sample size in health studies. WHO. Wiley. 1995.

Lendvay J, Rudas T. (1987) Bevezetés a panel adatok elemzéséhez. in: Váradi (szerk.) A panel adatok elemzése, 5-31. Tömegkommunikációs Kutatóközpont, Budapest.

Lestringant GG, Bener A, Frossard P, Townsend A. Association of Acanthosis nigricans with risk of diabetes mellitus and hormonal disturbances in females. INTERNATIONAL JOURNAL OF GYNECOLOGY AND OBSTETRICS. 2000 Dec;71(3):267-9.

Levine DH, Crisp BF. Venezuela: the character, crisis, and possible future of democracy. [Venezuela: disposición, crisis y posible futuro de la democracia.] World Affairs. 1999 Winter;161(3):123-65.

Levitas R, Guy W. Interpreting official statistics. Routledge. 1996.

Lewis PAW, Orav EJ, Uribe L. Enhanced simulation and statistics package. Wadsworth & Brooks/Cole. 1989.

Lewis DA, McDonald A, Thompson G, Bingham JS. The 374 clinic: an outreach sexual health clinic for young men. Sexually Transmitted Infections. 2004;80:480-483.

Lewis PAW, Orav EJ. Simulation methodology for statisticians, operations analysts, and engineers. Volume 1. Wadsworth & Brooks/Cole. 1989.

Lewis WE. Software testing and continuous quality improvement. Auerbach. 2000.

Lindsay JM. Techniques in Human Geography. Routledge. 1997.

Lindsey JK. Introductory statistics. A modeling approach. Clarendon Press. Oxford. 1996.

Liu J, Larsen U, Wyshak G. Prevalence of primary infertility in China: in-depth analysis of infertility differentials in three minority province/autonomous regions. Journal of Biosocial Science. 2005;37:55-74.

Lom AD. Demography and development. And if Malthus was right. Demographie et developpement. POP SAHEL. 1999 Dec;(28):35-7.

Longley JW. An appraisal of least squares programs for the electronic computer from the point of view of the user. JASA 1967(62):819-829.

Loranta V, Thomas I, Deliége D, Tonglet R. Deprivation and mortality: the implications of spatial autocorrelation for health resources allocation. Social Science & Medicine. 2001(53):1711-1719.

Louhenapessy M. 7th European Migrants Meeting: Access to HIV Care and Support for Migrants and Ethnic Minorities in Europe, Brussels, 19-22 September 2002. Report. Woerden, Netherlands, Netherlands Institute for Health Promotion and Disease Prevention [NIGZ], European Project AIDS and Mobility, 2003 Dec. 44 p.

Lowry C. Improving sexual and reproductive health services for especially vulnerable young people: a rapid assessment and response tool (RAR). Draft for field testing. [Unpublished] 1998 Sep. [95] p.

Ludbrook J. Repeated measurements and multiple comparison in cardiovascular research. Cardiovascular Research 1994(28):303-311.

Lukács O. Matematikai statisztika példatár. Műszaki K. Budapest. 1987.

MacKay DJC. Introduction to {M}onte {C}arlo Methods}. Learning in Graphical Models. M. I. Jordan. Kluwer Academic Press. NATO Science Series. 1998:175-204.

Mackin L. Promises to keep. Global AIDSLink. 2002 Oct-Nov;(76):10.

Magyar G. A radical voice in the science of science. TypoTEX. 1998.

Mahadevan K, Krishnan P. (ed.) Methodology for population studies and development. Sage Publication. 1993.

Maisel R. Persell CH. Hwo samplings work. Pine Forge Press. . Sge. 1996.

Makoha FW, Felimban HM, Fathuddien MA, Roomi F, Ghabra T. Multiple cesarean section morbidity. International Journal of Gynecology and Obstetrics. 2004;87:227-232.

Malcolm A, Aggleton P. Rapid assessment and response. Adaptation guide for work with especially vulnerable young people. Geneva, Switzerland, World Health Organisation [WHO], Department of HIV / AIDS, 2004 Sep. 67 p. WHO/HIV/2004.15

Management Sciences for Health. Philippines Program Management Technical Assistance Team Services. No-scalpel vasectomy: expanding options for male involvement in family planning. A guide for local government units. [Manila], Philippines, MSH, PMTAT, 2003a.:22.

Management Sciences for Health. Philippines Program Management Technical Assistance Team Services. Standard days method: a natural family planning option for couples. A guide for local government units. [Manila], Philippines, MSH, PMTAT, 2003b:12.

Manly BFJ. Multivariate statistical methods. A primer. 2nd ed. Chapman & Hall. 1994.

Manly BFJ. Randomization and Monte Carlo methods in biology. Chapman & Hall. 1991.

Manly BFJ. Randomization and regression methods for testing for associations with geographical, environmental and biological distances between populations. Researches on Population Ecology. 1986(28):201-218.

Manly BFJ. Randomization, bootstrap and Monte Carlo methodology in biology. 2nd ed. Chapman & Hall. 1997.

Manly BFJ. RT A program for Randomization Testing. Western EcoSystems Technology, Inc. Cheyenne, WY. 1996.

Manly BFJ. Statistics for Environmental Science and Management. Chapman and Hall/CRC. 2001. Boca Raton.

Manni F, Guérard E, Heyer E. Geographic patterns of (genetic, morphologic, lingusitic) variation: how barriers can be detected by "Monmonier's algorithm". Human Biology. 2004(76):173-190.

Manski CF. Identification Problems in the Social Sciences. Cambridge University Press. 1995. Cambridge.

Mantel N, Kryscio RJ, Myers MH. ables and formulas for extended use of the Ederer-Myers-Mantel disease clustering procedure. American Journal of Epidemiology. 1976(104):576-584.

Mantel N. The detection of disease clustering and a generalized regression approach. Cancer Research. 1967(27):209-220.

Many BFJ. Statistics for environmental science and management.. Chapman & Hall/CRC. 2001.

Maritz JS. Distribution-free statistical methods. 2nd ed. Chapman & Hall. 1995.

Masters T. Advanced algorithms for neural networks. A C++ sourcebook. Wiley. 1995

Maxwell SE, Delaney HD. Designing experiments and analysing data. A model comparison perspective. Brooks/Cole. Wadsworth, Inc. 1990.

May C. Project HOPE / Johnson & Johnson klinikai kiválósági központok az ápolási gyakorlatban. Nővér. 1994(7;5):11-16.

Mayhew SH. The impact of decentralisation on sexual and reproductive health services in Ghana. Reproductive Health Matters. 2003 May;11(21):74-87.

McDowell I, Newell C. Measuring heatlh. A guide to rating scales and questionnaires. 2nd ed. Oxford University Press. 1996.

McIntyre P. Facts for life: lessons from experience. New York, New York, UNICEF, 1996. 156 p.

McPherson MP. Population section strategy] [memorandum. [Unpublished] 1983 Mar 22. 9 p.

McQuarrie EF. The market research toolbox. A concise guide for beginners. Sage. 1996.

McWhinne W, Webber JB, Smith DM, Novokowsky BJ. Creating paths of change. Managing issues and resolving problems in organisations. 2nd ed. Sage. 1997.

Mead R, Curnow RN, Hasted AM. Statistical methods in agriculture and experimental biology. 2nd ed. Chapman & Hall. 1994.

Mehta, C. and N. Patel. StatXact. Computer program. 1991.

Mehta C, Patel N. StatXact 3.1. Cytel Co. 1998.

Merton RK. Társadalomelmélet és társadalmi struktúra. Gondolat. Budapest. 1980.

Mészáros J. A közvéleménykutatások néhány problémájáról. Budapest MTA Szociológiai Intézet 1991:28 o.

Mészáros J. A társadalmi döntéshozatal módszeréről, Budapest Szociológiai Kutató Intézet 1985:88 o.

Mészáros J. A társadalombiztosítási nyugdíjrendszerek, mint közjószágok, Közgazdasági Szemle 2005(3):275 - 288. o.

Mészáros J. A társadalombiztosítási nyugdíjrendszerek, mint közjószágok. Budapest, in. Társadalmi térben, Konferencia kiadvány, BME Szoc. Komm. Tsz . 2005:291-305. o.

Mészáros J. Az elosztási igazságosság néhány kérdése, Budapest, Szociológiai Szemle 1992/3. 95-98

Mészáros J. Bevezetés a társadalmi változások elméletébe, Budapest, MTA Szociológiai Intézet 1990:124 o.

Mészáros J. Egyéni hasznok és közjószágok (avagy meddig ér a láthatatlan kéz) Valóság 2006/2

Mészáros J. Egyéni racionalitás és a közjó (Társadalompolitikai tanulmányok)

Mészáros J. Estimation of distribution of parliament seats based on poll data, Budapest, Periodica Politechnia, 1998:105-128 o.

Mészáros J. Game theoretic explanation for absence of occurrence of public goods, Review of Sociology 2005(11, 2):1-15

Mészáros J. How do the social systems function? Connections between the subsystems, social solidarity and social safety, Budapest, Periodica Politechnica 1994:42-58. o.

Mészáros J. Játékelmélet, Budapest, Gondolat. 2004:226 o. (2. javított, átdolgozott kiadás,)

Mészáros J. Kereszténység és közélet, Budapest. Osiris, 1999:240 o.

Mészáros J. Racionális Döntések Elmélete és a Társadalomtudományok, Budapest, Társadalomkutatás 2004(4):427–451. o.

Mészáros J. Roles and Possibilities: The New Central-European Archives, 1999, .Univ of Essex, Colchester, in Information Dissemination and Access in Russia and Eastern Europe, 1999:122-129. o.

Mészáros J. Simpson Paradoxon (Intés a kereszttáblák aggregálásától), Budapest MTA Szociológiai Intézet 1990:32. o.

Mészáros J. Társadalombiztosítás és termékenység, Demográfia 2005(4)

Mészáros J. Területi statisztikai módszerek a választási adatok elemzésénél. (társszerző: Solymosi Norbert), Budapest Térinformatika 2005(2)

Miller RG Jr. Beyond ANOVA. Chapman & Hall. 1997.

Mohr LB. Impact analysis for program evaluation. Sage Publication, Inc. 1995.

Molnár DL, Benkő E. Kummerfett. Discrete discriminant analysis and loglinear models. Paper delivered at the Conference on Psychological dimensions of cardiovascular diseases. (In Hungarian). Budapest. 1990.

Molnár DL, Csizmás F. Spatial statistical analysis of nominal and ordinal health care data with geographic information system. 6th Conference of Hungarian Biometric and Biomathematic Conference. Budapest. 26-27 August, 2002.

Molnár DL, Kocsis S. Loglinear and association models of middle aged male mortality. 1st Conference of Public Health Scientific Committee, Budapest. 1992. A/5.

Molnár DL, Kocsis S. Mortality Model of Middle-Age Males in Budapest. (In Hungarian. English Summary) Statisztikai Szemle (Statistical Monthly). Budapest, 1992., December, 1048-1052; In Hungarian)

Molnár DL, Kovács I. Regional inequalities and project development. Contributing paper delivered at an international conference on social and regional inequalities. Barcelona. 1996. Sept.

Molnár DL, Kovács I. The old and the new. Changes in social care in Central and Eastern Europe. Ed. By B. Munday and G. Lane. EISS, University of Kent. 1996

Molnár DL, László K. Health status of homeless people in Budapest. (In Hungarian). Periferia Seria 6. Budapest, 1996. 33–61.

Molnár DL, László K. Homelessness and health status. (In Hungarian) Lege Artis Medicinae. (Medical Monthly) 1997 (11):746:752.

Molnar DL, Mészáros J. Improving ecological inference with survey data. Paper submitted to the European Journal of Research Methods for the Behavioral and Social Sciences

Molnár DL, Molnár B. Risk factors of stroke in the suburban region of Budapest. 4th Conference of Public Health Scientific Committee. Hévíz, Hungary. 1995.

Molnár DL, Móritz P. Is myocardial infarction manager's disease? 1st Conference of Public Health Scientific Committee, Budapest. 1992. A/1.

Molnár DL, Reiczigel J, Rudas T, Gárdos É. Monte Carlo and Bootstrap Methods for the Analysis of Multidimensional Contingency Tables Using Loglinear Models. Social Science Informatics Centre. Preprint 1992/4.

Molnár DL, Reiczigel J, Szendrő Z. Linear Dependence Analysis (LDA), its application in assessing risk factors of hypertension. (In Hungarian). Social Science Informatics Center. 1990:39-53.

Molnár DL, Simon P, Juhász B. Application of geographic information systems in the society of the future. Human Services Information Technology Applications (HUSITA5). Social Services in the Information Society: Closing the Gap. International Conference and Exhibition and Online NetConference. Social service provision supported by technology I. 29 August – 1 September, 1999. Parallel session PS4-4: Information for social policy planning, -T2: 31 August, 11.30-13.00.

Molnár DL, Solymosi N, Mészáros J. Területi adatok statisztikai elemzése 2005:37-42.o. In: Mészáros J. Magyarország Politikai Atlasza /társszerkesztő: Szakadát István/ Gondolat K. Budapest 2005)

Molnar DL, Suzuki K, Nagy Z. Comparison of Japanese and Hungarian vascular risk factors in healthy subjects, adjusting rates with loglinear parameters. Paper submitted to the European Journal of Epidemiology

Molnár DL, Szendrő Z. Mathematical statistical analysis of morbidity data. National Institute of Occupational Health. Methodological Publications. 10/1. (In Hungarian). 1989. pp. 1-62.

Molnár DL. Adjusting rates using loglinear models: application in mortality data analysis. TÁRKI preprint. 1994.

Molnár DL. Avoidable death. (In Hungarian) Esti Hírlap (Hungarian daily). 31 May, 1995.

Molnár DL. Basic ideas of software testing. Budapest, Hungary. Manuscript. 2006.

Molnár DL. Causes of high stroke morbidity and mortality in Hungary. (In Hungarian) Esti Hírlap (Hungarian daily). 7 July, 1995.

Molnar DL. Decomposition of aggregate data (the ecological problem). In: Mészáros J, Molnár DL, Reiczigel J, Solymosi N. Introduction to spatial statistics. Book in press

Molnár DL. Development of patient record and related services. John Neumann Medical Informatics Conference. Veszprém, Hungary. 1998.

Molnár DL. Development of portable patient record. (In Hungarian). OMFB, IKTA, Jahn F. Hospital. ÁSZSZ, Sociomed. 1997-2000.

Molnár DL. DiscDisc. Discrete discriminant analysis. In: DISTAN 2.0 (Statistical Software for the analysis of Multidimensional Contingency Tables) Manual, pp. 227-239. Ed. by T. Rudas. Budapest, 1992.

Molnár DL. Exact tests. SPSS User Conference. Budapest. 1995.

Molnár DL. ExpDim. Exploratory reduction of dimensionality. In: DISTAN 2.0 (Statistical Software for the analysis of Multidimensional Contingency Tables), Manual, pp. 240-250. Ed. by Rudas T. Budapest, 1992.

Molnár DL. Health care quality standards. (In Hungarian) Ministry of Health. 2002.

Molnár DL. Health care system browser. Inpatient and outpatient health financing and health care system software, a DHTML, Java, JavaScript program. 2002

Molnár DL. Health status of homeless people. (In Hungarian) Esti Hírlap (Hungarian daily). 24 May, 1995.

Molnár DL. Health status of homeless people. Final report. Grant OKTK 826. 1994.

Molnár DL. Hungarian healthcare: capacities and financing. Identification of crisis small region areas of the Hungarian healthcare system (In Hungarian). Ministry of Health. 2004.

Molnár DL. Kriging and smoothing. In: Mészáros J, Molnár DL, Reiczigel J, Solymosi N. Introduction to spatial statistics. Book in press

Molnár DL. Logistic regression. (In Hungarian). TÁRKI Információk 8. Budapest 1989:67 86.

Molnár DL. LOGLINDI: Log-linear Discriminant Analysis. The American Statistician. November, 1991, Vol. 45. No. 4. p. 339.

Molnár DL. Loglinear Discriminant Analysis. (In Hungarian) Social Science Informatics Centre. Preprint 1990/2.

Molnár DL. Loglinear discriminant analysis. Monte Carlo and bootstrap methods for the analysis of multidimensional contingency tables. Invited paper at the Czechoslovak Academy of Sciences, Institute for Informatics. Prague. 1990.

Molnár DL. Loglinear Discriminant Analysis. The American Statistician. 1991(45,4):339.

Molnár DL. Loglinear models of social mobility, asymptotic and approximate randomization tests. Hungary in the World Conference. Budapest. 1991.

Molnár DL. Multiple regression and regression diagnostics. (In Hungarian). TÁRKI Információk 8. Budapest, 1989:45 66.

Molnár DL. Nurses and midwifes. Research on health modernization. (In Hungarian). Phare HU9303. Social Science Informatics Center. 1996.

Molnár DL. Our life and blood. (In Hungarian) Esti Hírlap (Hungarian daily). 10 May, 1995.

Molnár DL. Quality assurance and quality improvement in healthcare. Institute for Health Promotion. (In Hungarian). Budapest. 2001.

Molnár DL. Quality assurance, quality improvement, statistical process control in health care. Paper read at the Technical and Economic University, Budapest. 2001.

Molnár DL. Regional differences of lung cancer, chronic obstructive lung disease mortality, and air pollution in Hungary. European Population Conference. Paris. 1991.

Molnár DL. Regional frequency of lung cancer and KALB mortality. (In Hungarian. English Summary) Statisztikai Szemle (Statistical Monthly) Budapest, 1994(7):577-583.

Molnár DL. Role of plagues in history. Orvosi Hetilap (Medical monthly) (In Hungarian). 1991(132/38):2105-2107.

Molnár DL. Second chance. Adult education: problems, prospects and solution proposals. Supported by the National Institute for Adult education. (In Hungarian, 150 pp) 2006

Molnár DL. Short term cash benefits in the case of sickness. Monitoring the development of social protection reform in the CEECs. Part 2. Phare Consensus Project. # ZZ-9710-0039, with ADECRI, Paris. 1999

Molnár DL. Social and health inequalities and quality of life measures in population-based Hungarian samples by using the EuroQol 5D instrument. Manuscript. 2001.

Molnár DL. Spatial inequalities in healthcare. Thematic maps and statistical analysis. Final report. Grant OKTK A1646/IIIb. 2001.

Molnár DL. Star Hotel, no heaven. VII. Annual Meeting of the European Society for Population Economics (ESPE). June 3-6, 1993. Budapest

Molnár DL. Statistical Process Control for Quality Improvement in Healthcare. Paper presented at the Technical University for the Clinical Biostatistical Society, Budapest. 18.02.2002.

Molnár DL. Statistics without tears. Permutation and exact test. Computer-intensive statistical methods. Paper delivered at the John Neumann Conference on Medical Informatics. Veszprém, Hungary. 1998.

Molnár DL. Survival analysis with the Kaplan-Meier method. (In Hungarian). Institute National Stroke Centre, National Institute of Psychiatry and Neurology. Budapest, Hungary. 2005.

Molnár DL. Testing Hypotheses. In: Mészáros J, Molnár DL, Reiczigel J, Solymosi N. Introduction to spatial statistics. Book in press

Molnár DL. The European Union and the Hungarian farmer. Ministry of Agriculture. 2004.

Molnár DL. The Hungarian pharmaceutical market, with international aspects. Pharmaceutical Marketing Conference. Institute for International Research. Hotel Hilton, Budapest. 10 February, 2003.

Molnár DL. The physician came but did not win. (In Hungarian). Esti Hírlap (Hungarian daily). 17 May, 1995.

Molnár DL. Time series analysis. In: Mészáros J, Molnár DL, Reiczigel J, Solymosi N. Introduction to spatial statistics. Book in press

Monmonier MS. Maximum-Difference Barriers: An Alternative Numerical Regionalization Method. Geogr. Anal. 1973(3):245-261.

Monroy de Velasco A. Reproductive health: contraceptive methods. [Salud reproductiva: metodos anticonceptivos.] In: Contenidos didacticos para el curso basico de orientacion sexual para personal multidisciplinario, [compiled by] Mexico. Instituto Mexicano del Seguro Social [IMSS], Subdireccion General Medica, Jefatura de Servicios de Planificacion Familiar. Mexico City, Mexico, IMSS, 1983. :[13] p.

Montlake S. Asia looks to Thailand's AIDS success story. Christian Science Monitor. 2003(Nov 20):4.

Moran PAP. Notes on continuous stochastic phenomena. Biometrika. 1950(37):17-23.

Morgan, BJT. Elementary Simulation. Chapman & Hall: London. 1984.

Morgan G. Images of organisation. Sage. 1997.

Móri FT, Székely JG. Többváltozós statisztikai analízis. Műszaki K. Budapest. 1986.

Möhner M. A global rank test for geographical clusters of disease. Biometrical Journal. 1991(33):317-323.

Mtika MM. The AIDS epidemic in Malawi and its threat to household food security. Human Organisation. 2001 Summer;60(2):178-88.

Muir Gray JA. Evidence-based healthcare. How to make health policy and management decisions. Churchill Livingstone. 1997.

Mukhopadhyay A. The kaleidoscope that is South Asia. Health for the Millions. 2004 Jan;30(4-5):37-44.

Mullin T. (ed) The nature of chaos. Oxford University Press. 1995.

Munasinghe RL, Robert DM Localization of disease clusters using regional measures of spatial autocorrelation. Statistics in Medicine. 1996(15):893-905.

Munday B (ed). European social services. EISS. 1993.

Murdoch A. Launching the Ministry of Health website "Medicine for You" and subsequent advocacy for electronic information dissemination throughout the MOH, Moscow, Russia, December 1996. Arlington, Virginia, Partnership for Child Health Care, Basic Support for Institutionalizing Child Survival [BASICS], 1996. 8, [75] p. Repor; USAID Contract No. HRN-C-00-93-00031-00

Murphy E. A quick history of health communication. In: Report from the Meeting on Changing Communication Strategies for Reproductive Health and Rights, December 10-11, 1997, Washington, D.C., [compiled by] Working Group on Reproductive Health and Family Planning. [New York, New York], Population Council, Health and Development Policy Project, [1998]. :3-5.

Murtagh F, Heck A. Multivariate data analysis. D. Reidel. 1987.

Murtha JA. Decision involving uncertainty. A @RISK Tutorial for the petroleum industry. Houston TX. 1995.

Müller B., Reinhardt J, Strickland MT. Neural networks. An introduction. 2nd updated and corrected ed. Springer. 1995.

MYSTAT Version 2.0. SYSTAT, Inc. 1988.

Nash A. Population geography. PROGRESS IN HUMAN GEOGRAPHY. 1994 Mar;18(1):84-91.

Naus JI. A power comparison of two tests of non-random clustering. Technometrics. 1966(8):493-517.

Naus JI. Some probabilities, expectations, and variance for the size of the smallest intervals and largest clusters Journal of the American Statistical Association. 1966(61):1191-9.

Naus JI. The distribution of the size of the maximum cluster of points on a line. Journal of the American Statistical Association. 1965(60):532-8.

Nearly two-thirds of world's people face water stress. POPLINE. 2003 Mar-Apr;25:3-4.

Ndamobissi R. Fertility preferences. [Preferences en matiere de fecondite.] In: Enquete Demographique et de Sante, Republique Centrafricaine, 1994-95, [edited by] Robert Ndamobissi, Gora Mboup, Edwige Opportune Nguelebe. Bangui, Central African Republic, Ministere de l'Economie, du Plan et de la Cooperation Internationale, Division des Statistiques et des Etudes Economiques, Direction des Statistiques Demographiques et Sociales, 1995 Dec. :101-10.

Némedi D. The intersts of knowledge. Jürgen Habermas: Knowledge and human intersts. BUKSZ. 2006. Tavasz. pp. 19-26.

Nemes Nagy J. Gazdasági-társadalmi súlypontok és mozgások az ezredvégi Magyarországon. Területi Statisztika. 2003(6;43;1):3-14.

Németh R, Rudas T. (2002) Mintavétel a Leslie Kish-kulcs alkalmazásával. Statisztikai Szemle, 80, 309-327.

New Economics Foundation. http://www.neweconomics.org/gen/

Newton HJ. Timeslab: A time series analysis laboratory. Wadsworth & Brooks/Cole. 1988.

Newton HJ. Timeslab: A time series analysis laboratory. Wadsworth and Brooks/Coole Advaced Books and Software. 1988. Belmont, California.

Noreen, E. Computer Intensive Methods for Testing Hypotheses. N.Y. John Wiley & Sons. 1989.

Norusis MJ. SPSS-X advanced statistics guide. 2nd ed. SPSS Inc. 1988.

Obádovics JG. Valószínűségszámítás és matematikai statisztika. Scolar K. Budapest. 2001.

O'Brien L. Introducing quantitative geography. Measurements, methods and generalized linear models. Routledge. 1992.

O'Brien SJ, Christie P. Do CuSums have a role in routine communicable disease surveillance? Public Health. 1997(111):255-258.

Oden N, Jacquez G, Grimson R. Realistic power simulations compare point- and area-based disease cluster tests. Statistics in Medicine. 1996(15):783-806.

Oden N. Adjusting Moran's I for Population Density. Statistics in Medicine. 1995(14):17-26.

O'Hagan A. Kendall's advanced theory of statistics. Volume 2B. Bayesian inference. 6th ed. Arnold. 1994.

Ohno Y, Aoki K, Aoki N. A. test of significance for geographic clusters of disease. International Journal of Epidemiology, 1979(8,3):273-281

Ohno Y, Aoki K, Aoki N. A test of significance for geographic clusters of disease. International Journal of Epidemiology. 1979(8):273-281.

OhnoY, Aoki K. Cancer deaths by city and county in Japan: a test of significance for geographic clustering of disease. Social Science Medicine. 1981(15D):251-8.

Okwesa A. How the message does not get through. Development Digest. 1983 Dec;21(2):95-8.

Oliveira-Cruz V, Kowalski J, McPake B. The Brazilian HIV / AIDS "success story" - can others do it? Tropical Medicine and International Health. 2004(2,;9(2)):292-297.

Olson J. Autocorrelation and visual map comlexity. Annals of the Association of American Geographers. 1975(65):189-204.

Oppenheim AN. Questionnaire design, interviewing and attitude measurement. Pinter Publishers. London and New York. 1992.

Ord JK, Getis A. Local spatial autocorrelation statistics: Distributional issues and an application. Geographical Analysis. 1995(27):287-306.

Oshi DC, Nakalema S, Oshi LL. Cultural and social aspects of HIV / AIDS sex education in secondary schools in Nigeria. Journal of Biosocial Science. 2005;37:175-183.

Overmars KP, de Koning GHJ, Veldkamp A. Spatial autocorrelation in multi-scale land use models. Ecological Modeling. 2003(164):257-270.

Page ES. Cumulative sum charts. Technometrics. 1961(3):1-9.

Pallangi J.Minőségbiztosítás az egészségügyben és a szociális ellátórendszerben. Vitéz János Római Katolikus Tanítóképző Főiskola. Kézirat. Esztergom. 2003.

Pande PS, Neuman RP, Cavanagh RR. The Six Sigma Way. How GE, Motorola, and other top companies are honing their performance. McGraw-Hill. 2000.

Parmar MKB, Machin D. Survival analysis. A practical approach. Wiley. 1996.

Patil GP, Stiteler WM. Concepts of aggregation and their quantification: a critical review with some new results and applications. Researches on Population Ecology. 1974(15):238-254},

Pavlik Z. Population and development. ACTA UNIVERSITATIS CAROLINAE: GEOGRAPHICA. 1995;30(1-2):43-51.

Pettigrew A, Ferlie E, McKee L. Shaping strategis change. Making change in large organisations. The case of the National Health Service. Sage. 1994.

Pérez-Escamilla R. Breastfeeding and the nutritional transition in the Latin American and Caribbean Region: a success story? [Lactancia materna y transición nutricional en la región de América Latina y el Caribe: ¿un éxito?] Cadernos de Saúde Pública. 2003(19 Suppl 1):S119-S127.

Phillips, L.D. [1973]. Bayesian statistics for Social Scientists. Nelson, London

Pielou EC. The interpretation of ecological data. A primer on classification and ordination. Wiley. 1984.

Pike MC, Smith PG. Disease clustering: a generalization of Knox's approach to the detection of space-time interactions. Biometrics. 1968(24):541-6.

Pikó B. Középiskolás fiatalok szabadidő-struktúrája, értékattitűdjei és egészségmagatartása. Szociológiai Szemle. 2005(2):88-89. pp.

Piotrow PT, Kincaid DL, Rimon II JG, Rinehart W. Health communication. Lessons from family planning and reproductive health. Praeger. 1997.

Plackett, R.L. The marginal totals of a 2x2 table. Biometrika, 1977(64):37-42.

Pocock SJ. Clinical trials. A practical approach. Wiley. 1995.

Pollock J. Performance-based contracting with NGOs in Haiti. [Une collaboration misant sur la performance avec des ONG en Haöti; [Haití: contratación de organisaciones no gubernamentales (ONG) basada en los resultados.] Performance Improvement. 2003 Sep;42(8):20-24.

Population Reference Bureau [PRB]. 2003 world population data sheet of the Population Reference Bureau. Demographic data and estimates for the countries and regions of the world. Washington, D.C., PRB, 2003. 13 p.

Population Reference Bureau [PRB]. Transitions in world population. Population Bulletin. 2004 Mar;59(1):[43] p.

Population Services International [PSI] Social marketing and communications for health. Washington, D.C., PSI, [1992]. [2], 32, [2] p.

Poverty. World Development Report 1990. World Development Indicators. World Bank. Oxford University Press. 1990.

Pratkanis és Aronson. A rábeszélőgép. (Élni és visszaélni a meggyőzés mindennapos mesterségével).Ab Ovo. 1992.

Prékopa A. Valószínűségelmélet műszaki alkalmazásokkal. Műszaki K. Negyedik Kiadás. Budapest. 1980.

Press WH, Flannery BP, Teukolsky SA, Vetterling WT. Numerical recipes in Pascal. The Art of Scientific Computing. Cambridge University Press. 1989.

Pyzdek T, Berger RW. Quality Engineering Handbook. Marcel Dekker, Inc. 1992.

Quality management in social welfare and health care for the 21st century. STAKES National Research and Development Centre for Welfare and Health. Finland. 1999.

Quality management in social welfare and health care. STAKES National Research and Development Centre for Welfare and Health. Finland. 1996.

Questionnaires from the National Health Interview Survey, 1985-89. U.S. Department of health and human services. CDC. 1993.

R Development Core Team. R: A language and environment for statistical computing. R Foundation for Statistical Computing. 2004. Vienna, Austria.

R: A language and environment for statistical computing R Development Core Team. ISBN 3-900051-00-3. R Foundation for Statistical Computing. Vienna, Austria. 2003.

Rabbani AK. Recent developments and programme for population census and surveys in Bangladesh. [Unpublished] [1985]. 40 p.

Radelet, M. Racial characteristics and impositions of the death penalty. Amer. Sociol. Rev. 1981(46): 918-927.

Ratzan SC. AIDS: when can the world rest? [editorial] JOURNAL OF HEALTH COMMUNICATION. 2000 Jul-Sep;5(3):193-4.

Ray HE. Incorporating communication strategies into agricultural development programs. Part two: agricultural communication in the context of agricultural development programs. [Unpublished] 1985 Oct. [6], 68 p. Contract No. AID/ta-C-147; Contract No. AID/DPE-1109-C-00-4081-00

Ravenholt B, Perla G, Vilarruz AQ. Proposed strategy for future USAID support to the Well-family Midwife Clinic franchise network. Washington, D.C., LTG Associates, Monitoring, Evaluation and Design Support Project, 2003 May. [64] p.

Reher DS. The demographic transition revisited as a global process. Population, Space and Place. 2004 Jan-Feb;10(1):19-41.

Reseau Africain de Recherche sur le SIDA. Women and AIDS in Africa. Scientific symposium report, 19-21 May, 1997, Abidjan, Cote d'Ivoire. [Femmes et SIDA en Afrique. Rapport du symposium scientifique, 19-21 Mai, 1997, Abidjan, Cote d'Ivoire.] Dakar, Senegal, Reseau Africain de Recherche sur le SIDA, 1999 Dec. 166 p.

Richardson, S. A method for testing the significance of geographical correlations with application to industrial lung cancer in rance. Statistics in Medicine, 1990(9):515-528.

Richardson S, Best N. Bayesian hierarchical models in ecological studies: of health-environment effects. Environmetrics, 2003(14):45-59.

Roberts L. Polio eradication effort adds new weapon to its armory. Science. 2005(1,14;307):190

Robinson AH et al. Elements of Geography. 6th ed. Wiley. 1995.

Rose G, Marmot MG. Social class and coronary heart disease. Br Heart J, 1981(45):13-19.

Radstats. http://www.radstats.org.uk/

Rasztrigin LA. A véletlen világa. Műszaki K. Budapest. 1973.

Ravenholt B, Perla G, Vilarruz AQ. Proposed strategy for future USAID support to the Well-family Midwife Clinic franchise network.

Rayner J. Risky business. Towards best practice in managing reputation risk. Institute of Business ethics. London. 2001.

Reher DS. The demographic transition revisited as a global process. Population, Space and Place. 2004 Jan-Feb;10(1):19-41.

Reiczigel, J. (1991 a). Investigation of some association measures by Monte Carlo methods. Social Science Informatics Center. Preprint 1991a/1.

Reiczigel, J. (1991 b). Monte Carlo methods in model testing. Social Science Informatics Center. Preprint 1991b/4.

Reimann J. Valószínűségelmélet és matematikai statisztika. Kézirat. Tankönyvkiadó. Budapest. 1975.

Rényi A. Valószínűűségszámítás. Tankönyvkiadó. Budapest. 1981.

Ribeiro PJ, Jr., Diggle PJ. geoR: a package for geostatistical analysis. ISBN 3-900051-00-3. 2001.

Rice JA. Mathematical statistics and data analysis. Wadsworth & Brooks/Cole. 1988.

Riihela M, Rutanen N (eds.) Visible child – invisible quality. Summary report on the International Conference 15.-18.11.1997 in Helsinki, Finland. Themes 5/1998.

Riley NE. China's population: new trends and challenges. Population Bulletin. 2004 Jun;59(2):[40] p.

Roberts L. Polio eradication effort adds new weapon to its armory. Science. 2005 Jan 14;307:190.
Robinson, AH, Morrison JL, Muehrcke PC, Kimerling AJ, Guptil SC. Elements of Geography. 6th ed. Wiley. 1995.
Rogerson PA. Surveillance systems for monitoring the development of spatial patterns. Statistics in Medicine. 1997(16):2081-2093.
Romesburg HC. Cluster analysis for researchers. Robert E. Krieger Publishing Company. Malabar, Florida. 1990.
Romesburg HC. Exploring, confirming and randomization tests. Computers and Geosciences. 1985(11,1):19-37.
Romesburg HC, DeGraff JV. Using the normal generated distribution to analyse spatial and temporal variability in geomorphic processes.
Romesburg HC, Marshall K. Lifetime publications. Belmont, California. Wadsworth. 1984.
Romesburg HC, Mohai P. Improving the precision of tree hight estimates. Can J For Res. 1990(20):1246-1250.
Romesburg HC. Chitest: A Monte-Carlo computer program for contingency table tests. Computers & Geosciences. 1985(11;1):69-78.
Romesburg HC. Exploring, confirming, and randomization tests. Computers & Geosciences. 1985(11;1):19-37.
Romesburg HC. Ftest: A computer program for "exact chi-square" goodness-of-fit significance tests. Computers & Geosciences. 1981(7):47-58.
Romesburg HC. Life: A computer program for stochastic life table analysis. The American Statistician. 1981(35;2):114.
Romesburg HC. Use of the normal generated distribution for estimating population survival. J Theor Biol. 1976(61):447-30.
Romesburg HC. Wildlife science: gaining reliable knowledge. J Wildl Manage. 1981(45;2):293-313.
Romesburg HC. Zorro: A Randomization test for spatial pattern. Computers & Geosciences. 1989(15;6):1011-1017.
Romics I, Molnár DL, Timberg G et al.: The effect of drotaverine hydrochloride in acute colicky pain caused by renal and ureteric stones. British J of Urology International, 2003(92):92-96.
Roos J. Backlash against prostitutes' rights: origins and dynamics of Nazi prostitution polices. Journal of the History of Sexuality. 2002 Jan-Apr;11(1-2):67-94.
Rosenfield A, Schwartz K. Population and development -- shifting paradigms, setting goals. New England Journal of Medicine. 2005 Feb 17;352(7):647-649.
Rosner B. Fundamentals of biostatistics. 3rd ed. PWS-Kent. Thomson Information/Publishing Group. Boston. 1990.
Rourke BP, Del Dotto JE. Learning disabilities. A neuropsychological perspective. Sage. 1994.
Rudas T, Bergsma P. On Applications of Marginal Models to Categorical Data. Metron 2004(42):15-37.
Rudas T, Bergsma W, Nemeth R. Parameterization and estimation of path models for categorical data. COMPSTAT 2006, to appear. 2006
Rudas T, Bergsma W. Letter to the Editor, Statistics in Medicine 2004(23):3545-3547.
Rudas T, Bergsma W. On applications of marginal models to categorical data. 23rd Biennial Conference of the Society for Multivariate Analysis in the Behavioral Sciences, Abstracts, 55-56, Tilburg. 2002
Rudas T, Bergsma W. On relationships between graphical and marginal modeling. Social Science Methodology in the New Millenium. Proceedings of the Fifth International Conference on Logic and Methodology, 308, University of Cologne. 2000
Rudas T, Bergsma W. On the parameterization of graphical models describing the association structure among several variables. International Conference on Methodology and Statistics, Abstracts, 46, University of Ljubljana. 2001
Rudas T, Bergsma W. On generalized symmetry. The Quasi Symmetry Project. 2001. http://www.ups-tlse.fr/PROJET_QS/PAPERS/ Rudas2/Rudas2.html
Rudas T, Clogg CC, Lindsay BG. A new index of fit based on mixture methods for the analysis of contingency tables. Journal of the Royal Statistical Society, Ser. B, 1994(56, 4):623-639.
Rudas T, Clogg CC, Lindsay BG. A new index of fit based on mixture methods for the analysis of contingency tables. Preprint 93-1, Center for Likelihood Studies, Department of Statistics, the Pennsylvania State University, State College, PA. 1993
Rudas T, Fekete-Miski A, Miski Z. Egy egyszerű mintavételi eljárás szimulációs vizsgálata. in: Kolosi T. (szerk.) Mérés a társadalomtudományokban, OMIKK-TARKI, Budapest . 1993:80-87
Rudas T, Leimer HG. Analysis of contingency tables with known conditional odds ratios or known log-linear parameters. in: Francis, B., Seeberg, G. U. H., van der Heijden, P. G. M., Jansen, W. (eds.) Statistical Modeling, Elsevier. 1992:313-322
Rudas T, Leimer HG. Analysis of contingency tables with known conditional odds ratios or known log-linear parameters. Proceedings of the 6th International Workshop on Statistical Modeling, Utrecht, Methods Series MS 91-2, University of Utrecht. 1991:271-282
Rudas T, Zwick R. Estimating the importance of differential item functioning. Journal of Educational and Behavioral Statistics 1997(22):31-45.
Rudas T, Zwick R. Measuring the importance of differential item functioning. Research Report, Educational Testing Service, Princeton, NJ. 1995
Rudas T. (ed.) DISTAN 2.0 Manual. Social Science Informatics Center, Budapest. 1992
Rudas T. (ed.) Handbook of Probability Theory with Applications, Sage (megjelenés alatt) 2007
Rudas T. A fast algorithm for some exploratory methods in categorical data problems. in: De Antoni, Lauro, Rizzi (eds.) COMPSTAT 1986, Proceedings in ComputationalStatistics, Physica Verlag, Heidelberg, Wien. 1986:49-54

Rudas T. A general framework for the analysis of surveys. 21st BiennialConference of the Society for Multivariate Analysis in theBehavioral Sciences,Abstracts, University of Leuwen. 1998

Rudas T. A latent class approach to measuring the fit of a statistical model, in Hagenaars J, McCutcheon A. (eds.) Applied Latent Class Analysis, Cambridge University Press. 2002

Rudas T. A Monte Carlo comparison of the small sample behavior of the Pearson, the likelihood ratio and the Cressie-Read statistics. Journal of Statistical Computation and Simulation, 1986(24):107-120.

Rudas T. A new algorithm for the maximum likelihood estimation of graphical log-linear models. Computational Statistics 1998(13):529-537.

Rudas T. A változók közötti kapcsolatok elemzése. in: Móri, Székely (szerk.) Többváltozós statisztikai analízis, Műszaki Könyvkiadó, Budapest. 1986:71-94.

Rudas T. A változók közötti kapcsolatok vizsgálata. in: Rejtő (szerk) Többváltozós statisztikai módszerek. Bolyai János matematikai Társulat, Budapest. 1984:174-225.

Rudas T. Assessment of Model Fit Based on Incomplete Data. Joint Statistical Meetings, Abstracts, 405, SanFrancisco. 2003

Rudas T. Assessment of model fit based on incomplete data. Proceedings of the 2003 Joint Statistical Meetings, San Francisco, American Statistical Association, 2004:3576-3582.

Rudas T. Canonical representation of log-linear models. Communications in Statistics (Theory and Methods). 2002(31):2311-2323.

Rudas T. Cluster analízis a BMDP programcsomaggal. in: A BMDP programcsomag rövid leírása. MTA SZTAKI Working Paper, Budapest. 1980

Rudas T. Conditional independence and conditional no-highest order association. Workshop on Conditional Independence Structures and Graphical Models. Abstracts, Fields Institute, University of Toronto. 1999:42-43

Rudas T. Contribution to the discussion of the papers by Wermuth and Lauritzen and Edwards. Journal of the Royal Statistical Society , Ser B, 1990(52):55-56.

Rudas T. Direkt loglineáris modellek maximum likelihood becslése. Alkalmazott Matematikai Lapok, 1986(11):349-362.

Rudas T. DISTAN for DIscrete STatistical ANalaysis, COMPSTAT 1990, Software Catalogue, 3-4, Dubrovnik. 1990

Rudas T. DISTAN for discrete statistical analysis. in: 5. Konferenz uber die wissenschaftliche Anwendung von Statistik-Software, Heidelberg, Abstracts 90, ZUMA, Mannheim. 1989

Rudas T. DISTAN for discrete statistical analysis. in: Faulbaum, Haux, Jockel (eds.) SoftStat'89, Fortschritte der Statistik-Software 2, Gustav Fischer Verlag, Suttgart, New York. 1990:144-154

Rudas T. DISTAN for discrete statistical analysis: an overview. Social Science Informatics Center, Budapest, Preprint 1989(2)

Rudas T. DISTAN for discrete statistical analysis: Help Text. Social Science Informatics Center, Budapest, Preprint 1990(1).

Rudas T. Exploratory methods for categorical data problems. in: 45th Session of the International Statistical Institute, Volume of Contributed papers, Amsterdam. 1985:107-108

Rudas T. Extension of measures: some statistical applications. Bull. of the Int. Statist. Inst., 47th Session, Paris, Contributed papers, Book 1989(2):276-277.

Rudas T. Faktoranalízis az empirikus társadalomkutatásban. Tömegkommunikációs Kutatóközpont, Budapest. 1979

Rudas T. Hogyan olvassunk közvélemény-kutatásokat. Új Mandátum, Budapest. 1998

Rudas T. Intersections of linear and multiplicative models. 7th European Meeting of the Psychometric Society, Trier, Abstracts, 1991:122.

Rudas T. Kontingencia táblák elemzése. Egyetemi jegyzet, ELTE, Budapest 1982. Újranyomás: 1993.

Rudas T. Kontingencia táblák loglineáris elemzése. in: Móri, Székely (szerk.) Többváltozós statisztikai analízis. Műszaki Könyvkiadó, Budapest 1986:191-207

Rudas T. Kontingencia táblák loglineáris elemzése. in: Rejtő (szerk) Többváltozós statisztikai módszerek, II. Bolyai János matematikai Társulat, Budapest. 1984:292-321.

Rudas T. Marginal and partial association models. Social Science Informatics Center, Budapest, Preprint 1989(1).

Rudas T. Maximum likeliood estimation of mixed linear and multiplicative models using DISTAN. in: Momirovic, Mildner (eds.) COMPSTAT 1990, Proceedings Computational Statistics, Physica Verlag, Heidelberg. 1990:127-132

Rudas T. Mixed linear and multiplicative models. in: T. Rudas (ed.) DISTAN 2.0 Manual, Social Science Informatics Center, Budapest. 1992:81-128

Rudas T. Mixture Models of Missing Data. Quality & Quantity 2005(39):19-36.

Rudas T. New modules in DISTAN 2.0. Proceedings of the International Conference on Social Science Methodology, University of Trento and ISA RC33. 1992

Rudas T. Odds and odds ratios, in: Everitt, B, Howell, D. (eds). Encyclopedia of Social Science Research Methods, Sage. (2005)

Rudas T. Odds Ratios in the Analysis of Contingency Tables. Quantitative Applications in the Social Sciences, No 117. Sage Publ., Thousand Oaks, California. 1998

Rudas T. Odds ratios in the analysis of contingency tables. Quantitative applications in the social sciences. A SAGE University Paper 119. 1998.

Rudas T. Odds Ratios in the Analysis of Contingency Tables. Sage Publ. Thousand Oaks. 1998.

Rudas T. On conditional independence interpretation of log-linear models. in M. Huskova, J. A. Visek, P. Lachout (eds.) Proceedinggs of Prague Stochastics 98. Jednota Ceskych Matematik a Fyzik, Prague, 1998(2):493-496.

Rudas T. Prescribed conditional interaction structure models with application to the analysis of mobility tables. Quality & Quantity 1991(25):345-358.

Rudas T. Probability Theory: a Primer. Sage Publ. Thousand Oaks. 2004.

Rudas T. Probability Theory: A Primer. Sage Publ., Thousand Oaks, California 2004

Rudas T. Probability, Prior probability, Probabilisitc, Probability value, Probability density function, Law of large numbers, in Byrman A, Liao TF, Lews-Beck M. (eds.) Encyclopedia of Social Science Research Methods, Sage. 2003

Rudas T. Stepwise discriminant analysis procedure for categorical variables. in: Havranek, Sidak, Novak (eds.) COMPSTAT 1984, Proceedings in Computational Statistics, Physica Verlag, Wien. 1984:389-394

Rudas T. The mixture index of fit and minimax regression. Metrika, 1999(50):163-172.

Rutherford A. Introducing ANOVA and ANCOVA a GLM approach. Sage. 2001.

Ryan B, Joiner B, Cryer J. Minitab Handbook. 2005. Duxbury Press. State College, PA.

Ryan TA Jr, Joiner BL. Normal probability plots and tests for normality. Statistics Department. The Pennsylvania State University. 1976. Technical Reports. Minitab Inc. November 1990.

Ryan, Joiner. Minitab handbook. 3rd edi. Duxbury Press. 1994.

Sackett DL, Straus SE, Richardson WS, Rosenberg W, Haynes RB. Evidence-based medicine. How to practice and teach EBM. Churchill Livingstone. 2000

Sagan C. Broca agya. Gondolatok a tudomány romantikájáról. Akkord K. Budapest. 2001.

Sarndal C, Swensson B, Wretman J. Model assisted survey sampling. Springer.1993.

SAS/STAT User Guide. Volume 1. ACECLUS-FREQ. SAS Institute. Version 6. Fourth Edition. 1990.

SAS/STAT User Guide. Volume 2. GLM-VARCOMP. SAS Institute. Version 6. Fourth Edition. 1990.

Scambler G (ed). Sociology as applied to medicine. 3rd ed. Bailliere Tindall. 1991.

Scott KD, Gilliam A, Braxton K. Culturally competent HIV prevention strategies for women of color in the United States. Health Care for Women International. 2005;26:17-45.

Searle SR, Rudson GFS, Federer WT. Annotated computer output for covariance (ACO:COV-SPSS). 1982.

Searle SR. Solutions manual for matrix algebra useful for statistics. Biometrics Unit. Cornell University. Ithaca, N.Y. 14853. 1983.

Shaddick G, Elliott P. Use of Stone's method in studies of disease risk around point sources of environmental pollution. Statistics in Medicine. 1996(15):1927-1934.

Sheldrake R. Hét kísérlet, amely megváltoztathatja a világot. Bioenergetic K. Budapest. 2003.

Schoen R, Jonsson SH. Modeling momentum in gradual demographic transitions. Demography. 2003 Nov;40(4):621-635.

Shoieb F, Abdel-Monem A, Khalil AM. The impact of internal migration on labour force in greater Cairo region. In: CDC 24th Annual Seminar on Population Issues and the Challenges in the 21st Century in the Middle East, Africa and Asia. CDC Annual Seminar, 1994, [compiled by] Cairo Demographic Centre. Cairo, Egypt, Cairo Demographic Centre, 1995. :29-52. Cairo Demographic Centre Research Monograph Series No. 24

Siegel S, Castellan NJ Jr. Nonparametric statistics for the behavioral sciences. 2nd ed. McGraw-Hill. 1989.

Siemiatycki J. Mantel's space-time clustering statistic: computing higher moments and a comparison of various data transforms. Journal of Statistical Computation and Simulation. 1978(7):13-31.

Simms A. http://www.neweconomics.org/gen/ecologicaldebt091006.aspx

Simon JL. Resampling Stats User's Guide: Resampling Stats, Inc. 1999.

Simon JL. Resampling: The new statistics. Resampling Stats, Inc. 1995.

Simon JL. Resampling: The new statistics. Resampling Stats, Inc. 1997.

Simon P, Molnár DL, Juhász B. Portable electronic patient record with special database functions (PATREC): preparation of the health card system application (1999). In: Proceeding on Health Cards '99. Milan. Ed. by. Sicurello F.

Simpson EH. The interpretation of interaction in contingency tables. J R Statist Soc B. 1951(13):238-241.

Skene AM, Wakefield JC. Hierarchical models for multi-centre binary response studies. Statist Med, 1990(9):919-929.

Slattery M. Official statistics. Tavistock. 1986.

Smith DP. Formal demography. Plenum Press. 1992.

Smith JQ. Decision analysis. A Bayesian approach. Chapman & Hall. 1992.

Smith PG, Pike MC. A note on a "close pairs" test for space clustering. Br J Prev Soc Med. 1974(28):63-4.

Smouse PE, Long JC, Sokal RR. Multiple regression and correlation extensions of the Mantel test of matrix correspondence. Systematic Zoology 1986(38): 727-732.

Snell EJ. Applied Statistics. A handbook of BMDP analyses. Chapman & Hall. 1987.

Sokal RR, Rohlf FJ. Biometry. The principles of practice of statistics in biological research. 3rd ed. W.H. Freeman and Company. New York. 2000.

Solt G. Valószínűségszámítás. Műszaki K. Budapest. 1985.

Solymosi N, Molnár DL, Mészáros J. Spatial statistical analysis of election data. In: Political Atlas of Hungary 2004. Gondolat K. 2005., pp. 37-41.

Solymosi N, Reiczigel J, Harnos A, Mészáros J, Molnár LD, Rubel F. Fidning spatial barriers by Monmonier's algorithm. Presented at ISCB Conference, Szeged, Hungary. 2005

Somlai P. Agol-magyar, magyar angol szociológiai szótár. Balassi K. Budapest. 1993.
Spadacini BM. Overcoming AIDS stigma and media fatigue. Global AIDSLink. 2003 Apr-May;(79):12-13.
Spector PE. Summated rating scale construction. An introduction. Series: Quantitative applications in the social sciences. A SAGE University Paper 82. 1992.
Speiser Ferenc, Mészáros József, Szakadát István: Tér-kép(elem)zés 11-17.o.
Spiegel MR. Statisztika. Elmélet és gyakorlat. Panem-McGraw-Hill. Budapest. 1995
Spira SC, Wainberg MA. Jewish religious ethics mandate access to antiretroviral drugs in developing countries. Journal of the International Association. 2004 Jan-Mar;3(1):7-11.
Sprent P. Data driven statistical methods. Chapman & Hall. 1998.
Spriet A, Dupin-Spriet T, Simon P. Methodology of clinical drug trials. 2nd, revised ed. Karger. 1993.
Srinivasan K. Policy perspectives on fertility regulation in developing countries. In: Population policy perspectives in developing countries, edited by V. Narain and C. P. Prakasam. Bombay, India, Himalaya Publishing House, 1983. :133-47.
Statistics in Behavioral Science, 1462-1467, Wiley.
Steer PJ, Little MP, Kold-Jensen T, Chapple J, Elliott P. Maternal blood pressure in pregnancy, birth weight, and perinatal mortality in first births: prospective study. BMJ. British Medical Journal. 2004 Nov 23;329:[7] p.
Steiner F. A geostatisztika alapjai. Tankönyvkiadó. Budapest. 1990.
Stevens SS. On the theory of scales and measurement. Science. 1946.
Stigler SM. Thomas Bayes's Bayesian Inference. J R Statist A, 1982(145):250-258.
Stimson GV, Donoghoe MC, Fitch C, Rhodes TJ, Ball A. Rapid assessment and response technical guide. TG-RAR, Version 1.0. Geneva, Switzerland, World Health Organisation [WHO], Department of HIV / AIDS, 2003 Jun. [325] p. WHO/HIV/2002.22
Stone RA. Investigations of excess environmental risks around putative sources: Statistical problems and a proposed test. Statistics in Medicine. 1988(7):649-660.
Stuart A, Ord JK, Arnold S. Kendall's advanced theory of statistics. Volume 2A. Classical inference & the linear model. 6th ed. Arnold. 1994.
Stuart A, Ord JK. Kendall's advanced theory of statistics. Volume 1. Distribution theory. 6th ed. Arnold. 1994.
Study confirms HIV viral load lower in women than men; implications for therapy. AIDS WEEKLY. 2001 Mar 19;:6-7.
Success stories. Improved services in Egypt. Safe Motherhood. 2003a;(30):2.
Success stories. National insurance in Bolivia. Safe Motherhood. 2003b;(30):3.
Sváb J. Többváltozós módszerek a biometriában. Mezőgazdasági K. Budapest. 1979.
Sz.K. Caldwell JC, Schinndlmayr T. Historical population estimates: Unravelling the consensus. A népesség hosszú távú idősorainak becslése. DesL(ed.) Epidemiology in Medicine4). 1987.
Szalai J. Az egészsépgügy betegségei. KJK. Budapest. 1986.
Szeles P. A hírnév ereje. Image és Arculat. STAR PR Ügynökség, Worldcom Hungary. 1998.
Szeles P. Public relations a gyakorlatban. Geomédia szakkönyvek. 1999.
Szende Á, Molnár DL. Socio-economic variations in health related quality of life based on Hungarian population surveys using the EUROQOL instrument. 7th International Conference on System Sceince in Health Care, Sustainable structure for better health; Budapest, Hungary, 29 May – 2 June, 2000. University of York, United Kingdom, Semmelweis Medical Univer4sity, Budapest, Hungary
Szende Á, Molnár L. Inequalities in health status and inequity in the delivery of health care in Hungary. Archives of Hellenic Medicine. 2001, 18(2):169-179.
Szivós P, Rudas T, Tóth IGy. (1998) Mikroszimuláció. Tárki Tanulmányok 8.
Szoboljeva L, Molnar DL. Bezdomnoszty i Alkoholizm v Vengrii. Obrozrenyije Pszichiatrii i Medicinszkoj Pszichologii Imenyi V. M. Bechtyereva. 1995 (1):127-131. (In Russian)
Tango T. The detection of disease clustering in time. Biometrics. 1984(40):15-26.
Tanne JH. Abstinence only programmes do not change sexual behavior, Texas study shows. BMJ. British Medical Journal. 2005 Feb 12;330:[2] p.
Tanur J, Mosteller F, Kruskal WH, Lehmann EL, Link RF, Pieters RS, Rising GR. Statistics. A guide to the unknown. 3rd ed. Wadsworth & Brooks/Cole. 1989.
Taren DL, Duncan B, Shrestha K, Shrestha N, Genaro-Wolf D, Schleicher RL, Pfeiffer CM. The night vision threshold test is a better predictor of low serum vitamin a concentration than self-reported night blindness in pregnant urban Nepalese women. Journal of Nutrition. 2004;134:2573-2578.
Tarter ME, Lock MD. Model-free curve estimation. Chapman & Hall. 1993.
Telematik im Gesundheitswesen. Perspektiven und Entwicklungsstand. AKA. 2005.
Területi Statisztika. 2005(8;45;1):15-32.
Thind A. Analysis of health services use for respiratory illness in Indonesian children: implications for policy. Journal of Biosocial Science. 2005;37:129-142.
Thisted RA. Elements of statistical computing. Numerical computation. Chapman & Hall. 1996.
Thompson JR, Koronacki J. Statistical process control. The Deming paradigm and beyond. 2nd ed. Chapman & Hall/CRC. 2002.
Thompson SK. Sampling. Wiley. 1992.
Thorngate W, Ferguson T. Behind the eyeball: some popular misuses of information in human decision making. Canadian J of Information, Science, 1977(2):1-11.
Tiefelsdorf M, Griffith DA, Boots B. A variance-stabilizing coding scheme for spatial link matrices. Environment and Planning A. 1999(31):165-180.

Tilanus EW. Working with the SAS system. SAS Institute Inc. 1994.

Torres Parodi C. Actions to achieve health equity for ethnic / racial groups. Regional workshop: adoption and implementation of affirmative action policies for Afro-descendants in Latin America and the Caribbean, Montevideo, Uruguay, May 2003. [Washington, D.C.], Pan American Health Organisation [PAHO], Governance and Policy Area, 2003 Aug. 27 p.

Torrico F, Alonso-Vega C, Suarez E, Rodriguez P, Torrico M. Maternal Trypanosoma cruzi infection, pregnancy outcome, morbidity, and mortality of congenitally infected and non-infected newborns in Bolivia. [Infección materna por Trypanosoma cruzi, resultado del embarazo, morbimortalidad de neonatos con infección congénita y no infectados en Bolivia.] American Journal of Tropical Medicine and Hygiene. 2004;70(2):201-209.

Toubia N. Caring for women with circumcision. A technical manual for health care providers. New York, New York, Research, Action, and Information Network for Bodily Integrity of Women [RAINBO], 1999. 95 p.

Townsend N, Madhavan S, Tollman S, Garenne M, Kahn K. Children's residence patterns and educational attainment in rural South Africa, 1997. Population Studies. 2002 Jul;56(2):215-225.

Towsend P, Davidson N (eds). The black report. Penguin Books. 1988.

Tölgyesi, J., Rudas, T. (1980) A SIMULA programozási nyelv alkalmazása a társadalomtudományban.Tömegkommunikációs Kutatóközpont, Budapest.

Tsafack M, Wakou R. Family planning. [Planification familiale.] In: Enquete Demographique et de Sante, Cameroun, 1998, [by] Medard Fotso, Rene Ndonou, Paul Roger Libite, Martin Tsafack, Roger Wakou, Aboubakar Ghapoutsa, Samuel Kamga, Pierre Kemgo, Michel Kwekem Fankam, Antoine Kamdoum. Yaounde, Cameroon, Bureau Central des Recensements et des Etudes de Population, 1999 Mar. :59-82.

Tu X, Cui N, Lou C, Gao E. Do family-planning workers in China support provision of sexual and reproductive health services to unmarried young people? Bulletin of the World Health Organisation. 2004;82(4):274-280.

Tudor K. Mental health promotion. Paradigms and practice. Routledge. 1996.

Tufte ER. Envisioning information. Graphic Press. Cheshire, Connecticut. 1991.

Tuiran R, Partida V, Mojarro O, ZúAiga E. Fertility in Mexico: trends and forecast. In: Expert Group Meeting on Completing the Fertility Transition, New York, 11-14 March 2002, [compiled by] United Nations. Department of Economic and Social Affairs. Population Division. New York, New York, United Nations, Department of Economic and Social Affairs, Population Division, 2004. :483-506.

Turmen T. Gender and HIV / AIDS. International Journal of Gynecology and Obstetrics. 2003 Sep;82(3):411-418.

Understanding GIS. The ARC/INFO Method. Environmental Systems Research Institute, Inc. 1990.

University of North Carolina at Chapel Hill. Carolina Population Center [CPC]. MEASURE Evaluation, Associates for Community and Population Research. Evaluation of impacts of the Rural Service Delivery Partnership (RSDP) Chapel Hill, North Carolina, University of North Carolina at Chapel Hill, Carolina Population Center [CPC], MEASURE Evaluation, 2003 Feb. 42 p.

Upton, G. J. G. (1991). The exploratory analysis of survey data using log-linear models. The Statistician, 40, 169-182.

Upton GJG. The analysis of cross-tabulated data. John Wiley & Sons, New York. 1978.

Upton GJG, Singleton. Spatial data analysis by example. Volume 1. Wiley. 1985.

Upton GJG, Singleton. Spatial data analysis by example. Volume 2. Wiley. 1989.

Upton GJG. On Mead's test for pattern. Biometrics. 1984(40):759-766.

Urban Hjorthe JS. Coméuter intensive statistical methods. Validation model selection and bootstrap. Chapman & Hall. 1994.

VanDevanter NL, Messeri P, Middlestadt SE, Bleakley A, Merzel CR. A community-based intervention designed to increase preventive health care seeking among adolescents: The Gonorrhea Community Action Project. American Journal of Public Health. 2005 Feb;95(2):331-337.

Varga CA. Introduction. In: Fertility. Current South African issues of poverty, HIV / AIDS and youth, compiled by Human Sciences Research Council. Child, Youth and Family Development Research Programme. Cape Town, South Africa, Human Sciences Research Council, HSRC Publishers, 2003. :1-6.

Vargha A, Rudas T, Delaney HD, Maxwell SE. (1996) Dichotomization, partial correlation, and conditional independence. Journal of Educational and Behavioral Statistics, 21, 264-282.

Varkey LC, Mishra A, Das A, Ottolenghi E, Huntington D. Involving men in maternity care in India. New Delhi, India, Population Council, Frontiers in Reproductive Health, 2004 Apr. [72] p. USAID Cooperative Agreement No. HRN-A-00-98-00012-00

Velleman PF. Learning data analysis with data desk. W.H. Freeman and Company. New York. 1989.

Verdes E, Rudas T. The pi star index as an alternative for assessing goodness-of-fit of logistic regression. Social Science Methodology in the New Millenium. Proceedings of the Fifth International Conference on Logic and Methodology, University of Cologne. 2000:240-241

Verdes E, Rudas T. The pi-star index as a new alternative for assessing goodness-of-fit of logistic regression. In: Gregori D, Rozbowsky P, Luisa L, Torelli N, Gori E. (eds.) Proceedings of the Fifth Youngs Statisticians Meeting, Edizioni Universita di Trieste. 2001:45-54

Vetterling WT, Teukolsky SA, Press WH, Flannery BP. Numerical recipes in Pascal. Example book [Pascal]. Revised edition. Cambridge University Press. 1989.

Vetterling WT, Teukolsky SA, Press WH, Flannery BP. Numerical Recipes. Example Book [Pascal]. Revised Edition. Cambridge University Press, Cambridge, Massachusetts. 1990.

Vincze I. Matematikai statisztika ipari alkalmazásokkal. Műszaki K. Budapest. 1975.

Vincze I. Matematikai statisztika. Kérirat. Műszaki K. Budapest. 1981.

Vitez M, Koranyi G, Gonczy E, Rudas T, Czeizel A. (1984) A semiquantitative score system for epidemiologic studies of fetal alcohol syndrome. American Journal of Epidemiology, 119, 301-308.

Von Eye A, Clogg CC. Latent variables analysis. Applications for developmental research. Sage. 1994.

Vose D. Quantitative risk analysis. Wiley. 1996.

Wakefield J. Ecological Inference for 2x2 tables. J R Statist Soc A 2004(167):1-42.

Wakefield J. Ecological Inference for 2x2 tables J R Statist Soc A 2004(167): 385-445.

Wakefield JC, Kelsall JE, Morris SE. Clustering, cluster detection, and spatial variation in risk. Ecography. 2000(25):558-577.

Wakefield JC, Kelsall JE, Morris SE. Clustering, cluster detection, and spatial variation in risk. In Spatial epidemiology: methods and applications. Elliott P, Wakef, JC, Best NG, Briggs DJ (eds). Oxford University Press Inc. New York. 2000:128-152.

Wakefield, J. Ecological inference for 2 x 2 tables. J. Roy. Statist. Soc. A 2004(167):385-445.

Walker MA. Some critical comments on " An analysis of crimes by the method of principal components" by Ahamad. Appl. Stat. 1967(16):36-39.

Ward RC, Davis GJ and Kane VE. Algorithm 633. An algorithm for linear dependency analysis of multivariate data. ACM TOM 1985(11,2):170-182.

Waldhör T. The spatial autocorrelation coefficient Moran's I under heteroscedasticity. Statistics in Medicine. 1996(15):887-892.

Wallenstein S. A test for detection of clustering over time. American Journal of Epidemiology. 1980(111):367-72.

Wallgren A, Wallgren B, Persson R, Jorner U, Haaland J. Graphing statistics & data. Creating better charts. Sage. 1996.

Walsh SJ, Page PH, Gesler WM. Normative models and healthcare planning: network-based simulations within a geographic information system environment. Health Serv Res. 1997(32(2)):243-260.

Walter SD. A simple test for spatial pattern in regional health data. Statistics in Medicine. 1994(13):1037-1044.

Walter SD. The analysis of regional patterns in health data. I. Distributional considerations. American Journal of Epidemiology. 1992(136):730-741.

Walter SD. Visual and statistical assessment of spatial clustering in mapped data. Statistics in Medicine. 1993(12 (14)):1275-1291.

Washington, D.C., LTG Associates, Monitoring, Evaluation and Design Support Project, 2003 May:64.

Weber RF, Dohle GR. Male contraception: mechanical, hormonal and non-hormonal methods. World Journal of Urology. 2003 Nov;21(5):338-340.

Weinstock MA. A generalized scan statistic test for the detection of clusters. International Journal of Epidemiology. 1981(10):289-93.

Weissberg RP, Gullotta TP, Hampton RL, Ryan BA, Adams GR. Healthy children 2010. Establishing preventive services. Sage 1997.

Westfall PH, Young SS. Resampling-based multiple testing. Examples and methods for p-value adjustment. Wiley. 1993.

Wetherill GB, Glazerbrook KD. Sequential methods in statistics. 3rd ed. Chapman & Hall. 1986.

Whitehead J. The design and analysis of sequential clinical trials. 2nd ed. Ellis Horwood. 1992.

Whitehead M. The health divide. Penguin Books. 1988.

Whittemore A, Keller JB. A letter to the editor. On Tango's index of disease clustering in time. Biometrics. 1986(42):218.

Whittemore AS, Friend N, Brown BW, Holly EA. A test to detect clusters of disease. Biometrika. 1987(74):631-5.

Wickman D. Bayes-statisztika. ELTE Eötvös Kiadó. Budapest. 1990.

Wilkinson RG. Unhealthy societies. The affliction of inequality. Routledge. 1996.

Winston WL. Operations research. Applications and algorithms. 3rd edition. Duxbury Press. 1994.

Winston WL. Simulation modeling using @RISK. Duxbury Press. 1996.

Wolfe DA, McMahon RJ, Peters RdeV (eds). Child abuse. New directions in prevention and treatment across the lifespan. Sage. 1997.

Woolgar S. Science the very idea. E. by Hamilton P. Routlege. 1993.

World Bank. Integrating Rural Development and Small Urban Centers: an Evolving Framework for Effective Regional and Local Economic Development, March 18-19, 2003. [Integración del desarrollo rural y de los pequeÃos centros urbanos: marco dinámico para el eficaz desarrollo económico regional y local, marzo 18-19, 2003.] Washington, D.C., World Bank, 2003. 20 p.

Yamada S. Latin American social medicine and global social medicine. [Medicina social latinoamericana y medicina social mundial.] American Journal of Public Health. 2003 Dec;93(12):1994-1996.

Yarnold, J. K. (1970). The minimum expectation in X2 goodness of fit tests and the accuracy of approximations for the null distribution. J Amer Statist Assoc 65, 864-886.

Yates BT. Analysing costs, procedures, processes, and outcomes in human services. Sage. Applied Social Research Methods Series. 1996:Volume 42.

Yavuzalp O. On the front line. NATO Review. 2002 Winter;49:24-5.

Yue TX, Wang YA, Liu JY, Chen SP, Tian YZ. SMPD scenarios of spatial distribution of human population in China. Population and Environment. 2005 Jan;26(3):207-228.

Zeldovics JB, Miskisz AD. Az alkalmazott matematika elemei. Gondolat K. Budapest. 1978.

Zeldovics JB. Ismerkedés a felsőbb matematikával és fizikai alkalmazásaival. Gondolat K. Budapest. 1981.

Zimon J. Not Knowing, Needing to Know, and Wanting to Know, in When Science Meets the Public. In: Bruce VL. (ed.) 1992.

Zupan J, Gasteiger J. Neural networks for chemists. An introduction. VCH. Weinheim, New York, Basel, Cambridge, Tokyo. 1993.

Zupan J. Algorithms for chemists. Wiley. 1989.

Zwicker C, Ringheim K. Commitments: youth reproductive health, the World Bank, and the Millennium Development Goals. Washington, D.C., Global Health Council, 2004. 30 p.